THE BEATING HEART

THE BEATING HEART

Exploration of Jewish Communities around the World

An Anthology by
Leading Tour Educators

Ya'acov Fried

Yishay Shavit

gefen publishing house בית הוצאה לאור
JERUSALEM ◆ NEW YORK   Est. 1981

Typing: Tami Dekel
Hebrew editing: Amnon Jackont
Initial English editing: Sorelle Weinstein
Editor: Kezia Raffel Pride
Cover design: Leah Ben Avraham/Noonim Graphics
Cover art by Larry Abramson, courtesy of Gordon Gallery
Typesetting: www.optumetech.com

ISBN: 978-965-7801-19-2

1 3 5 7 9 8 6 4 2

Gefen Publishing House Ltd.
6 Hatzvi Street
Jerusalem 9438614,
Israel
972-2-538-0247
orders@gefenpublishing.com

Gefen Books
c/o Baker & Taylor Publisher Services
30 Amberwood Parkway
Ashland, Ohio 44805
516-593-1234
orders@gefenpublishing.com

www.gefenpublishing.com

Printed in Israel
Library of Congress Control Number: 2022917002

Contents

North Africa and the Middle East

Preface
We All Stood at Mount Sinai
Ya'acov Fried

I reached Tushita Meditation Centre, located in northern India between the slopes of the Himalayas, as a young backpacker in my late twenties. Dharamsala and the villages surrounding it – Bhagsu, Dharamkot, and McLeod – are home to the exiled Tibetan community led by the Dalai Lama.

I can't articulate why I felt such a strong pull to visit the region; it was as if an inner force magically lured me. A full week of practicing Buddhist meditation in steely discipline while sitting opposite a wall exposed me to inner worlds that I had never known existed. During the meditations, my mind raced with thoughts that slowly dissipated, to the point that even the mosquitoes around me could not disturb my tranquility.

At the end of the retreat, I returned to Dharamsala to visit the monastery where the Dalai Lama resides and the museum adjacent to it. The museum tells the painful story of the Tibetan community in exile, who were persecuted by the Chinese authorities and found a safe haven in northern India.

During the tour, I chatted with friends as we deliberated which restaurant to go to that Friday night. In the end, we decided to visit the Bayit Hayehudi (Jewish home) at the bottom of the village alleys. The Jewish home was founded specifically for backpackers in the Far East and in South America with the purpose of opening the hearts of the Jewish young adults who visit it and connecting them to Jewish sources and culture. "We do this through positive experiences, love, and happiness," said the woman who welcomed us at the entrance with a broad smile. We joined the Shabbat dinner meal and feasted on traditional Jewish foods, recited the Kiddush over wine, and topped it all off with joyous, soulful singing of traditional Jewish and modern Israeli songs.

After the meal, we went up to the roof and settled ourselves in hammocks and comfortable pillows. Our lively and impassioned conversation took the following turn: What had we discovered about ourselves in India? What was the significance of our existence as Jews? What was our spiritual destiny? Which songs had felt especially meaningful to each of us during the trip? Most of all, what did we all have in common – this group of young Jews on the rooftop of the Jewish home on a Friday night on a forlorn hilltop of the Himalaya Mountains?

Late at night, I walked to the guest house where I was staying, and I will never forget the thought that firmly planted itself in my mind that Shabbat night: Home is not a place. Home is a feeling. A Jewish home is first and foremost an emotional sensation of togetherness and belonging to an extended family.

Throughout history, until today, the basis upon which Jewish identity is founded all over the world is the same. Jewish identity draws upon religious, national, and cultural characteristics. Inside every Jew, wherever a person may be in the world, there is a feeling of Jewish experience that connects both to the past and the present. It is a feeling of belonging to a broad global family that extends beyond one's physical place of residence. Yet every Jewish community has dealt with challenges related to its Jewish identity, as impacted by the external circumstances of history, politics, religion, and society. As a result, each community develops its own unique character. But despite the stark differences between the communities, there was and still is a broad common Jewish foundation.

For many years, I have been curiously studying, discovering, researching, and participating in the worldwide Jewish space. I've witnessed the magic that occurs when Jewish communities meet with each other, whether outside or inside of Israel. I have visited numerous communities, including some that were very distant, geographically and culturally. In almost every place, the Jewish element rose to the surface. I tried to discover and understand the situation of the communities and their needs with a sense of empathy, respect, partnership, and recognition that Jewish existence is like an enigma that we must decipher, understand, and perpetuate. I always came to these places wearing my "Jewish glasses," in search of the Jewish perspective.

The majority of the journeys that the writers and I focus on in this book are a result of my exposure to the Jewish journeys developed by Da'at Educational Expeditions. The mission of the company, which I founded and was blessed to have led for over thirty years, was to create inspirational Jewish journeys around the world for the North American Jewish community.

However, on a journey, it is difficult to absorb the wealth of Jewish culture that exists around the world. It is just too overwhelming to grasp the tremendous impact Jewish culture has on the world. In this book, all of the contributors delve deeply into communities with which they are intimately familiar. By accompanying them, the reader can visit various destinations around the world while wearing "Jewish glasses."

The Beating Heart is not a travel guide, nor a book about Jewish history, Jewish community institutions, Jewish sites, or kosher restaurants. It is a book that is intended to pique your curiosity to take a Jewish cultural journey, as a family member peering into your own family home. My hope is that the reading experience will echo the historical and creative expanses that have shaped and continue to shape our lives, here and now. We bring you, the reader, the lives and struggles characteristic of individual and communal Jewish existence in the modern world. Essentially, we are attempting to build a bridge between the American Jewish population and Jewish communities around the globe, and to be the connecting link that will help preserve the Jewish continuum.

For each chapter of the book, we selected a central local personality from near or distant history, or a modern personality. We chose to focus on these personalities because they enabled us to shine a light on a unique phenomenon or process. In many cases, the local personality illuminates distinctive elements or trends that go beyond the scope of the local community. The local personality – the insider – is the vessel through which you can explore a reality that is often concealed and distant from the naked eye.

Reading the book – whether you are in Detroit, Michigan, New Jersey, or San Francisco – will allow you to connect to your Jewish home inside your heart. If you decide to travel to one of these Jewish communities, we hope that reading *The Beating Heart* before your journey will allow you to experience, feel, learn, and enjoy the layers beneath the surface of a typical trip.

The contributors offer thoughts, approaches, and angles developed over many years of work on the ground. Their fresh, unconventional attitudes are the product of thousands of tours in both classic destinations and creative ones; of encounters with community leaders, opinion shapers, and community members; as well as of historical study and research.

All of the authors share the strong desire, as educators, that curiosity will be your inner guide as a tourist. My wish for you is that this book will serve as a map, allowing your curiosity to serve as a compass that will lead you to your Jewish home.

Central Europe

Czech Republic

1. Jewish Alchemy – Prague, Czech Republic
Local Personality: Rabbi David Maxa
Ya'acov Fried

On any trip, to any city in the world, I visit the historical Jewish quarter and the area where the Jewish community lives today. In Prague, the historical Jewish quarter contains major parts of Prague's royal city center. There is a strong sense of dissonance between the opulent past of the Jewish community that once lived in Prague and its bleak reality today. Once, Prague was home to a flourishing, successful Jewish community of about 150,000 Jews, of whom only a few thousand remain.

My special relationship with the city began during my first trip in the winter of 1990. It was my last night in Prague. On a break during a concert held in the elaborate Rudolfinum hall, home of the local philharmonic orchestra, I went down to the lobby to drink a glass of champagne and nibble on caviar canapes, in keeping with the finest Russian culture. Just a year earlier, the Velvet Revolution had taken place here in Czechoslovakia, ending without bloodshed and heralding the end of Communist control and liberation from the oppressive Russian stranglehold. It was the beginning of an age of democracy, finally giving Western tourists the opportunity to discover the mysteries of this enchanted city.

During the first part of the concert, I listened to the cheerful piece *Slavonic Dances* by Czech composer Antonin Dvorak, played four hands

3

at the piano in a moving rendition. I eagerly awaited the second part of the concert to listen to the symphony *From the New World*, composed after Dvorak moved to the United States, and to discover the changes that this move had made on the style of his compositions.

While listening to the symphony, I envisioned images from my various trips to the city. From the very beginning, when I visited Prague Castle, which soars above the city with its golden turrets, I realized why Prague is considered one of the most beautiful cities in the world. I later visited St. Vitus Cathedral, built in the fourteenth century and embellished with gold and deep blue stained-glass windows, and I climbed to the top of its bell tower, from which I took in a panoramic view of the city in all its glory.

Prague, as beautiful as Paris in its eclectic architectural style, is similar to Budapest with the river running through it. It also reminds me of Jerusalem; its golden rooftops are similar to those of the Dome of the Rock and the Church of Mary Magdalene.

From there, I continued to the ornate Charles Bridge. As I crossed it, I gazed down at the waters of the Vltava River underneath it and at the arches and baroque statues. Once I reached the other side, I turned toward the main square of the old city, where I encountered the beating heart of Prague, with its collection of architectural styles. The tower of the old municipality building featured a humongous clock that was installed on the tower in 1410. I patiently waited to see the magic of this mechanical astronomical clock, which chimes on the hour, accompanied by moving figures.

The Jewish quarter of Prague piqued my curiosity due to its historical traditions and its structures, which remained intact during World War II. A feeling of sorrow washed over me as I walked through the alleyways of the quarter, thinking of the Jewish world that once was and had disappeared. In the Old-New Synagogue (the Altneuschul), built in 1270 and attended today by a handful of Jews, I obviously searched for the Golem of Prague, still buried in its attic, according to legend. Next to this synagogue, I discovered the four additional syna-gogues in the city, as well as the old Jewish cemetery, Josefov, which was used for hundreds of years and in which thousands of Jews are buried in twelve layers, one on top of the other.

Although this is a Jewish quarter that was fully preserved, I felt as if I were visiting a Jewish museum void of all modern-day Jewish life. This feeling was exacerbated by the contrasting vibrant liveliness in the city surrounding it, the extensive infrastructure work, the restorations of the ancient buildings, the cultural life, and the abundance of new restaurants that had opened. I walked toward the Jewish community building. The clock affixed to it was built in 1586 in Renaissance style, and the hours were marked with Hebrew letters. As if that weren't strange enough in the local environment, I discovered that the clock's hands were moving counterclockwise, as if to say: *Here in Prague, in the Jewish community, time is not progressing, but rather moving backwards.*

Following the concert, I decided to celebrate the end of my first visit to Prague with a beer at the historic tavern U Fleku, which has been open continuously since the fifteenth century. While I drank, with folk music playing in the background, I wondered about the rea-sons I had fallen in love with the city. I think the core of it was that I felt Prague had a secret to tell. What was that secret? I didn't know, and thus I returned excited and curious from my first visit with the feeling that I hadn't solved the enigma of the city's soul and that I had to delve deeper.

The German poet Goethe said that "Prague is the prettiest gem in the stone crown of the world." This sentence reverberated in my mind and reminded me how much my heart had been enchanted by the city's magic. This magic brought me back to the city several times and even led to my establishment of an office for educational tour-ism there, which was the headquarters for our operations in Eastern Europe.

My subsequent visits to the city conjured up in my mind the words "Prague of gold." I heard the expression on my first visit to Prague Castle, situated on a high hilltop above the city. From this vantage point, overlooking the golden-edged rooftops, I noticed that the Vltava River cuts through the city in something of a question-mark formation, an apt shape for this enigmatic city. What makes Prague the city of gold? A bit of gold at the edges of the rooftops? The golden entrance to the castle? I heard many explanations, but when I visited the mysterious world of the Golden Lane, or the Street of Alchemists, I discovered that there is not a bit of gold on this street. Indeed, this street provides a better explanation of the city's nickname.

Prague's Golden Lane developed during the reign of Emperor Rudolf II in the sixteenth century, which is considered one of Prague's most interesting and captivating periods. Rudolf II dabbled in occult sciences, astrology, astronomy, divination, and especially alchemy. He was interested in the economic aspect of creating gold from cheaper metals, as well as the mystical aspect of alchemy. He considered the process of producing gold a spiritual process, a process of inner human development, to the extent that gold was created on a symbolic level.

I was extremely interested in mystical alchemy, which deals with the attempt to create something from nothing or to initiate metamorphism. During the Holy Roman Emperor's era, from 1576 to 1612, he encouraged the study of occult sciences, astrology, astronomy, divination, and especially alchemy. During his reign, many scientists were involved in the practical side of alchemy as well as the spiritual elements. Did the fact that spiritual alchemy was practiced in Prague influence the overall Czech national character, and particularly the character of Czech Jews?

During every visit to Prague, I dived into the magnificent Jewish past of the city, the Jewish community that has since disappeared. Over the years, I had come across many different local rabbis and leaders in Prague but had always felt something was missing. As soon as

I spoke to Rabbi David Maxa, a young, dynamic, and charismatic Jew who was appointed as the Reform rabbi of the Etz Hachaim community, I knew I had found what I was missing in the other rabbis and leaders. Authenticity. As soon as I started to talk to Rabbi Maxa, I could hear the genuineness in his voice. "Whether you're a tourist or you were born here," he explained to me, "the city captures you with its magic. If you're a tourist, you'll probably come back to visit again. If you were born here, you'll probably continue to live here."

"I was born in Prague in 1990," he shared, "immediately after the end of Communist control. Judaism was perceived as a negative stigma among Czech Jews, and its very mention was accompanied by deafening silence. The silence existed among Jewish families and was even expressed in the relationships between Jews and non-Jews. The Jews felt the need to escape from the stigma weighing them down, and soon after World War II was over, they left Czechoslovakia in waves. Many of those who remained hid their Jewish identities. For me, as a son of Holocaust survivors, the frightening silence that shadowed our Jewish identities at home and outside was often interrupted by short memories that my parents shared, by leafing through the few faded photographs from the past, by wandering through the local Jewish cemetery, and by a random visit to Pinkas Synagogue, which became a museum commemorating the names of eighty thousand local Jews who perished in the Holocaust.

"I grew up with the feeling that I needed to run away from the shame of being Jewish. My father hid from the Nazis during World War II, and when he was liberated, the Communist regime led him to once again conceal his Judaism. He was a famous opera singer but was prevented from performing, due to his Jewish identity. His stories of anti-Semitism during those years, expressed in newspapers filled with hatred, jokes about circumcision, statements about the Jewish attitude toward women and about allegedly contemptible Jewish practices seeped into my consciousness. In retrospect, Communism seemed to me like the forty-year journey of the Children of Israel through the desert – they only became free people when it was over. Communism sought to eradicate our religious, national, and cultural affiliation, and so as a boy and a teenager, I was not exposed to the richness of Jewish culture.

"After my father's death, I decided to research the Jewish life that had existed in Prague prior to the Holocaust and during the Communist regime. When a friend took me to a Seder night event at the Jewish community building, it was my first time experiencing a 'living' Judaism. Over a long process, I realized a few things: first, I had to break the silence, for myself and for others, that leads to the feeling that Judaism is a 'dead' religion, and to make my religion a source of pride. Second, the tiny Orthodox community that exists in Prague is not appropriate for the spirit of the times. Judaism, in my opinion, is a celebration of joy. It is a framework for belonging to a family and to a community. It is like a spark of gold.

"In my community, we bring back the meaningful prayers according to the Jewish calendar. The Jewish calendar, which is based on the cycle of nature throughout the year and on Jewish history and culture, helps us live in the present. We celebrate the Jewish holidays, we learn the Jewish traditions, integrating Jewish music from various sources, and in this way, we create a community and new customs. We have developed a sense of shared fate and mutual responsibility through conversations, events, joint learning, and celebrations. We even brought back and upgraded the traditional Jewish foods of Eastern and Central Europe at our Friday night meals. We are creating a living Judaism and trying to engender a feeling that a Jew is a worthy person. Jewish holidays inspire our discussions and value-based experiences. We celebrate Purim by focusing on the subject of Jewish survival. We celebrate Passover by clarifying the values of freedom. We celebrate Rosh Hashanah by emphasizing the opportunity for personal introspection. We arouse the motivation for self-searching and Jewish life, corresponding to our distant Jewish memories.

"In the past, Jewish culture was at the center of Czech culture," the rabbi adds. "My grandfather's generation lived in a state of congruence between their Jewish and Czech identities. The synagogue was a musical center, and the community members went to the synagogue to enjoy a Jewish concert. Composers such as Lewandowski and Rubin created music in the general music world and in the Jewish world. Playing on the organ in the synagogue, brought directly from the world of Czech culture, was Frantisek Skroup, who even wrote the Czech national anthem. Our identity is also shaped by music today, through intensive study and involving the young children. Learning the values of the Jewish religion is very important. But a living, vibrant Judaism that we talk about and that we aren't ashamed of, which we share with our environment, is the key to breaking that negative stigma of the past. I try to give Jews the feeling that we are normal. We are not a minority, despite our numbers. We are part of a global Jewish family. When people come to us today, they share that their grandparents were Jewish and that they don't know what to do about that fact. So we invite them to join a vibrant Jewish community that is relevant to them. We created new practices of progressive Judaism that are suitable for the time and place, which are used by this generation and will also allow future generations to feel that they are part of the family."

Rabbi Maxa continues, "After the Holocaust, the number of Jews in Prague dropped drastically. The synagogues stood empty, and the Torah scrolls were given away to different communities around the world. As a teenager, I visited the United States to attend a Jewish summer camp, where I touched a Torah scroll for the first time. The summer camp closed down about five years ago, and the scroll, which had originally come from Czechoslovakia, was returned to my community. During the summer, we hold our Friday night prayer services on the hilltop next to the castle, with the golden city of Prague spread before our eyes. We gather outside opposite the golden sparks of the city. Praying outside is a statement we want to make to the non-Jewish world: 'We exist.'

"Judaism needs to come out into the open, under the skies. Praying outside opposite the sky, as it kisses the earth, represents the feeling that the spiritual and the earthly are becoming one. We create a sense of peace within ourselves, between our internal soul and the outside world. When I look at our study groups learning about Jewish culture, at our family events, at the friendships that have been forged, at the spirit that we have created at our celebrations of the Jewish holidays, at the shining faces of the young families, I feel that we are on the right path to creating a live, vibrant Judaism that is, most importantly, free of negative stigmas."

The story of the establishment of the Etz Hachaim community led by Rabbi David Maxa introduces me for the first time to a Prague where a local Jewish leader is not flying on autopilot. My encounters with him bring me back to my thoughts about the world of alchemy in general, in the context of Prague specifically. The purpose of alchemy on a practical level was, of course, to create gold out of cheap metals. On a spiritual level, the purpose of alchemy was to cultivate a spiritual-metaphysical development that would lead to wholeness and inner balance.

Psychologist Carl Jung, who was the first to study and understand the psychological significance of alchemy, said, "I am not what happened to me. I am what I choose to be." The alchemists viewed themselves as the "redeemers" of simple material in the process of turning it into gold. I am reminded of them when I think of Rabbi Maxa's educational approach. This is the first time I have met a local Jewish leader who is not engrossed in nostalgic stories or trying to force a reality of Israeli Jewish culture or American Jewish culture onto the members of the community. Rather, his goal is to "redeem" and refine the components of Czech culture and of Jewish traditions, to create an authentic local Jewish culture. This is also the first time I have met a Jewish leader who is not busy lamenting the bitter fate of the historical community, but instead demonstrating a sense of personal responsibility and spreading a message about the ability to change one's circumstances and oneself with the inner strengths used to realize what a person "chooses to be," in the words of Jung.

The more I become familiar with Rabbi Maxa's authentic approach to guiding the Jewish community, the more impressed I am. I connect to the sense of local pride and authenticity that he has nurtured and the desire to be relevant in today's world. I think that perhaps the time has come for the alchemy of Prague to finally produce gold.

Hungary

2. Children Teaching Parents – Camp Szarvas, Hungary
Local Personality: Zsuzsa Fritz
Ya'acov Fried

Summer 2019. The evening was warm, and a pleasant breeze caressed my face and the faces of my friends. We walked from our hotel on the banks of the Danube toward the entertainment complex at Gozsdu Court, sprawled across seven huge buildings in the heart of Budapest. On either side of the street, there were pubs, cafés, bars, and restaurants. Music in a range of styles echoed in all directions. Some of it was from live performances. Earlier, when I had asked the concierge at the hotel where we should go to experience the beating heart of Budapest at night, we were recommended a bar called Vicky Barcelona. We found the spot during our nighttime stroll of the complex. Sitting on the high barstools, we ordered wine and listened to a Big Band ensemble, which played a few instruments that I had never seen before. Suddenly, I grabbed my head with both hands and exclaimed to my friends, "I visited this spot almost thirty years ago, on my first visit to Budapest. We're in the heart of the old Jewish quarter!"

We couldn't hear each other over the intense volume of the music, so we decided to continue the evening somewhere else. We entered a club called Bar 360, located on the roof of one of the tall buildings on the boulevard opposite Vicky Barcelona. The regal landscape of the city was spread out before our eyes. We were taken aback by the Buda Hill, the Citadella, the old parliament building, and the boats sailing down the Danube River, which crosses the two parts of the city – Buda and Pest.

"You know," I said to my friends enthusiastically, "in November 1990, I visited Budapest for the first time. In this area of the city, where the music and cultural scene is one of the best in Europe, the Jewish quarter once stood. On that cold winter night, bundled up from head to toe, I took a nighttime tour of Budapest with my friend Yuri Stern. We saw a desolate city, ornate buildings that were falling apart with concrete monster buildings alongside them, a testament of 'glorious' Communist architecture and the regime that had just left Hungary and Eastern Europe a few months prior to our visit."

Two weeks before that first visit to Budapest, I had received a phone call from Barry Shrage, director of the Jewish Federation of Boston. I learned to appreciate and love Barry over the years because he challenged me with his unconventional worldview and his educational approach. Barry told me, "I would like your help in organizing a visit to Budapest for a select group from Boston. Could your company organize a jumbo plane for a private flight from Budapest to Tel Aviv? The Jewish Agency won't do it for us." He explained, "As you are aware, the Soviet Union is in the process of falling apart. Russia has opened its gates and is allowing Jews to leave freely. But it won't permit direct flights from Moscow to Tel Aviv. Thousands of Jews are making their way from all over the Former Soviet Union by car, bus, and any other means of transportation, to Budapest. There, they are being taken care of by the Jewish Agency, who are putting them on planes to Israel."

Barry continued, "We are about to witness a new world. The entire map of the Jewish diaspora is going to change, and this process will have a decisive impact both on Israel and on the Jewish communities in North America. I would like your help in organizing this visit to Budapest, which will enable us to familiarize ourselves with the local Jewish community – which has also just started to free itself from the shackles of Communism – so that we can see how they have chosen to rebuild their community. We will also arrange opportunities for an unmediated encounter with the Russian Jews on their way to Israel, to support them emotionally during this brave step in their lives and physically fly with them to Israel."

I said to Barry, "You are giving me a chance to take part in one of the most important and meaningful projects of my life." Before putting down the receiver, I promised him that within a few days, the project would start to come together. I recommended that my dear friend Yuri Stern accompany the group. He had immigrated from Russia to Israel fifteen years earlier, had spent time with Prisoners of Zion Anatoly Shcharansky (now Natan Sharansky) and Ida Nudel prior to his immigration, and was one of the leaders of the struggle for free Jewish existence in the Soviet Union and for free immigration to Israel. Yuri could talk to the members of the group from Boston about the complexities of the immigration process, the responsibility of Jewish leadership, and about the huge challenge at hand – all while simultaneously supporting his old friends from Moscow on their journey to Israel.

Two weeks after that phone call, we joined the members of the group from Boston in Budapest. For two days, we toured Budapest and discovered why it is considered one of the most beautiful cities in Europe. In a few places, some of the members of the group remarked that they could feel the special charm and romance of good old Central Europe. Strolling through the streets, I was beginning to imagine that a carriage might suddenly appear, and two princes would get out for a walk down the banks of the Danube. When I mentioned this to the group's guide, he replied that Budapest was indeed a romantic city and that there were more poets than places to eat goulash. We of course discussed the fact that Budapest was Herzl's birthplace, and quite a few conversations revolved around the Holocaust, during which over half of this community, which dated back to the eleventh century, was wiped out. During our visit, we participated in a few moving encounters with the local community, who shared the feeling of free-dom and Jewish awakening that they had just started to feel in recent months after the long period of Communist control had ended, as well as the new challenges that were developing.

On the evening of the third day, we traveled to Keleti pályaud-var (Eastern Railway Station), which is located in a historic building. Hundreds of Jews from all over the Soviet Union had arrived here. Throughout the station, we met the immigrants, standing next to their belongings packed into torn suitcases and sacks tied with rope. Their faces expressed worry as they constantly attempted to calm their frightened children. I never saw so many Siberian Huskies in my life. I later learned that the dogs would be sold once in Israel as a way of transferring money. My dear friend Yuri started to talk to them and translate their life stories for us and what they hoped to find in Israel. Their concerns about dealing with the new climate and language came up in every conversation. I remember a comment, which I will never forget, from Sasha, a train engineer from Moscow: "I am running away from Russia and going to the Jewish state. My mother is Jewish. But I don't know a thing about Judaism. Communism wiped out all of the memories and did not allow Hebrew culture to develop. I am not sure that a Jewish state is the right thing for me." Yuri, who was standing next to me, responded to him, "The group and I are just finishing up touring Budapest for a few days, which also just parted ways with the Communist regime. They too are grappling with questions of identity. Only time will tell us the answers to these questions."

Just a day earlier, we had met with Zsuzsa Fritz, who was intro-duced to us as a representative of the Joint Distribution Committee in Budapest and director of the educational center. She was in her mid-twenties, dynamic, cheerful, and a born leader. "I was born in Budapest in 1966 in a neighborhood next to the parliament building," she shared. "In proper Communist tradition, we lived in an apartment shared by my grandfather, grandmother, and parents. I remember a small room without any windows facing the street. I was the only daughter to an older father, who was a taxi driver, and a younger mother, who worked as an engineer. I had a regular childhood with trips and a public school education. In 1981, when I was fifteen, my father passed away. Suddenly, I found myself at his funeral at the Dohány Street Synagogue, affiliated with Neolog Judaism. It was there that I discovered that I was Jewish. In retrospect, there were a few earlier signs that I was Jewish, but I hadn't paid any attention to them. Judaism wasn't present in our family, not even with a mezuzah [a piece of parchment called a *klaf* contained in a decorative case and inscribed with specific Hebrew verses from the Torah] on the door-post. I only remembered that in Yiddish, there was an expression '*fin unzere,*' which means 'one of us,' and my parents sometimes used it when we had guests at home."

"During the shivah (week of mourning), each of us hid in our rooms with our own personal trauma. On one of the days, a Christian woman came to visit and told us about how she saved my mother and her family during the Holocaust, hiding them in a Carmelite monastery for a few years. Even the intense pain that my mother experienced during the Holocaust did not result in dialogue or shared emotions. As per Hungarian tradition and culture, all pain was kept inside."

During those years, under Janos Kadar, Hungary was under a softer Communist government than the Soviet Union. This permitted, for example, the opening of a limited number of private stores, and even limited religious identification.

"My father's death," Zsuzsa continued, "was a turning point in my life as a Jew. A few months after his passing, my mother told me about youth activities held in the rabbinical seminary building. I started participating in the social activities with a small group. I didn't know what Kiddush or prayers were. My first Jewish experience was drinking hot chocolate in the seminary building with Jewish friends. A few years later, while with friends at Café Donna in Budapest, I met Jews of Hungarian descent for the first time; they had immigrated to Israel and were given permission to visit family in Budapest. In the mid-eighties, the feeling began to spread that Communism was crumbling. The scent of freedom was in the air. Years later, I realized that during this period, there were Jews among us who reported our allegedly 'Zionist' activities to the Communist authorities. That year, I participated in my first Passover Seder with friends. Immediately after the Seder, we were summoned to the Interior Ministry for interrogations about our forbidden Jewish activity. This was the first time that I understood that the Communist regime attempted to erase any hint of Jewish, religious, and of course nationalistic identity.

"In 1988, I started studying English at the public high school. The social group that I associated with was Jewish. I remember the feeling of being part of a small group within a broader family. Everything I did during that period was part of my search for identity. I remember long days of discussions – would my friends have circumcisions? What could we do to feel more Jewish?

"In 1989, I was recruited as a counselor on the first trip of local high school students to Israel. We spent a few weeks on Kibbutz Kfar Szold, and two things stand out in my mind: I fell in love with the Galilee, and I was exhilarated by learning Hebrew. The landscapes of the Sea of Galilee are etched deep in my heart. During my first visit to the Western Wall, all I could think of was that my father would have been happy to be there with me. When I returned to Budapest, I started volunteering in the Jewish community. I met *shlichim*, representatives of the Jewish Agency and of the Joint, and they were all involved in building this community from nothing."

Zsuzsa concluded by saying, "We are responsible for building the community. Our reality is that parents can't teach their children a thing about Jewish heritage and culture. We decided to be the pioneers and involve ourselves in building the Jewish community in Budapest. Tomorrow, you will meet Russian Jews on their way to

Israel. Remember that both they and we have no Jewish background. Communism did not allow us to learn and experience Judaism. Not culturally, religiously, or nationalistically."

I kept in touch with Zsuzsa over the years and met her many times during several subsequent visits to Budapest. Zsuzsa became one of the leaders of the summer camp in Szarvas, which was established in the format of an American summer camp and is dedicated to bringing Jewish children from all over the former Communist bloc to have a meaningful Jewish experience.

In 1994, I visited Camp Szarvas for the first time. It is about a three-hour drive from Budapest. There, I met Zsuzsa again, and she explained to me, "We need to build a new tradition, teaching children about Jewish heritage and tradition through the camp. We need to create a reality in which children will teach their parents. Our camp is meant to make the campers' Judaism accepting and open to everyone. We help campers find their Jewish identity and encourage them to create a sense of community. At first, we brought some of the finest teachers and counselors from Israel and the United States to teach us how to experience Judaism, so that campers could take their first steps on the Jewish path. Our mission is to create a community that cultivates and strengthens personal development. We believe in educating with a pleasant, encouraging, and diverse attitude. We created a method that allows people without any background to explore and strengthen their identities, by presenting many different possibilities of cultural, religious, traditional, and community styles through which they can identify as Jews.

"You need to understand," Zsuzsa added, "that teaching children who come from homes where their parents were part of the Communist system for decades to talk about emotions, to share and explore as a group, is very challenging, to put it mildly. Through adventures and activities involving sports, art, culture, ceremonies, and social life, our campers experience what it feels like to be part of a group, and simultaneously get to know themselves better, open up to others, and learn what it means to have mutual respect. Our programs are based on openness to Jewish traditions and values, which are interactively taught through discussions, debates, conversations, art, games, and most of all, the principle of freedom of choice.

"These children's parents are not proficient in Jewish culture or tradition and are not accustomed to this type of thinking or education. For this reason, we created a paradigm – 'children teaching parents.' The leaders of the camp today were once seven-year-old campers, who acquired more and more skills. Today, they are the leaders of the Hungarian Jewish community and other communities in Central and Eastern Europe."

When the camp opened, the campers were from Hungary and Ukraine. The educational aspect was provided by people from the Jewish Agency and by the *shlichim*. The local camp leaders had no Jewish background or knowledge that they could utilize in managing or leading the camp. Zsuzsa and other camp leaders acquired the educational and Jewish education necessary to run the camp. Together with Zsuzsa, there were and still are unique personalities such as Itzko, the legendary camp director from Israel; Sasha, the camp director for the past fifteen years who immigrated from Ukraine to Hungary; and Mina from Serbia. They have all become role models, and thanks to them, the camp has become professional and modern. They understood their responsibility to build a laboratory for education and leadership, and that they were being entrusted with children who would later return to their original communities with a strong desire to be part of the Jewish community. Today, there are campers from Central and Eastern Europe, Israel, the United States, Turkey, and Germany, and it has become a unique example of how to build young leadership and impact communities.

During my most recent encounter with Zsuzsa, about a year ago, I visited her at the Jewish community center, which she is involved in managing today. We recalled our first meeting in Budapest about thirty years earlier and spoke about the fact that in the United States, Judaism is sometimes taken for granted. A person who chooses to continue to live as a Jew in the United States feels that all options are open, without any special effort necessary. In Israel, the Hebrew calendar dictates the Jewish lifestyle, the Hebrew language is the language of the Jewish nation, nationalism is intertwined with Jewish culture, and of course, Jews in the country live a sovereign Jewish life as a Jewish majority.

Zsuzsa replied, "Even after the fall of Communism in Central and Eastern Europe, one still needs to make an effort to be a Jew. Parents do not encourage Judaism. To preserve the communities, the children need to initiate living as Jews. In addition, we don't have a critical mass here of Jews. The memory of the Holocaust alone is not sufficient to preserve Judaism here. The connection to Israel and Israeli culture isn't enough either. Our summer camps, where hundreds of Jewish children learn, create, sing, and dance together, aren't sufficient either. But each of these elements is one part of the overall feeling that the Jewish nation has a future. My role, as a Jewish educator, is to contribute my part."

Our conversation ended with my reminder of our first meeting, during the trip with the group from Boston and my friend Yuri Stern. I told Zsuzsa that Yuri had become a social and political leader in Israel, and even a member of Knesset, and that issues related to Jewish culture and identity were very close to his heart. "It is possible," I told her, "that in the United States and Israel as well, like in Hungary, no single element is enough to guarantee Jewish continuity. I believe that what you said about the need for an arsenal of components to continue Jewish existence holds true for the United States and for Israel." These components are also expressed in the fact that Camp Szarvas transformed from being a camp for children from a few countries in Central Europe to an international camp where Jewish adolescents meet from all over the world, including from the United States and Israel. "You succeeded in creating a sense of family between the generations of campers. This is a central part of your goal of imbuing that feeling that we are all one international Jewish family."

3. A Family of Orphaned Jews – Budapest
Local Personality: Kata Erdelyi
Gilad Peled

We do not choose our family story; we are born into it, and the story has its own ways of perpetuating itself in our lives. Budapest is full of family stories, even if you didn't eat Gesztenyepüré (chestnut puree with whipped cream) at family get-togethers when you were a child. The stories jump out at you from the street corners, from the bus stops, or on the banks of the beautiful Danube at dusk, sending regards from distant relatives – even those you didn't know existed.

Hungarian, for example: soft, rolling, foreign. When I hear young people speaking Hungarian, I am struck by how wrong it sounds. Growing up, Hungarian was the language of old people sitting in green suede chairs with frayed edges, chandeliers hanging from the ceiling above their heads, a low glass coffee table for refreshments, and old oil paintings on the walls. That was the décor of Grandpa's house, and the soundtrack was warm and completely incomprehensible Hungarian chatter.

Other memories are hidden on the city's ancient streets. During my most recent visit, I heard about a new Jewish site that was now open to the public. A soft rain pattered lightly on the umbrella that I clutched with frozen fingers as I walked around Castle Hill. Moistness seemed to be penetrating everywhere: my forehead, nose, neck, ankles. I walked down the small, winding streets, passing shops with souvenirs from

China, the type that can be found anywhere in the world, with just the name of a different city printed on them. The light and friendly atmosphere at Castle Hill in the summer months was replaced by the introverted grayness of winter. The few tourists around me hurried from store to store to fulfill their familial obligations before fleeing back to their hotels or to the next tourist attraction.

I would not have ascended the hill that day had I not been searching for the entrance to an ancient synagogue that was recently renovated and had started to operate again, 350 years after being destroyed by the Christian coalition that conquered the city from the Turks. During that period, the Jews of Buda settled in the streets surrounding the castle, a reality that seems completely preposterous today. Yet like an old family necklace forgotten at the bottom of a jewelry box, or a beloved children's book that brings back memories of safety and warmth, at the bottom of the street, the modest façade of the synagogue suddenly appeared, hidden between the picturesque neighborhood homes that are attached to one another. My heart pounded as I stepped inside.

On a different day and in a different year, I strolled leisurely alongside the tranquil Danube. For anyone who calls the Jordan a river, the Danube looks like an unsatisfied lake, trying to move itself determinedly and ambitiously from one side of Europe to the other, amidst bridges, forests, and castles. A lazy sun set in the west and the promenade along the length of the river bustled with men and women running in fashionable sports apparel, groups of teenage girls and boys whispering and giggling on the many benches scattered along the promenade, and mothers calmly pushing baby strollers. A cool breeze chilled the heat of the day, which had finally started to dissipate, and gulls flew and squawked above our heads. The pastoral atmosphere was disrupted in just one place, where rows of bronze shoes are affixed to the bank of the Danube – small and large, women's and men's, high-heeled and flat – all telling the story of the Jews who were murdered and whose bodies were tossed into the river during World War II. So out of context at this twilight hour, the shoes unrelentingly cry out to the pedestrians: *Remember!*

Unfortunately, it is not truly possible to share memories. Memories are not words; they are feelings, smells, sounds, and tastes. Shared memories are what create a family. It can be Grandma's Dobos torte, with copious amounts of chocolate, honey, and sugar to frustrate any nutritionist. It can be the memory of music flowing out of Grandpa's room, igniting a longing for a hug mixed with day-old beard stubble, or a memory of persecution and discrimination that creates an unmediated connection with strangers. What is certain, as Kata told me, is that "it is necessary to create memories so that there will be a shared future."

I first met Kata one autumn morning at the entrance to Dohany Street Synagogue, the most prominent Jewish monument in Pest. We didn't know each other until then, and we were searching for very different things: Kata was looking for her future, while I was looking for my past. I was on a family heritage trip, and Kata was our "local family": Fülop (Philip), Kata's great-grandfather, and Zigmond, my great-grandfather, were brothers. Zigmond was murdered at Auschwitz; Fülop passed away before the Holocaust. We didn't know them, but thanks to them, we met each other that morning at the entrance of Dohany Street Synagogue. Such is the power of family memory.

Every tour of Jewish Budapest begins here. The huge Neolog synagogue, the largest synagogue in Europe, is so rich in embellishments and interplaying architectural styles, so tall and so prominent compared with its surroundings, that it seems as if the entire Jewish story revolves around it. But the synagogue, like monuments of magnificent proportions, is just a flamboyant façade for a deeper, more complex story – the family story of a large, ancient community that is constantly searching for its way in an ever-changing world.

There are many communities in the world, and each one of them is a family story in itself. Why talk about family specifically in Budapest? Family is the home we were born into; family is the people who accompany us and the compass that directs us at the crossroads of our lives. Family can give meaning to our actions, a source of closeness and warmth, assistance and security. It is a source of strength. Family can also be a source of heartbreak, pain, strife, and tension. The reason is one and the same: we care about our families. One thing is common to all families: family is for life. Even if you think that you left, even if you changed your name, moved away, and deleted your contacts, family remains with you. Likewise, a family cannot get rid of its children – even if it thought they had forgotten it, even if the children ignore it or choose to focus their gaze elsewhere. They will chisel their way back with fingers and soul, looking for their home, looking for their family. The Jewish community in Budapest underwent 150 years of tossing and turning: from modernism to schism, from the Holocaust to Communism, from democratization to increasing nationalism – but its very existence was never doubted. What preserved this living, vibrant community is a deep sense of family, mutual responsibility, belonging, and a need to create appropriate frameworks for every Jew according to his or her beliefs and outlook. In Budapest, multiplicity is strength, and flexibility is power.

If Judaism is one big family, then Hungary – and Budapest in particular – is the cool aunt. Even at age fifty, she shows up to family occasions with purple highlights in her hair and revels in the shock on the faces of everyone present. She dresses a bit differently, reinvents herself time and time again, driven by curiosity and the originality of a free spirit. She chooses her own path with a self-confidence reserved for older siblings.

While the rural areas of Hungary are where a reaction to modernism gave rise to the most introverted Orthodox Jewish groups, Budapest is the city where innovative experiments in shaping Jewish identity are constantly being performed. It is a city where family and national memories are blended in a rich goulash stew that warms the stomach but burns the mouth. Only here, it was the Orthodox and not the progressives who split away from the lap of the community. This is where Theodor Herzl, architect of the Jewish national movement that eventually founded the State of Israel, grew up, but up until World War I, the community rejected the Zionist idea vehemently. And only here, the prominent Jewish denomination to this day is one that does not exist anywhere else in the world: the Neologs.

Like all the Jewish denominations that were formed in hopes of promoting national-social improvement in modern history – from Chassidism to Zionism – the Neolog movement strove to strengthen the Jewish family by adapting it to the changing reality. The movement was established in the early nineteenth century during a period when the winds of modernism and nationalism were sweeping through Europe, and Jews were offered equal rights. The Neolog movement, which wanted to bring closer those who had accepted this offer and started to drift away from Jewish life, focused primarily on ritual changes (and less on Bible criticism) – such as the design of the synagogue, the language of prayers, and secular studies – in hopes of making the rituals more pleasant. Although there were barely any theological differences between the different groups of Jews in Budapest, the tension between the Neologs (who strived for optimal integration into their surroundings) and the Orthodox (who wanted to protect the old customs) constantly increased. In 1869, the Orthodox Jews established their own community, separate from the Neologs. The schism gave rise to a third group that did not identify with the religious zeal of Orthodoxy but did not agree with the changes implemented by the Neologs either. It was called the "status quo." More than it indicated weakness, the schism testified to the community's strength: a strong family knows how to offer each family member the path that allows him or her to remain part of the family, without forcing uniformity on everyone. Over the years, the community honed its ability to develop a diverse range of frameworks for Jewish belonging, and today, Budapest offers a dizzying selection of organizations and social groups that offer the depth and style of Jewish life that best suits each person's needs.

Our family – Kata's and mine – came from the rural areas to Budapest at the beginning of the twentieth century. The family was very religious, but in the big city, each of the brothers chose his own path: some lived as long-bearded Orthodox Jews who were stringent about religious observance. My great-grandfather, who was an officer in the Hungarian army and one of four Jewish judges in the Hungarian judicial system, attended synagogue every day but wore modern clothing. Kata's great-grandfather left religious life completely, to the extent of eating pork. All of them, without exception, made sure to marry Jewish women; in other words, they didn't leave the family. The Jewish community of Budapest succeeded in giving each of them the Jewish framework that suited him, and thus did not disconnect from any of them, regardless of their Jewish lifestyles.

Next to Dohany Street Synagogue is the seventh district, the center of Jewish life in Pest for the past two hundred years. Quiet streets intersect with each other between old residential homes with inner yards, and the atmosphere is intimate. In recent years, the Jewish district has undergone an accelerated process of renewal, with the opening of new restaurants, upbeat pubs, and the speedy renovation of old homes. Hungarian Jewry, which was suppressed for almost eighty years by an authoritative Hungarian government, the Nazi regime, and then Communism, is peeking out again from every corner, like small flowers pushing their way out between the pavement cracks. The city's Jewish memory is reinventing itself in a multiplicity of expressions and with characteristic flexibility. It is a surprising and creative process in a surprising and creative city. Not only is the physical Jewish home being renewed in Budapest with the opening of new synagogues and the development of social initiatives and community centers, but Jewish life itself, composed of thousands of personal stories of discovery and connection, is redefining and reshaping the concept of the Jewish family in Budapest.

Kata is also part of the renewed Jewish memory of Budapest. Babi, Kata's grandmother, and Eva, my grandmother, were cousins. When they returned from the camps and the ghettos after the Holocaust, my grandmother fought to immigrate to Israel, while Kata's grandmother decided to stay in Hungary. The two grandmothers were in their twenties, and although their social circles were composed primarily of Jews, whom they tended to trust more than the Hungarians, Kata's grandparents made the decision to assimilate into Hungarian society. They lived as atheists and baptized their children in order to protect them from anti-Semitism. It was only when Kata's father came home one day and cheered for the Arab armies during the Yom Kippur War that his father divulged to him that he was in fact a Jew. He was twenty-three years old. "I'm lucky," Kata added when she told me this story, "because I found out that I was Jewish when I was nineteen."

Kata's father married a woman from a Protestant family, who was an atheist like himself. "But," says Kata, "looking back, I realize that my closest friends as a child were all Jewish." Similar to the Neolog denomination, for Kata's atheist family as well, assimilating into Hungarian society never meant giving up the Jewish family. Most of Babi's friends were survivors of the same camp that she had survived, and they made sure to meet up every year. They felt more comfortable among Jewish friends, and even today, Kata says that "Jews receive ten extra points from me for security." Within the family, you don't need to introduce yourself. The same is true of the Jews in Budapest – when they meet, they won't smile and say to each other, "Nice to meet you, I'm a Jew." They feel that they are meeting a family member. To be safe, they might say something like, "My aunt lives in Israel."

When she was nineteen, Kata wanted to travel to a summer camp in the United States, but on the registration form, she was asked, to her surprise, to write her religion. She turned to her father for advice, and he suggested that she write Jewish – "because we are Jewish." At the camp, she met Israeli teenagers and encountered Jewish culture for the first time. "For years, an enticing gift had been sitting in my room, and I never noticed it," she says of that period in her life. "Only once I started to tear off the wrapping paper did I start to become truly interested. From that moment, I wanted to know more and more about what was hiding inside." Kata started to ask questions about her Judaism. She dug for information wherever she could: from family members, Jewish summer camps, Jewish student organizations, religious organizations. "My father told me that Judaism is part of my life and my history – a part of who I am. But I didn't understand. What is this thing that I am a part of?!" She became closer to her grandmother, but it was only before Kata's first trip to Israel that Babi started talking to her about the family. "Until then, the photographs on the dresser were just old items belonging to an old woman," she said. The puzzle pieces started to come together.

During the following years, Kata traveled to Israel at least once a year, sometimes more. She traveled the country, studied Hebrew, met new friends, and spent time with new family members. "It was probably the only time in my life that I could give my parents something that they couldn't obtain themselves," she recalls today, "by showing them that we had more family. Our family is very small, and I always wanted a bigger family. Cousins are like bonus family – they aren't close like siblings, so there's no tension, but they're close enough to be there for you when you need them."

Kata reclaimed her family history and thus rejoined the Jewish family. "There are certain things that you need to understand in order to understand yourself. A family transmits to its children hopes and fears that are rooted in the collective family memory. For children, it's a given – they're born into it – but if they don't understand where it all came from, they will never be able to understand who they are."

Kata says that memories are passed down in the family even when no one speaks about them. Just as Holocaust survivors make sure their shelves are always stocked with food, their children will do so as well.

Kata calls Jews who grew up without knowing that they were Jews "orphaned Jews," because they did not know that they were part of the family. She views her renewed connection with the Jewish family as a miracle that is the result of coincidences, openness, and acceptance. Today, this family is already a part of her, "like being Hungarian," and although she is not actively involved in the Jewish community, she prefers knowing what she's choosing to refrain from over not knowing at all. For the same reason, Kata also chose to live in one of the three areas in Budapest where there is a large concentration of Jews. She chooses the Jewish frameworks that suit her, even if they are not religious ones, and also decides how much she wants to be involved – without disconnecting. The abundance of different programs, their diversity on the spectrum of Jewish existence, and the flexibility of the Jewish community in Budapest allow her to choose how she wants to be part of the family.

In addition to the underlying principles of multiplicity and flexibility of the communal family, there are two more external factors that make Budapest's Jewish community unique and captivating. The first is the huge size of the community. In Poland, whose modern history resembles that of Hungary to an extent, there is also an extensive phenomenon of "orphaned Jews" who keep discovering their connection to the Jewish family, on the personal and national levels. However, while the number of Jews in Poland is only a few thousand, there are tens of thousands of Jews in Budapest alone. The established Jewish communities in Budapest are numerous and diverse; almost every international Jewish organization runs a program in the city. Resources invested in reviving Jewish life are enormous, and correspondingly, the options for connecting to the family are extensive.

The second factor is the fact that Hungary is trapped between the European regions that speak Latin, Germanic, and Slavic languages. Hungarians speaks a language from a different family and view themselves as belonging to a separate ethnic group – the Magyars (in Hungarian, *magyarok*). This gives them the character of a cultural island isolated from its surroundings. As part of a cultural enclave with its own unique lifestyle, Hungarians tend to keep to themselves and enjoy their own rich culture. Hungarian Jews feel very connected to Hungarian culture, and most of the young people who connect to Judaism do not do so through religion, but rather through social or family ties. In a family, you do not need to prove that you belong; it is enough to feel that you are part of it, or in Kata's words, "The Jewish community is like a social club. You go there for companionship…the meaning of being a Jew is not to express your Judaism, but to feel Jewish." This is one of the reasons Jews in Budapest are concentrated in areas where other Jews tend to live. In those districts, Jewish identity is a sense of familiarity that is not necessarily based on Jewish institutions or religious observance. The neighborhood is the Jewish family of its residents: they meet at the park, at cultural events, at the bus stop, and at the kosher shop selling Elite chocolate and Bamba snacks. They know that most of the people around them in the neighborhood are probably also Jews, and the sense of partnership and common identity connects them to Judaism.

The large number of Jews in Budapest – and their identification with the cultural Hungarian island on which they live – creates unique social phenomena. In recent years, one of the most interesting of these is a social hub called Auróra, which expands the definition of family and includes additional, surprising circles. Marom, the organization that operates Auróra, is a Jewish young adults' organization dedicated to bringing young people closer to the Jewish world through relaxed social encounters and *tikkun olam*.

Auróra meets both needs. In an old building renovated in the neglected eighth district of Budapest, there is a pub, various cultural events, and live performances by local artists in the evenings. During the day, the building hosts a range of social organizations that represent minorities, human rights groups, and LGTBQ organizations. Though there are Jewish cultural events at the site, it does not limit itself to the Jewish circle alone, opening its gates to any person or organization promoting *tikkun olam* and a struggle for justice in the city and in the country. The focus on *tikkun olam* in Marom's vision means that from their place in the Jewish family, they are able to look outward at the world around them. This is a worldview that is in contrast with most of the established Jewish organizations in Hungary, which focus on strengthening Jewish life, which means "keeping it in the family." At Auróra, the ideals are synthesized: the coalitions forged with non-Jewish organizations that share similar worldviews – the need to protect the rights of minority groups as an important element of community life – are what strengthen the sense of belonging to Judaism. Lending a hand to your neighbor is, if you will, what strengthens the sense of belonging to the family, in the shared home where the Jews of Hungary live. For the members of Auróra, the day-to-day tasks common to Jews and non-Jews in order to build a more just society reflect the realization of the values upon which their Judaism is based, making it relevant, alive, and more meaningful than ever. On the other hand, in the political reality of Hungary today, this type of activism is not welcomed warmly. The authorities are constantly threatening to close Auróra's operations, not because of the Jewish content, but because of the civil-social nature of its activities. In certain places, there is a price to opening up the family.

In the Torah, we are called the Children of Israel, a name that encapsulates the way that Jews perceive themselves as family to this day. It is no coincidence that the word *familiarity* comes from the word *family*. Within a family, we enjoy a sense of intimacy and informal atmosphere.

The informal manner in which many of Budapest's Jews relate to the Jewish family – as a connection that is organic, social, and based on friendships rather than religious ceremonies – is clear evidence of the community's strength. The phenomenon of the "orphaned Jews" is exceptionally widespread and intense in Budapest, but the fact is that neither these people nor the community have given up on each other. Although it seems like an act of choice, both sides understand that this is not the case. You are born into your family without choosing it, even if many years pass before you become aware of its existence. The question with which Jews grapple all over the world – what connects us as a group? what makes us a people? – has a simple answer in Budapest. We are family. In Budapest, the answer to the question of what preserves the family is a multiplicity of options and social flexibility.

Poland

4. A Celebration of Jewish Melodies – Krakow
Local Personality: Janusz Makosz
Ya'acov Fried

I visited Poland for the first time in the summer of 1990. I had been on a business trip in the United States, and while watching television one night, I discovered that a government had been established in Poland under the leadership of the Solidarity movement. This was part of an accelerated process of transition to a democratic government and increased freedom. I immediately decided to change my return ticket to Israel so that I could visit Poland for the first time.

I boarded the Pan Am aircraft and landed in Warsaw about three days before Yom Kippur, hoping to meet with local tourism professionals and organize future trips to Poland. I also planned on visiting Bialystok (my family's city of origin), observing Yom Kippur in Krakow, and visiting the nearby death camp, Auschwitz.

It was my first encounter with the collapsing Communist world. I walked down Poland's gray, dark streets. The stores were barely stocked, and the minimarkets displayed a few half-rotten potatoes and onions. Money changers stood on the street corners, trying to convert local currency into dollars, which could be obtained from the few tourists in the city.

On the second day of my visit, in the Jewish cemetery in Warsaw, a young man approached me wearing clean but old clothing that had seen better days. He introduced himself to me in broken English as a

Jew named Olek who organizes tours for the Jewish public who had started visiting Poland over the past few months. I quickly hired him for the next few days, and he took me in a broken-down, rusty car on a six-hour drive toward Krakow. We went straight to Kazimierz, which was a vibrant Jewish district prior to the Holocaust. I walked between the houses of the quarter, the elaborate but dilapidated synagogues, and the tombstones in the Rema Jewish Cemetery. Neglect was rampant. There were broken streets, crumbling sidewalks, streetlights that no longer shined, and most of all, the stench of overflowing garbage filled the air.

Exiting the cemetery, I met a few people who introduced themselves, with the assistance of Olek's translations, as Jews. They invited me to participate in the Kol Nidrei prayer at the adjacent synagogue. We prayed together, a small group of eight worshippers. I learned from them that they knew they were Jews all their lives, but had no knowledge of the Jewish culture, tradition, or religion. They shared stories about their grandparents, fathers, or mothers who had identified themselves as Jews at home but had hidden their identities throughout the past generation. One of the participants read Kol Nidrei in broken Hebrew without the communal singing to which I was accustomed.

A sense of sorrow overcame me. I knew that these people were my brothers, but I missed the excitement and the family-style participation that I experienced every year, when the Kol Nidrei prayer is sung together out loud. That singing was much more important to me than the words of the prayer in creating that sense of togetherness as part of a greater Jewish family.

Twenty-seven years went by. I again traveled to Krakow, this time to uncover the secret of the success of the Jewish music and culture festival in Kazimierz. The event took place on Szeroka Street, which is also the location of the Rema Synagogue, the Jewish cemetery, and restaurants that offer Jewish foods on their menus – which are written in Hebrew. One after another, the artists who appeared here throughout the days of the festival got up on stage. From Israel, the festival was attended by Dudu Tassa and the Kuwaitis, Neta Elkayam, Shye Ben Tzur and the Rajasthan Express, and Gili Yalo, and they were joined by performances from American musician Paul Shapiro and a local Klezmer ensemble. The audience of over twenty thousand people stood up, sang, and danced for hours on end.

At ten o'clock at night, the time that the Sabbath ends in Krakow, a group of rabbis from different denominations ascended the stage together for a joint Havdalah ceremony (a ritual farewell to Shabbat), complete with a cup of wine, sweet-smelling spices, and a candle that was held by Kasha, a convert and member of the local Jewish community center. Everyone joined in the singing of the traditional Jewish tune for "Shavua Tov" (a good week).

A few days earlier, at the entrance to a café called Cheder (which means "room"), whose sign was also written in Hebrew letters, I had met Janusz, the driving force behind the festival and its manager, along with his team. "Tonight, there will be a Jewish Persian music concert," Janusz told me. A few hours later, I was enjoying a performance by Rajasthan Express, a band from Israel, in the hall of the beautiful synagogue known as the Tempel, one of the seven synagogues in the district. Later, I listened to music mastered by the DJ Gili Yalo, an Ethiopian immigrant to Israel, at the dimly lit Alchemia bar.

For about twenty-five years, this festival, featuring mainly Jewish music, has been taking place here. The festival also features a range of lectures, workshops, and exhibitions related to Jewish culture. Throughout the days of the festival, the streets of Kazimierz are filled with cafés and pubs playing Jewish and Israeli music, as well as cultural events – thirty thousand people celebrating a renewed jubilee of Jewish music and culture. "We breathe the old Jewish music and are even more excited about modern-day Jewish music," Janusz told me.

The team managing the festival is composed almost entirely of non-Jewish Poles. My conversation with Janusz is conducted in English, with the occasional Hebrew word thrown in. In Janusz, I discovered a bubbling, sharp, cheerful, and very humorous man. Janusz himself was, most surprisingly, from a non-Jewish Polish family, with an astonishing affinity for Jewish culture. "My rabbi is Rabbi Nachman of Breslov," he said. "He said, 'The entire world is a very narrow bridge. The most important thing is not to be afraid at all.' We stand today in Poland, in Europe, and around the world facing anti-Semitic and anti-Israeli sentiments. We will stand together with Israel and with the Jews, wherever they are, and we will never give up. Our festival is meant for entertainment too, but first and foremost, it is a manifest of identification with Judaism through song. I know what happened here between 1939 and 1945, and I know what Poland did during those years. I was born fifteen years after the end of World War II. I cannot know how I would have behaved if I was alive during the war, but the least I can do today is what I am doing now. I am not responsible for what happened. I cannot change the past. I can only change the present."

Our conversation took us back to the small village where he was born. "I didn't know a thing about Jews, not from my home or from my school. At the age of fifteen, I met a Catholic friend who taught me the first facts about history and about the Jewish culture of his neighbors in the village. When I was twenty, I moved to Krakow. I started studying Yiddish at the Tempel Synagogue and connecting with Polish Jews, who were initially wary of me. 'The crazy Polish guy who came to learn Yiddish from us,' they would call me, as they shared with me the horror stories their families endured in the Holocaust.

"I slowly realized that the Jewish world is something global, and that if I wanted to define my Polish identity, I needed to include Jewish culture. Judaism played a very important role in the creation and development of Polish culture, and music is a central element of my culture and of the people here.

"When I was twenty-eight, I decided to get up and do something, together with a few of my friends – to establish a festival dedicated to the culture of Jewish music, in Krakow. That was in 1988, when the country was still under Communist rule, and we didn't ask for anyone's permission. The first festival was local and small and took place in a theater with about a hundred seats. But something happened there. When we opened the panel discussion dedicated to Polish-Jewish relations, I suddenly noticed a few young men in the audience who were wearing *kippot* [skullcaps worn by Jews]. In 1988, that was a brave thing to do. A statement that they were Jews and proud of it. During those days, I thought the festival would be a one-time event. A year later, though, the Communist regime collapsed, and a new, free government was established, which encouraged us to continue this tradition. Since then, twenty-seven years later, we have been celebrating Judaism in Krakow."

During our conversation, a group of young Israelis entered the room. Janusz excitedly introduced them. "Do you know who they are? This is Nitai Hershkovitz, and this is Eyal Talmudi, two musicians who performed yesterday. Eyal has been here many times. The older Jewish generation comes to the festival, as well as amazing young people like them. I believe in culture, and I believe in living culture. The heritage that is left from the Germans is death, and the heritage that is left from the Jews is life itself. So we remember them via the authentic, cultural, genuine, living world, and I think that these musicians and this festival represent that idea."

There is a common perception among Jews and non-Jews alike that Jewish culture is expressed through old Jewish customs and Klezmer music. The festival is a breakthrough in the sense that it has introduced many different types of Israeli music, including eastern, Mediterranean, and ethnic Israeli music into the Jewish music arsenal at the festival. Janusz added, "We are aware of the tensions that exist in Israel between these communities. We want to show people that the Jewish-Polish culture that has developed here is only one of the options, and we encourage them to break the stereotype about Jewish culture that it is only composed of Ashkenazi culture. Another common stereotype is that Jewish culture is something ancient, historical, like *Fiddler on the Roof*, the shtetl, and the Golem of Prague. We say no, Jewish culture isn't only all of those things. Jewish culture today is also avant-garde and constantly developing, and it includes Israeli culture, with its many different styles. I feel that it is my obligation to introduce this culture to the Jews here and to the non-Jews.

"Jews have lived in Kazimierz since the fourteenth century, for hundreds of years. There was a tragic pause in the period of the war and the decades that followed it, and the festival created the possibility of continuing the Jewish tradition of the district. Jewish culture is intrinsically connected to Polish culture, so we are simply presenting something that we see as local. Jewish culture belongs here. Sometimes, people ask why we organize a festival for a different culture and not for Polish culture, and we say, is this not part of Polish culture? If you look at Polish literature, you can see how many of the names are Jewish. If you look at the names of Polish artists, you can see how many of them are Jewish. In many senses, it is impossible to separate Jewish culture and Polish culture. Therefore, the festival is not only important for Jews, but for Poles as well, so that they can gain a better understanding of their Polish heritage."

During the festival, I participated in a symposium with a Jewish-Polish author and journalist, who was asked why the Polish are attracted to Jewish culture. He replied, "Sometimes people feel phantom pains. Like after a leg or hand is amputated, when a person continues to feel pain in the limb that doesn't exist. The Jews are part of our body, and they were cut off from us in the Holocaust. We feel pain in the limb that was cut off of us."

After the lecture was over, I asked Janusz if that feeling of something missing is also related to guilt over the responsibility of the

Poles for what happened in the Holocaust. He thought for a moment and then answered, "I don't think so. Those who feel guilty want to escape from it. In the Polish mentality, the common way of dealing with a problem is running away from it and saying that it doesn't exist, instead of confronting it. When we create this Jewish renaissance, we do so with positive feeling and emotions. We want to contribute, to learn, to study – not because we feel guilty, but because we are really missing something. At the festival, a lot of young people partic-ipate, and for them, that feeling of guilt doesn't exist; they know that everything happened in the past. It is clear that historically, we are to be blamed. But today, we cannot change anything. It's important to know what happened in the past and to take note for the future, to try to create something positive out of the complex and terrible things that happened. This is also a process of making peace with the past. But the main thing is current Jewish cultural music."

The Jewish center is managed by Jonathan Orenstein, whom I met several times while organizing our delegations. He spoke to me in flu-ent Hebrew with a slight American accent but spoke to the employees and visitors to the site in fluent Polish. Jonathan was born and raised in New York, immigrated to Israel as a lone soldier, and after completing his service, traveled to Poland because of a woman he met. "The rela-tionship ended, but I fell in love with Krakow and decided to stay," he says. "Since then, it's been fifteen years, and I'm still here."

The Jewish community center has hundreds of members who attend events throughout the year. It hosts hundreds of cultural activi-ties, music events, Sabbath meals, a student club, a school for learning Hebrew, Yiddish lessons, kindergartens, and a newspaper.

Members of the JCC community can be anyone who has Jewish roots, whether on the maternal or paternal side. Jonathan shares that since the collapse of the Communist regime in Poland, and especially in recent years, many young people in Poland have been discovering that they have Jewish roots and have come to the Jewish center in Krakow.

"After the war, some of the survivors stayed in Poland, changed their names, and didn't tell their children that they were Jewish because of persecution by the Communist government. In recent years, many of these children are discovering the truth. Sometimes, the grandmother decides to tell them before her death. Sometimes they remember Jewish customs that they saw as children and start doing research, or they find a box at home with photos of rabbis and Jewish items, such as candlesticks…"

Later, I participated in a music workshop by Neta Elkayam entitled "From Morocco to Jerusalem," and I smiled at the sight of the Polish participants singing Moroccan songs with quite some effort. After the session, some of the participants approached the instructors and asked questions. In front of me stood a Polish woman who hugged Elkayam, cried, and spoke to her with great emotion for several minutes. She shared that her parents never spoke at all about what had happened in the war, but recently someone in their neighborhood spray-painted in English on the empty Jewish homes in their neighborhood, "We miss you." "Since then, I have been preparing Jewish foods on your holidays," she said, bursting into tears.

On the last day of the festival, before returning to Israel, I met Janusz once again. "For ten days, we've gotten used to the masses of people on the streets of Kazimierz," he said, "but suddenly, everything's empty. Nevertheless, even on regular days, there is genuine Jewish life here, and the Jewish community is gradually growing. Once, when a group of tourists would arrive in Kazimierz, the guide would tell them that they were standing in the historic Jewish quarter of Krakow. Now, he says that we are in the Jewish quarter of Krakow. Because it's not history anymore; Jewish life has returned here. Kazimierz is becoming more and more Jewish, and it's wonderful." Janusz concludes, "My message is that we don't want to rebuild the past. We want to build the future."

My visit to the Jewish festival showed me how music can serve as the basis of a small but vibrant Jewish community and unify it around the unique social center. The Jewish music festival has restored the site's former glory, in the sense of promoting Jewish culture even among the general Polish public, for whom Jewish music and culture were an almost inseparable part of its culture in the past.

5. Let the Dead Tell Their Story – Okopowa Cemetery, Warsaw
Local Personality: Meir Balaban
Mike Hollander

Can the Okopowa Jewish Cemetery be the place in Warsaw that is most full of life? I have guided over fifty trips to Eastern and Central Europe, and on each trip, I endeavor to focus more on life than on death. With that in mind, it may seem unusual that I choose to begin guiding my trips in Jewish cemeteries. Why do I do that?

It all began on my first trip to Poland over twenty-five years ago. Immediately after landing at the Warsaw airport, my colleagues and I climbed onto a bus to drive around and orient ourselves with the city and the sites we would be guiding the next day. Much to my surprise, our first stop was the Okopowa Street Jewish Cemetery. Unfortunately, it was a Polish national holiday, and the gate was locked. As we decided to surreptitiously climb the wall, a number of thoughts ran through my mind, namely the old joke: "Why is there a wall around the cemetery? Because people are dying to get in," and the ancient rabbinic adage of "Do not climb the walls," i.e., do not forcibly emigrate to the Land of Israel. I also heard my late grandmothers who had emigrated from Eastern Europe to Canada after the First World War warning me about going to Poland, since "Nothing good ever happened in the Old Country."

One of the major educational challenges when guiding in Europe is the dichotomy between the rich thousand-year Jewish presence and the small size of contemporary Jewish communities. There are an estimated five to ten thousand Jews living in Poland today, in contrast to before the Second World War, when there were 3.25 million Jews (10 percent of the entire country's population), and Warsaw's population was one-third Jewish.

To try to understand the present budding Jewish community in Poland, I encourage groups to visit one of the small but growing Jewish institutions, organizations, or communities. Most prominent of these are the Nozyk Synagogue and the Lauder Jewish School in Warsaw, the university student Hillel organization, and a growing number of Reform and Liberal communities, as well as the decade-old Krakow JCC and its new preschool.

Many Jewish visitors have told me that they visit Poland largely to say Kaddish for lost relatives, or because of what they describe as a moral or theological imperative to visit Auschwitz-Birkenau or other sites of mass murder during the Shoah. I encourage them to take a step back and recognize the rich Jewish presence in Poland over a thousand years, with periods of prosperity as well as persecution, successes as well as setbacks, opportunities as well as obstacles. I remind them of the line from the Joni Mitchell song "Big Yellow Taxi" about realizing what you have only after it's gone. How can one mourn the loss of Jewish life if one doesn't comprehend the significance of the former Jewish presence that is today largely absent?

My first suggestion is that to best understand our experience in Jewish Europe, visitors should put on a new set of lenses, with a three-sided prism, representing the three components of our journey: learning about the thousand-year story of the Jews in Poland, the Shoah, and the challenges and complexities of Jewish life after 1945.

Although a Jewish cemetery, which in Hebrew is called *beit hachayim* (house of life), may seem to be an unusual choice to start our journey, it is often the only logical place. Cemeteries can provide a rich collection of stories of people, giving visitors an understanding of the depth and breadth and legacy of life. A visit to the cemetery is often the key to appreciating the rich legacy of these communities.

I try to transport visitors back to the era before the Shoah and introduce them to the rich heritage of Polish Jewish life in the Okopowa Cemetery, the ultimate place to learn about the dreams, ideas, achievements, and failures of what was the most significant Jewish community in Europe until the outbreak of World War II. Here, I begin to paint the picture of the rich Jewish life that was.

Okopowa Cemetery is one of the largest Jewish cemeteries in Europe, with over 250,000 people buried here since the early nineteenth century. Although somewhat rundown, over 60 percent of the tombstones are identifiable. The small landscaping staff struggle valiantly to prevent the thick natural growth from overtaking and destroying the cemetery, which surprisingly was not destroyed by the Nazis. It functioned during the years of occupation between 1940 and 1943, when 100,000 Warsaw Jews were buried here. Concerned about the spread of disease, the Germans kept the cemetery, on the edge of the ghetto, open for burial in mass graves. As my group meanders through the vast, seemingly never-ending rows of tombstones, I am reminded of the words of Yehuda Amichai, the late Israeli poet, who wrote about the Warsaw cemetery: "Here it is the roots that are seeking. They burst from the ground, overturn gravestones, and clasp the broken fragments in search of names and dates, in search of what was and will never be again." He beautifully describes how nature seems to be in the process of overtaking the cemetery.

My challenge is to uncover and unravel the amazing story of a millennium of Jewish life in Poland buried here. The labyrinthine rows and aisles of graves lean in every direction, and through the wonderful diversity of funerary art, we can see how those close to the deceased perpetuated their legacy.

I have heard many stories of people who want to find the graves of their family who lived in Poland before the war. Some conduct research before they come, and others only realize that there may be a grave of a family member in the cemetery when they walk around. Often, people pass graves with their family's name and wonder if they were relatives. There is a couple buried there who bear my family name. Each time I visit, I wonder if they could be long-lost relatives.

As we wander the cemetery, one can sense the dramatic richness of Polish Jewish life, through the diversity of tombstone styles and some of the more well-known personalities buried there. A quick search on the internet yields a list of dozens of prominent Jews who were interred here between 1800 and 1939. One of the most colorful graves is that of the Bialystock-born Ludwig Zamenhoff (1859–1917). As a teenager, before he became an ophthalmologist, he developed a new language, Esperanto (from the Latin root "to hope"). Concerned with the tensions and divisions in the world during the period of imperialism, nationalism, and xenophobia, Zamenhoff wanted to create a means to allow people to communicate more effectively and bring people together to create a world without war. His grave is a pilgrimage site for people from all over the world who want to celebrate his utopian dream of uniting humanity.

Not too far away are the graves of the triumvirate of late nineteenth-century Yiddish writers, Shlomo Ansky, I. L. Peretz, and Yaakov Dinezon. This beautiful monument celebrates the particularism of Yiddish culture, so different from Zamehoff's idea of inventing a language to foster universal communication. One can begin to grasp the diversity of Jewish life in Poland before the Shoah merely by contrasting these opposing ideas emerging during the same milieu.

To further appreciate the creativity and diversity of Polish Jewry, one should also visit the graves of Esther Rachel Kaminska, the "mother of Yiddish theater" and aunt of actor Danny Kaye; Adam Czerniakow, the head of the Warsaw ghetto Judenrat who took his life rather than send Jews to their death in Treblinka; and great rabbis including Naftali Zvi Yehuda Berlin (the Netziv), dean of the great Volozhin Yeshiva, and the great Rabbis Yosef Dov and his son Chaim Soloveichik.

For me, the most important grave is that of Meir Balaban, one of the few people buried in an individual grave from the Warsaw ghetto in 1942. A significant historian of Polish and Galician Jewry, he was one of the first to use objective scholarship to chronicle Jewish history. The idea of Jewish history, rather than Jewish memory, which is a more theological interpretation of past events of the Jewish people, only began to emerge in the modern era. Balaban was one of the most important early proponents of this new discipline of Jewish history, explaining events through the prism of human rather than divine actions. His extensive use of personal stories shed tremendous light on the history of the communities of Lwow, Krakow, and Lublin over centuries, as he artfully described how Polish Jewry had become one of the most creative Jewish communities in the world.

He was born in 1877 in Lwow/Lemberg/Lviv in Galicia in the Austro-Hungarian Empire into a family hostile to Chassidism. He studied in a German-language high school and afternoon Hebrew schools, and later learned law and history in university in Lviv. His prolific research and writing are considered a major historical source for Jewish life over hundreds of years in Poland.

Balaban was one of the first to take up the plea of one of the earliest Jewish historians, Simon Dubnow, who urged Jews in the late nineteenth century to collect and chronicle Jewish sources. One of the torchbearers of the second generation of historians, Balaban had a growing interest in methodologically studying history, using documents and archival sources.

Balaban helped turn Warsaw into the center for Jewish historians in Eastern Europe through his diverse career, during which he directed secular studies at the Mizrachi Tahkemoni Rabbinic School in Warsaw, lectured at the University of Warsaw in Jewish history (he was the only Jewish academic to be an assistant professor in interwar Poland), and together with colleagues, founded the Institute for Jewish Studies, the first Jewish research and educational center in Europe. Active in Zionist circles, he twice unsuccessfully ran for parliament. His last role was the director of the Judenrat archive in the Warsaw ghetto. In 1942, he died of a heart attack in the ghetto.

His colleague David Assaf eulogized him at his funeral as a great historian, saying, "escorting you to your eternal rest are…generations of Polish Jews, for whom your books are an everlasting memorial, a monument to the holy Jewish communities of Lvov, Lublin and Krakow, their leaders and their people. Your great mission is over. You, Balaban, chronicler of the history of the Jews of Poland, have no work left to do…. The Jews of Poland are no more…. Only broken shards remain…. An era has ended – an era of glorious Jewish life. Polish Jewry is destroyed and gone" ("Only Broken Shards Remain," *Haaretz*, May 2, 2003, https://www.haaretz.com/1.4688620).

As my group stands around Balaban's grave, hurriedly dug and shoved in a crowded area during the darkest period of the Warsaw ghetto, I remind them of this man's centrality to this place and the story of Polish Jewry. Even as he was approaching death, he was documenting life in the ghetto. His students created a group, the Oneg Shabbat, to surreptitiously collect and chronicle life in the ghetto. The "Chronicler of the history of the Jews of Poland" spread the idea of historical research, tracing the individual stories of the generations that live on through the tombstones in the cemetery.

A few years ago, I arrived in Poland a day before my group and went with my wife to Kolbuszowa, the village in Galicia where her paternal grandmother had grown up. In 1920, the young woman was sent to the United States in order to flee anti-Jewish sentiment and look for a better future. My wife's grandmother and father never desired to visit Poland. Almost a century after she left Poland, her granddaughter (my wife) went to her small village, barely an hour outside of Krakow, to walk the streets and see the sights that had been an important part of her family's story.

One of our first stops was the cemetery, and as we walked through the dilapidated ruins (no Jews had lived there since 1941), I realized that my wife was having a profound transformational experience. Her father and grandmother never wanted to visit a place of persecution and death, whereas she was trying to imagine the rich fabric of Jewish life over centuries in this little town that had been half Jewish. Which of her relatives were buried here, and who had attended a funeral or said Kaddish here?

I will continue to visit the grave of Meir Balaban in the Warsaw Okopowa Cemetery. His and other Jewish historians' work allows us to learn the story of Polish Jewry. I see myself as a link in the long chain of the Jewish people, from Dubnow to Balaban, through me and down to others. We must continue to connect the chain by telling the meta-narratives of Jewish memory as well as Jewish history, understanding the central role of individuals in the story of our people. I hope to be able to introduce you to some of those amazing people in the Okopowa Cemetery, so that you can find your link in the continuing chain and story of our people.

6. The Auschwitz Phoenix – Oswiecim
Local Personality: Maciek Zbiarovsky
Hillel Meyer

"*Jeden, dwa, trzy, cztery,*" I repeat after the teacher. One, two, three, four. "*Dobrze, Hillel!* Very good," says Gosia, my Polish teacher, on the Zoom screen. This is my first Polish lesson, and I feel that despite having visited Poland countless times, I am closing a circle that was open for so many years – starting a new journey that is no less captivating.

Fifteen years earlier. "LOT Flight 303 from Chicago O'Hare to John Paul II Krakow departing from gate 5 on schedule." I hurried my seventeen-year-old students through the terminal toward the departure gate, giving them a few minutes to visit the restroom and pay a visit to Starbucks for the last taste of home they would be having for a while before we boarded the plane. "Don't forget to stay with your partner!" I shouted, "and get me a tall dark coffee please." I approached the airline representative to check that the kosher meals we ordered would in fact be served to us on the flight. The company representative was named Maria, according to the name tag on her blue uniform, and she had blue eyes as clear as the sea on a chilly day. Maria examined the list and replied with a polite smile and a heavy Polish accent, "Yes, Mr. Meyer, kosher food has been ordered for you, twenty-four meals." The way she pronounced the word *kosher* made me feel inexplicably uncomfortable. In English, it sounds fine to me; in English with a Polish accent, it sounds like a nuisance. I couldn't wait for the flight to be over and for us to be on the ground.

On the ground, everything was in Polish. The porters, the signs, the announcements made in the airport. I carefully made sure that the instructions I received from my contact at March of the Living were being followed. The kids were not allowed to spend time in the city on their own, talk to the locals, or waste money. As far as they saw it, Poland was a blood-soaked country composed of camps and ghettos. We'd keep the fun and joy for our next stop – Israel. After I nervously made sure the entire group was present, I reminded them of the instructions about staying together at all times and not talking to the locals, who aren't too pleased about the masses of groups coming to remind them of the dark period that took place on their soil. We went to meet the staff members, the ones whom we were allowed to talk to: the guide, the driver, and the security guard. They were all polite; the driver and the security guard didn't speak English. The guide, Jankes, who was about sixty, spoke broken English, with a heavy accent. With an official air, he led us to our bus, nodding to his fellow tour guides on the way and calling out to them in words I didn't understand. I assumed it was something along the lines of, "Good luck to us this week with this group of wacko Jews."

On the way to the hotel, I started thinking about Jankes. If he was already sixty, that meant his parents were probably in their twenties at the time of the Holocaust. What were they doing at that time? Did they hide Jews or report them? Perhaps they were silent while these atrocities were happening? Driving next to the forests, the signs in Polish, slowing down before crossing the train tracks, the noisy conversation in Polish between the guide and the driver – all of these conjured up memories that I didn't even know existed inside of me. These memories weigh heavily on my heart. I was glad that our instructions had been not to look right or left, but to concentrate exclusively on the Holocaust, on 1939–1945. Contemporary Poland was not on our agenda, only World War II Poland and the glorious Jewish life that had been extinguished.

The next morning, on the same bus, we headed toward Auschwitz. On the way, I described to the students how the timeline unfolded, from the Nazi rise to power until the Final Solution. Every time I mentioned the Holocaust in Poland, I looked out of the corner of my eye to see how Marek was reacting. He was listening with one ear and the rest of the time chatting with the driver in a whisper. I was very cautious, making sure there was nothing in my comments that connected the Poles to the Holocaust. When we reached Auschwitz I, we met Beata, our local guide. In snowy winter weather, she led us through the camp that was turned into a museum for preservation by the Soviets. We passed through the sign that reads "*Arbeit macht frei*" (work sets you free) and continued to the barracks, which are now exhibit halls according to topics: the history of the invasion of Poland, photographs of political prisoners, piles of looted items, maps, diagrams, photos. Beata told us the precise numbers, dates, and events. She used the word *prisoners* – political prisoners, Jewish prisoners, war prisoners – and I exploded inside. What do you mean, Jewish prisoners? Political prisoners? War prisoners??? This Holocaust was ours! The Jews! They are holy, captives, slaves. The war captives weren't killed with gas, there weren't children among the political prisoners. Prisoners? Children who were prisoners? Not prisoners, murder victims. I couldn't bear to listen to her. As we walked quietly between the barracks, with only the sound of our steps on the stone in the air, I tried and failed to organize my thoughts. The ease and laconic way in which she described life in the camp made me lose my mind. The tour over, Beata parted with us, wishing us a pleasant time in Poland, and we continued alone to the second camp, Auschwitz II, also known as Birkenau.

Birkenau is an extension of Auschwitz. This was where the systems of destruction – the gas chambers and the crematoriums – were built. This is where Dr. Josef Mengele stood and waited for the incoming groups of Jews arriving by train, so that he could wave his hand to decide who would be sent to live, for harsh labor or medical experiments, and who would die. In contrast with Auschwitz I, which became a museum, Birkenau remained in ruins, remnants of wood barracks destroyed by fires and weather conditions. Only the stone chimneys remained, silent witnesses of the horrors that occurred there. The rain stopped, and we walked along the train tracks, and I spoke. Finally, I got to be alone with my students without a Polish person accompanying us, and in this terrible place, I felt freedom for the first time. Freedom to blame, freedom to be angry, freedom to cry and hug, freedom to lead. This was the first time I felt that it's my Holocaust, my memories, and that no one is coming to twist my reality. The reality of the Jewish Holocaust, and the evil of those people who stood by, including the Polish. All of them, especially those who are trying to cheapen my Holocaust.

After a ceremony in the crematorium, reciting Kaddish and singing "Ani Ma'amin" and "Hatikvah," we left Auschwitz and traveled to Oswiecim, the town next to the camp, from which the camp's name originated. It's Oswiecim in Polish, Ushpizin in Yiddish (which means inviting guests), and Auschwitz in German. The town had a vibrant Jewish community as far back as the fifteenth century. Before the outbreak of World War II, Jews comprised more than 50 percent of the local population of about ten thousand residents. It was a cultural, political, rabbinic, and Zionist center. During the war, the Nazis took control of the town, burned all the synagogues except one, expelled the Jews to nearby ghettos, and then took those same Jews to Birkenau, where they were gassed. The pastoral landscape of the town, located near part of the Vistula River where swans swim, reminded me of the poem "Ashes and Dust," by Yehuda Poliker, which begins with the words "A perfect day to fish in the brook; in my chest, my heart still breaks."

At the entrance to the museum, we were greeted by a tall, smiling young man with glasses by the name of Maciek Zabierowski. He began by welcoming us and then took us on a short tour of the museum, which ended at the synagogue. From everything Maciek said, including his intonation, he sounded like a local Jewish young man whose father once lived there, perhaps as the local milkman or butcher. But I wasn't not sure. Maciek described the story of the town from its golden years to its destruction in the Holocaust and focused on the story of the site's renovation.

The Jewish museum was built inside one of the only Jewish homes that remained in the town and next to the only synagogue that survived the war, the Chevrat Lomdei Mishnayot synagogue, which the Nazis used as a warehouse during the war. The interior of the synagogue is restored almost exactly the way it was then: rows of dark wood benches that reach the raised bimah, and at the front of the synagogue, the Ark with the Tablets of the Law. The walls are repainted, the inscriptions partially restored, and the lighting in the ornate chandelier is electric. But one can feel the presence of past worshipers.

Throughout Central and Eastern Europe, there are synagogues that rose phoenix-like from the ashes and were renovated. In Poland, Jews made up 10 percent of the population, and in some towns, they were even the majority. Until World War II broke out, there were about seventeen thousand active synagogues in Europe, of which about three thousand synagogue buildings survived, and seven hundred of them are active (Ofer Aderet, "From a Place of Worship to a Bakery: European Synagogues Are Changing Their Role," *Haaretz*, February 26, 2018, tinyurl.com/4p2a54vt). Those that survived were used as storage rooms, workshops, and stables. At the end of the war, with no Jews left in the towns, the synagogues were still used for various purposes other than their original one as houses of worship. In the large cities, renovations and restorations began a few years after the war ended, but in the small towns, where there was no Jewish community or representation, the synagogues and cemeteries remained in ruins. Once the gates of Central and Eastern Europe were opened, the desire to protect what was destroyed and taken away was aroused. Funding for renovating the Polish synagogues came from the Polish government, the State of Israel, foundations set up by descendants from the towns, and private donors. It is common to find, in certain towns, that the non-Jewish residents of the town themselves were the ones who financed the renovation. This is what happened in Oswiecim.

I now felt comfortable talking with the local Poles about "then and now" and started chatting with Maciek, asking him what brought a non-Jewish young man to work at this museum. He tells me about his father's trauma as an academic from Krakow, who feared the Germans as a child during World War II and to this day trembles when he hears the German language. It brings him back to that dark time when his Jewish neighbors and friends disappeared overnight. Maciek spoke of his first trip to Berlin, in his twenties, when he couldn't understand how German could be such a commonly spoken language without any connotation of the Holocaust, and how he felt uncomfortable about it. He completed his degrees in history and started working in Oswiecim in a temporary student position. Since then, preserving Jewish awareness in Oswiecim became the center of his life.

Maciek's story is not rare. In every town, museum, and Jewish commemoration site in Central and Eastern Europe, most of the guides and staff members in preservation positions are not Jewish. "I feel a need and obligation to preserve the culture of the Jews of Poland who were part of my nation," Maciek told me.

"What about the Poles who helped destroy Jews?" I challenged him.

"Like there were good and bad Jews, good and bad Germans, there were good and bad Poles," Maciek replied. "I can't take responsibility for the bad ones. I can only do good from now on, on behalf of the future generations." He doesn't just speak; he acts. He has visited Israel several times, is learning Hebrew, and is active in curbing anti-Semitism and hatred of all types.

According to the records at Yad Vashem, the number of Righteous Among the Nations (non-Jews who saved Jewish lives without any monetary compensation, putting their own lives in danger) in Poland is over seven thousand, the highest number for any country, but in terms of the proportions in comparison with the size of the Jewish population that was killed (three million, about 90 percent of the Jewish population of Poland at the beginning of World War II), the number isn't too impressive. The Netherlands, for example, boasts over five thousand Righteous Among the Nations, for the 140,000 Jews who lived in the country at the beginning of World War II.

In 2018, the Polish parliament passed the "Holocaust Law," under which anyone who accuses the Polish of taking an active part in the Holocaust is punishable with three years of imprisonment. It was preceded by the storm that revolved around the story of the Jedwabne pogrom. In 2001, a Jewish-American-Polish historian named Jan Tomasz Gross published a book called *Neighbors*, in which he describes the massacre committed by the residents of the Polish village of Jedwabne against their Jewish neighbors in 1941. They tortured their neighbors, locked them all into a barn, and set it on fire, without the Germans' involvement. Sixteen hundred Jews were murdered in this massacre, and only seven survived to tell the story. Despite the fact that in 2001, the then president of Poland recognized Polish responsibility for the massacre, over time, the discussion continued to develop. The Polish residents of the town claimed that they had nothing to do with the affair and that the perpetrators had been German. Add to that the fact that former president of the United States Barack Obama mentioned the "Polish death camps" in a 2012 speech awarding the Medal of Freedom to Polish resistance fighter Jan Karski. The expression was met by angry reactions from senior members of the Polish government and led to an apology and correction from the president.

In snowy Auschwitz, the teenagers had a powerful experience. They stood, shivering from the cold in the latrine (the bathroom barrack), huddling next to each other and listening to the chilling testimony of a Holocaust survivor who had survived the camp. On the bus, they sat in silence, each engrossed in his or her own thoughts. Occasionally, someone burst into tears. Marek turned around and said to me, "They're sad. Children aren't supposed to be sad." Suddenly, I looked at him with a different pair of eyes, as an adult, a grandfather, looking at children and feeling upset at their sorrow. "Marek," I asked him, "how can we cheer them up? Can we stop somewhere on the way and buy them chocolate?" Marek asked the security guard whether we were allowed to stop and received a negative answer. I didn't give up. "There must be somewhere we can stop, to do something." Suddenly Marek became a partner in cheering up children who just came out of Auschwitz. He thought, contemplated whether to tell me, and then finally said, "They opened a new shopping mall in Krakow, and there's a Starbucks. Would that work?" "But security," I said. "I'll talk to him," Marek replied. He spoke with the security guard in Polish, and I only understood the words "*nyah*" (no) and Starbucks. Marek raised his voice uncharacteristically, and the security guard gave in. Marek smiled at me triumphantly and said that we were going to stop there, but we needed to stay together as a group. Who would have believed that visiting a Starbucks in Krakow would be the turning point in my relationship with Poland and the Poles?

Since the students didn't have zloty or credit cards, I offered to pay for hot cocoa and whipped cream for all of them; the only condition was that they needed to talk to the cashier and order it themselves. The cashiers, students just a year or two older than my students, started a conversation with them, asked for their names on the orders, and taught them how to say thank-you in Polish. It was the first time that the teens had any interaction with a Polish person, especially Poles their own age. Slowly, I watched as they chatted with some of the other people in the coffee shop, telling them about their experiences from the flight, the hotel, and Auschwitz. The locals expressed interest, asked questions, and expressed sorrow and compassion, thanking the teenagers for visiting Poland and talking to them. They see groups come and go, but they have no dialogue with them. They were so eager to talk, to tell them about Poland from before, during, and after the war. On the bus, the energy was refreshed. The teenagers were talking, laughing, looking out the windows, and admiring Wawel Royal Castle, which has stood there for so many years, but they only noticed it now. I asked Marek to explain to me what we were seeing, and I suddenly discovered that he was a wonderful guide and storyteller. We reached the hotel; I felt an urge to hug Marek but instead sufficed with a hearty thank-you for this meaningful day. The day that I discovered Poland, and the first step of the bridge that was built – at Starbucks.

Ever since, whenever I visit Krakow, I make my own personal pilgrimage to the mall and drink coffee.

Poland is a beautiful country. A land of lakes and rivers, mountains, castles, and evergreen forests. A country of musicians such as Chopin and Huberman, poets such as Szymborska and Szlengel. The country with the oldest university in Europe, with the largest library. A country where Jews found a safe haven and established their homes for a thousand years, the foundation of Hebrew and Yiddish literature and theater, the center of the yeshiva world on the one hand and cradle of secular Jewish culture on the other hand. Poland is also the country that suffered the most losses and destruction in World War II. Ninety percent of the city of Warsaw was destroyed down to the foundations, and in addition to the Jewish murder victims, another three million non-Jewish Polish citizens were murdered by the Nazis. Poland's history books have recorded that during World War II, six million Poles were murdered, of whom three million were Polish Jews. Like in other countries in Europe, the nationalistic movements in Poland are gaining momentum, and recently, the governors of about eighty districts in the country declared that their regions were free of LGBTQ people.

"Why do I judge Poland more than Germany, for example?" I ask myself. "Why do I feel more comfortable walking around Berlin than I do in Warsaw?" The answer is simple yet complex. When the war ended, Germany was destroyed, divided, and a new Germany was built, in which the Holocaust is present and mentioned without any attempt to blur or deny it. In Poland, when the war ended, they transitioned from being conquered by one government to another, and the entire subject of the Jewish Holocaust was swept under the carpet; the Polish people had other problems to handle. The Soviet influence aggrandized the Soviet victory over Germany and overcame the memory of the Jewish Holocaust, to the point that there was very little testimony or memories. By contrast, in my national consciousness as a child who grew up in Israel, Poland was a synonym for the Holocaust.

Since that trip, the educational philosophy of the March of the Living has changed. On every trip, there is an encounter with local high school students, Polish foods are tasted, there are local tours, and free time is provided to explore the markets and shops. Attitudes in Poland have also changed, and the Jewish Holocaust has a more distinct and respectful status than ever before. I believe that the Polish nation is undergoing a process of acceptance and healing and understands the atrocities that took place. Polish soil was indeed the most extensive location of the Nazi crimes, and Poles were victims of the war as well, but that does not erase the anti-Semitism and persecution of Jews that was rampant in Poland for hundreds of years, including during World War II. Laws and opinions regarding the involvement of the Polish people during the Holocaust or the right of return of Jewish possessions will be implemented and changed. However, I believe that most of the Polish nation would like to forget about anti-Semitism and the Nazi atrocities and to focus on the future, while preserving the rich Jewish culture that constituted an integral part of the country's cultural and social fabric. The proof is that while classic anti-Semitism is once again awakening in Europe, there is also a huge revival of preservation of the Jewish memory. There are people like Maciek and Marek who are looking forward and building a bridge in my direction – a grandson of Holocaust survivors and nephew of victims. The question is: Am I obligated to cross that bridge? Time will tell. In the meantime, I will continue to visit this magical country, meet and talk to the locals, enjoy the wonderful pierogi, drink amber-colored vodka, and study Polish, so that on the day that I do reach that meeting point, I will be able to present them with the word *wybaczam* – I forgive.

7. The Tablecloth – Krakow
Local Personality: Rabbi Moshe Isserles
Gilad Peled

Reb Yisrael owned a textile shop in the center of the Jewish quarter of the small Kazimierz district. He managed his shop with the same level of devotion as his prayers. He was the first in the quarter to open shop in the morning, and the last shop in which a candle burned at night. He was careful about cleanliness and order, warmly welcomed every person, and was a fair boss to his employees. He never missed a day of work. Yet every single day, a few minutes before noon, he would close his books, exit the store, and lock the door behind him.

Reb Yisrael put on his hat, buried his head in his coat, and without turning or delaying for even a short exchange of words, walked briskly down the city streets until he reached the *beit midrash* (study hall). He entered, hung up his coat, took off his hat, sat down in his regular seat, and opened a volume of the Talmud whose pages were worn due to excessive use. He did the same thing day in, day out, for his entire life.

One day, God and Satan ran into each other. After their regular exchange, Satan started to boast about his recent achievements, as usual. He shared stories of evil and corruption with glee, describing the envy and violence spreading on earth. "Soon," he announced misty-eyed, "the entire world will be mine."

God looked back at him with a small grin and shrugged his shoulders in pity. "My dear brother," he said quietly, "I've just returned from Kazimierz, next to Krakow. In the city square, there is a small textile shop whose owner is an honest man of pure heart. You will never succeed in corrupting him, even if you try with all of your might."

Lightning flashed in Satan's eyes, and sparks flew out of his horns. "There is no person I cannot corrupt!" he cried out furiously. "Humans are evil from birth! You will see!" and he disappeared in a storm, leaving scorch marks in the spot where he had stood.

It was 11:30 a.m. the next day when Satan entered Reb Yisrael's shop, dressed as a high noble in expensive clothing, surrounded by a group of servants. "Hello and welcome," Reb Yisrael greeted him warmly.

"I have come to buy fabric! A lot of fabric!" Satan announced.

"With pleasure," replied Reb Yisrael, "but we have just thirty minutes, because at 12:00, I will have to close the shop." He started spreading out his wares before Satan, who examined each and every roll carefully. It was 11:45 when Satan asked to see what else was in the back warehouse, and at 11:55, he was still standing and deliberating between the blue and the azure.

When Reb Yisrael tried to put the rolls of fabric aside and go on his way, Satan bellowed, "This is the opportunity of a lifetime! With the money that I pay you, you will be able to close your store and take a vacation for the rest of your life. What could be more important than a sum of money as big as this?"

But Reb Yisrael could not be budged, and at 12:00 precisely, he escorted Satan, who had thin curls of smoke emanating from his ears, out of the shop, locked the door, and walked toward the *beit midrash* as usual.

From His seat in heaven, God watched the events with interest. He smiled to Himself with satisfaction and at that moment decided that as a token of thanks to Reb Yisrael, He would give him a righteous son who would be a great scholar and a leader, famous in all Jewish communities. That night, Reb Yisrael's wife became pregnant, and nine months later, the Rema, Rabbi Moshe Isserles, was born.

It's been years since Reb Yisrael's shop stood on Szeroka Square in the center of Kazimierz, the Jewish quarter of Krakow. Today, the only shops here are a bookstore, selling spiritual and tourist guidebooks about Krakow and Judaism, and a small souvenir stall at the entrance of the Rema Synagogue. A few restaurants bearing signs that read "Kosher" are open on weeknights, serving meaningless, warped versions of classic Polish dishes, lacking butter and cream. Around the square, there are four synagogues just a hundred meters from each other, testimony of the rich Jewish life that once existed here. I don't think there is another place in the world where one can find such a tight cluster of synagogues, not even in the Jewish state.

On Friday afternoon, Szeroka Square is very quiet. There is no commotion of preparations for the Sabbath, no Jews walking back and forth loaded with shopping bags, and none of the excitement reserved for sanctity that awaits you just around the corner. A few tourists, engrossed in paperback travel guides, stand in the corners of the square, and one tour guide walks between the desolate synagogues with his group.

Although Warsaw has been the capital of Poland for the last four hundred years, during the six hundred years that preceded them, the capital was Krakow. The Rema's Krakow was a multicultural city where culture, arts, architecture, scientific research, and commerce flourished. It was the capital city of one of the largest, wealthiest, and strongest countries in Europe. It is no wonder that the sixteenth century was the first golden age in the history of Polish Jewry, while the second took place from the middle of the nineteenth century until World War II. These were periods of prosperity, when Jews were allowed to develop extensive autonomy, which included rich spiritual, cultural, and social life. However, while the Jewish story in Warsaw disappeared among the modern skyscrapers and the few relics that remain from the bombed-out city after the war, in Krakow, the Jewish story of the golden periods peeks out from every corner.

In 1495, about thirty years before the birth of the Rema, Jews were expelled from Krakow and forced to live in nearby Kazimierz. This was due to the jealousy and resentment of the city's merchants and the scholars of the Jagiellonian University. To this day, the university stands in a region that was previously Jewish. Most of the stores surrounding the central square of the old city today, the Sukienice, were owned by

Jews at the beginning of the twentieth century, and the bridge featured in photographs of Jewish families loaded with packages on their
way to the ghetto still stretches across the Vistula River. In Kazimierz,
the center of Jewish life since the sixteenth century, there are five-
hundred-year-old synagogues alongside marketplaces that rested on
the Sabbath. Jewish schools where Zionism was taught are adjacent
to the tombs of authorities of Jewish law who influenced the entire
Jewish world. In a few places, the remains of Hebrew inscriptions
above empty *batei midrash* are still visible, as are the rusty Yiddish
street signs that tell the story of this vanished world.

Not much remains of the glorious age of the sixteenth century:
a few books and manuscripts, empty synagogues, a small cemetery,
and quite a few legends that shroud the visit to Krakow with a light
aura of mystery and longing. These legends come in different shades
and sizes, but always captivate the heart, and as opposed to the fairy
tales on which we grew up, the legends of Krakow tell of people and
places that really existed. Sometimes, they tell the story of an ancient
tombstone, smooth from the caresses of countless hands over the
centuries. Sometimes, they are modern stories based on events that
really happened, such as the film *Schindler's List*, which was filmed in
the alleyways of Kazimierz.

Like any product in high demand, these legends aren't always
authentic, and you need to examine them carefully before opening
your heart to them. Not far from Szeroka Square, there is a small sec-
ond-hand market on Sundays. The Judaica items offered for sale on
wooden tables covered with worn carpets coax the Jewish heart and
whisper their own legends. Once, I paid an exorbitant sum for a charming miniature "travel *chanukiyah*." I thought that I was redeeming a
small Jewish story from the abyss of oblivion. How great was my disap-
pointment when I discovered later on that I had fallen into the trap of
a successful forgery. *My chanukiyah* turned out to be a tale that never
was.

In the past, people told legends around the bonfire, at the fair, or around the family table. Today, we are told legends in color and sound on the big screen and on television. Films and TV series offer us a window to a wondrous world, as did legends, ballads, and folk tales in the past. Heroes of legends are blessed with an abundance of humanity so that we can identify with them and superhuman qualities in order to inspire us. They are quicker, smarter, better, or more deadly than we can ever be. They surmount challenges that we can only dream of withstanding and deal with questions that we thankfully don't have to face. A successful legend enables us to play the heroes of the story, to get emotional, and then resume our regular lives with a new perspective.

It is no wonder, then, that the stories about Rabbi Moshe Isserles, the son of Reb Yisrael, owner of the fabric store, are among the most well-known legends of Krakow. The Rema was the superhero of Krakow Jewry throughout the generations. He was wealthy, wise, original, and successful. He led the local community but was renowned by Jewish communities worldwide. He introduced new ideas, aroused polemics, stood by his opinions, and was blessed with a sensitive heart. The Rema was part of the first golden age of Polish Jewry and was the most prominent Jewish leader in Poland in the sixteenth century. One legend notes that he lived for thirty-three years, passed away on the thirty-third day of the Omer (Lag BaOmer), and wrote thirty-three books. While most of the historical facts known about the Rema do not support this legend, for hundreds of years, Jews from all over Poland have been coming to Krakow on Lag BaOmer to pray and hold festive meals at his grave. They meet at the small cemetery hidden behind the synagogue that bears his name. The gravesite is concealed by a huge tree, and legend has it that the tree shielded him throughout the generations, to the extent that even the Nazis didn't dare touch his grave.

One legend attributes the Rema's heightened moral qualities to a poor water carrier. Because of an act of charity that the water carrier performed, he merited to be returned to this world as an emissary from heaven. His task was to tell the Rema that he should ask every Jew – not just the wealthy members of the city – to contribute charity, an important commandment that earns great rewards in the World to Come. According to the legend, after he did so, the Rema was blessed with long life.

However, the many legends surrounding the life of the Rema are nothing compared with his true-life story. If you are inclined to learn about just one Jewish leader from Poland, the Rema should be the one. The decisions that he rendered established ethical standards that were relevant not only to Jews but to every human being to this day. Two stories that almost became legends – but actually happened – illuminate his extraordinary character.

The first story is about a young woman whose father lost everything he had and then passed away together with her mother, leaving her alone in the world. Before his death, her father arranged her marriage to a worthy man, but when the time came for the wedding, there was no one to provide her with a dowry. The date set for the wedding was a Friday, and on that morning, the young woman decided that she would not give up on her wedding plans, out of a strong sense of faith that God would provide a solution for her. She immersed herself in a ritual bath, and kind women helped her with the wedding dress, but there was still no one to provide her with a dowry. The groom refused to proceed with the marriage. Despite the cries from the people of the city begging him not to embarrass his future wife, the groom would not budge from his decision. The argument continued for hours and was settled at long last – alas – only after the Sabbath had started.

The Rema, who was called to officiate at the wedding ceremony, faced a difficult decision: to make a lonely young woman happy on her big day, or to protect the sanctity of the Sabbath. Loyal to his practical, sensitive approach, the Rema permitted conducting the ceremony on the Sabbath, in order not to shame the bride. This decision was met with harsh criticism. The people in the city were so worried that such a precedent might repeat itself that from that day onward, the custom in the city was not to hold weddings on a Friday. It took a great deal of courage, as well as modesty and practical wisdom, for the Rema to reach this decision. Thus, the Rema marked himself as a cultural super-hero, enabling each of us to follow our hearts on issues related to dealings between one person and another.

The second story is nothing less than amazing. Traditional Judaism is a religion of practical commandments that encompass all areas of life. Since the reality of life changes from generation to generation, a collection of halachic compositions (expositions of Jewish law) was compiled over the years to summarize the proper practices of Jewish life during the relevant period. The last work in this series was written about two hundred years before the Rema was born. Thus, the Rema decided to dedicate his life to writing a work that would constitute an updated guide for the Jews of his generation. Without Google to help him, he immersed himself in the holy books. He used his phenomenal memory to analyze the massive quantities of information scattered across hundreds of books and rendered decisions between the different opinions appearing in the books that preceded him. For years, he worked day and night writing this magnum opus. Right before the book was finished, his entire world collapsed. He received a copy of a book called the *Beit Yosef*, written by Rabbi Yosef Karo of Tzefat, in the Land of Israel. To his dismay, it turned out that Rabbi Yosef Karo had also worked on an identical book and published it just a few months before his own work was ready. The Rema, utterly devastated, shut himself in his study and didn't come out for days on end. Yet after thoroughly reading Rabbi Yosef Karo's work, he reached the conclusion that his interpretations of Jewish law followed the Sephardic customs, while the Rema's book followed the Ashkenazi customs. Therefore, he dedicated the next few years to pinpointing the differences between the two methods of rendering Jewish law. The years went by, and when he was finally ready to publish his revised book, he received, again to his astonishment, a copy of the abridged version of Rabbi Yosef Karo's book, which was entitled the *Shulchan Aruch*. Once again, the Rema faced a difficult decision: Should he publish his life's work as a separate book under his own name, which would inevitably cause a schism in Judaism between Sephardic and Ashkenazi Jews?

He stepped down. Instead of publishing his life's work under his own name, the Rema decided to add his notes to the *Shulchan Aruch*, reflecting his rendering of Jewish law in the spirit of the customs of Ashkenaz. He called these additions the *Mapah* (tablecloth), which he spread on top of the *Shulchan Aruch* (set table). These notes still appear in every printed version of the *Shulchan Aruch* throughout the entire Jewish world. In this way, the Rema preserved the unity of the nation, at the cost of his own renown and personal glory. Every time I tell this story, I am moved to tears. It is difficult to imagine how the Jewish world would look today if the Rema had not made the brave and humble decision that he made. What immense strength of character must a person have to give up his entire life's work on behalf of future generations – people whom he would never even meet. Would I have made the same decision? Would you?

Krakow, the legendary capital of Poland, gives the visitor a different perspective on Jewish life. At the basis of the Jewish story of Krakow, there are no impressive numbers, no technological achievements or national awakening. The Jewish heart is the driving force behind the tale of Krakow – and if you just listen to it carefully, it will whisper to you a different tale of Jewish heroism.

Romania

8. Man Is But the Imprint – Transylvania and the Maramures Region
Local Personality: Tzipporah Friedman (née Hager)
Doron Wilfand and Yishay Shavit

The poet Shaul Tchernichovsky was one of the cultural giants of the Zionist movement in its early days. He was among the founding fathers of modern Hebrew literature and raised generations of poets and authors who followed in his footsteps. His influence on Hebrew culture is still very significant, and idiomatic phrases that many Israelis use in their daily lives today can be attributed to him. One such famous line is "Man is but the imprint of his native landscape." Those of you who speak Hebrew or visit Israel frequently may find this line quoted in Israeli newspapers, written on monuments and at national landmarks, or simply used in conversation by Hebrew speakers. What a beautiful idiom! According to Tchernichovsky, it is impossible to understand people, their culture, and their manner of thinking without recognizing the fact that all of these are rooted in the landscapes where they grew up as children. One's homeland influences the trajectory of one's entire life.

How is it possible, for example, to deeply understand the soul of a French-born person without being familiar with the landscapes, the history, and the culture of his or her homeland? Even more difficult, how is it possible to understand the soul of refugees, forced to leave their homeland and essentially relinquish their grasp of the soil that they were born upon and the culture in which they were raised? The connection between land and the human soul is one of the complex and meaningful questions that touch upon the roots of human existence. When discussing the history of the Jews in Europe in the twentieth century, these questions become critical in order to understand the thought processes and nature of Jewish identity to this day.

Tchernichovsky's statement places anyone interested in the history of Eastern European Jewry in a quandary. The Holocaust – which destroyed Jewish communities throughout all of Eastern Europe, together with the social and geographic processes that the countries of the region subsequently underwent – prevents us from understanding the imprint of the native landscapes on those Jews who were born in Eastern Europe and were fortunate enough to escape before the Nazi beast arrived. These processes changed the face of Europe forever; what we are left with is the history, the literature, and the culture, which help us understand those communities a bit more deeply.

In our humble opinion, there are very few regions in Eastern Europe today where it is possible to encounter the imprint of the native landscapes on Ashkenazi Jewry. One of them is in the northern part of Romania, in Transylvania and the Maramures region. We would like to share two very different stories with you that will hopefully help you understand Tchernichovsky's saying.

Doron's Story

On the night of our wedding, under the canopy, as the Klezmer band played Chassidic melodies, I couldn't help but notice my wife's grandmother, Tzipporah Friedman (née Hager), well up with tears. Tzipporah was a woman of short stature who was always dressed simply, her head covered in a traditional white kerchief. She survived the Holocaust and underwent several major crises, but managed to build a home of her own and celebrate the births of thirty-seven grandchildren. My wife, Yael, was the eldest of them. After the wedding ceremony, I approached Grandma Tzipporah and asked her why she had cried. She didn't try to evade the question, but replied, "They were all here with us under the canopy. I miss them so much and that world that once was, in Romania, which no longer exists."

Tzipporah was born in 1927 in the city of Oradea, in Transylvania, not far from the Hungarian border in northern Romania. As in many cities in the region, Romanians lived alongside Germans, Hungarians, and Jews. Essentially during those years, the city was known by its German name, Grosswardein, and was recognized for its extraordinary beauty. The city is situated on the banks of a river and surrounded by green mountains and hills, with many homes built in the Baroque style. Even several decades of Communist architecture did not succeed in tainting its beauty. The combination of the nineteenth-century vibe on the streets and the landscape's pastoral flavor transformed Oradea into a popular tourist spot.

During the years between the two world wars, Oradea became a vibrant, diverse Jewish center. The political instability of the adjacent areas of Ukraine made Transylvania an attractive location for many Jews. The Jewish community that had been living in the city for many generations expanded with the arrival of large numbers of Jews who sought a place where they could live their lives in peace and quiet. Thus, Tzipporah was born into a highly developed Jewish world. Satmar Chassidim lived alongside Maskilim (members of the Jewish Enlightenment movement), Zionists, and completely assimilated Jews. This diversity in their lifestyles existed not only on the streets, but within families as well. In almost every family, there were representatives of the different sects. Today, it may be difficult to imagine, but this was the reality in many Jewish communities during the years prior to the Holocaust.

Tzipporah was no ordinary girl. She was the youngest granddaughter of Rabbi Yisroel Hager, the Grand Rabbi of the Vizhnitz Chassidic dynasty, who moved the Chassidic group from its birthplace in the city of Vyzhnytsya, Ukraine, to Oradea, Romania. When the rabbi passed away in the mid-1930s, he was succeeded by his son, Rabbi Chaim Meir Hager, Tzipporah's father. This was a decisive point in her life. Being the daughter of the Grand Rabbi, the uncontested leader of the Chassidic group, meant growing up in a home to which myriads of Chassidim flocked in order to be near the rabbi, learn from his ways, consult with him, and request his blessing. Although she was the youngest of the rabbi's six children, all eyes followed her as she went outside to play, when she ate her meals, and when she was sent to school.

Anyone familiar with the Vizhnitz Chassidic group (as the city of Vyzhnytsya is called in Yiddish) – in Bnei Brak, Israel; in Monsey in the United States; in Montreal; or in other locations – knows that it is a prominent group with tens of thousands of Chassidic followers. It is characterized by deep Torah study and strict adherence to the Grand Rabbi's directives. Openness to non-*charedi* society, especially on subjects related to education, is not customary in this Chassidic group today. The group manages a large network of educational institutions in the spirit of its beliefs and does not encourage pursuit of a secular education, which deviates from the boundaries of this outlook. Therefore, it is surprising to discover that in the home of the Grand Rabbi in Romania during the years prior to the Holocaust, things were different. At the age of ten, Tzipporah was sent to a Bais Yaakov Jewish school for girls, where German was the primary language of study. In addition, the girls at the school learned Hungarian and modern Hebrew. This fact is especially interesting because among many Chassidic groups, the study of Hebrew for use in holy contexts is considered a positive thing, but turning Hebrew into a secular, spoken language is prohibited.

The curriculum at Bais Yaakov in Romania provided a secular education as well toward the end of the 1930s. The girls read the works of Dostoevsky, Tolstoy, and even poems by the Zionist author Bialik. In theory, the Vizhnitz Chassidic group was opposed to Zionism and the Enlightenment movement, but in practice was in fact quite tolerant toward people who held these views. In almost all of these Chassidic families, including the family of the Grand Rabbi himself, there were those who supported and actively pursued Zionism and the ideals of the Enlightenment movement. Their family members did not excommunicate or shun them, and the conversations around the dinner table must have been very interesting.

Tzipporah's father, Grand Rabbi Chaim Meir Hager, developed a strong affinity for classical music, and when he traveled to the hot springs in Carlsbad, Czechoslovakia, in the summer, he would listen to concerts by philharmonic orchestras. Ironically, his favorite composer was Richard Wagner (later known to be a vicious anti-Semite and vociferous supporter of the Nazi party and its leader), and it seems that many of the melodies that the rabbi composed and that are still sung today by the Chassidic group were inspired by this music. Tzipporah notes that there was no separation between the Chassidic courtyard and other Jews, and Jews of all types would come to the Grand Rabbi's home to hear his advice and sometimes ask for blessings. This included men who were involved in the underworld and women who worked as prostitutes.

The connection with the non-Jewish world was more complex. On the one hand, there were good relationships and even friendships, especially with the Romanian-speakers who mostly lived in this rural area. Some of them were even willing to resolve disputes that arose with Jews in the rabbinical court, where the Grand Rabbi presided as the judge, and in quite a few of these cases, he ruled in favor of the Christian claimant. On the other hand, Tzipporah relates that almost every walk outside in the city itself, especially around the time of a Christian holiday, was fraught with fear of curses, spitting, and often physical violence as well.

In 1940, the city of Oradea, like all of Transylvania, was annexed by Hungary. While in the first stage, ghettos were not built and there were no deportations to death camps, the Jews lost the sense of security that they had once enjoyed. In March 1944, after the Germans occupied Hungary, the Jews of Oradea were expelled to a ghetto, and following two and a half months of living under horrific conditions, more than half of the city's Jewish population was sent to Auschwitz. Tzipporah's family succeeded, with the help of the local underground, in escaping to Bucharest, where the Romanians did not permit the Nazis to conduct deportations to the death camps. Tzipporah relates that upon arriving in Bucharest, she couldn't stop crying for an entire week. The devastating collapse of the world where she had grown up and the trauma of the ghetto led to a severe crisis of faith. These feelings were intensified when she met Yisrael Friedman, a distant relative who was himself a descendant of the Ruzhin Chassidic dynasty and had already abandoned his religious observance and joined the secular, Zionist, and socialist Hashomer Hatzair movement in Romania. Their shared Chassidic background and subsequent crisis of faith, combined with their Zionist fervor and sense of deep loss, forged a connection between the two. It didn't take long before they fell in love and resolved that they would marry as soon as possible. During those two years in Bucharest, Tzipporah still lived and dressed like a *charedi* girl, while Yisrael walked around bare-headed. In a manner that is almost incomprehensible today, not only did Tzipporah's father, the Grand Rabbi of Vizhnitz, not shun his daughter or demand that she abandon the relationship, he even loved and respected Yisrael, the secular socialist.

After the war ended, Tzipporah and her spouse Israel immigrated to Israel, as did the rest of Tzipporah's family. But they soon discovered that the Chassidic group that they had known all their lives changed dramatically in Israel. It seemed that upon leaving Romania, the special mosaic of Romanian Jewry before the Holocaust, without partitions and walls, had vanished, and in its place, Vizhnitz, like other Chassidic groups, chose an isolated, protective lifestyle.

When Tzipporah immigrated to Israel and joined a kibbutz, her father decided to shun her and would not agree to see her until she started a long process of returning to religious observance, first with a move to the national religious Kibbutz Sa'ad and eventually toward the end of her life, readopting almost all of the Chassidic customs and traditions of her youth.

A few years ago, Tzipporah passed away. I and the other participants at the funeral walked in complete silence through the dark streets of Kiryat Vizhnitz, the place of residence of the Grand Rabbi in Bnei Brak, not far from Tel Aviv. In the name of that isolated lifestyle, Tzipporah was brought to eternal rest, and not even one of the melodies that we sang together on almost every holiday or family occasion was sung. Not even one word of eulogy was spoken, and not even her granddaughters or daughter were present to accompany her on her last journey. When we reached the cemetery, where there was not even a single patch of greenery in sight, I understood what Tzipporah meant at my wedding, when she spoke and cried about the world that was lost. It is difficult to imagine such a glaring contrast as Vizhnitz in the sea of asphalt that is Bnei Brak, which is closed off and isolated from the rest of the sects and Jewish life, and the vibrant, open Chassidic group that viewed itself as an inextricable part of the life of every Jew, cultivated between the green hills and expanses of Transylvania.

Yishay's Story

The old steam engine began to emit deafening noises, thick smoke spiraled above it, the wheels screeched, and the Carpathian Forest Steam Train left the station. The last steam train in Europe made its way on a pleasant summer's day into a narrow valley in the heart of the Carpathian Mountains. A light rain added a hint of mystery to the slow ride on the narrow tracks. The train crawled out of the village of Vişeu de Sus and entered a forest that could have been taken straight out of a fairy tale.

I sat in one of the somewhat spartan train cars with my family and looked out at the landscape. This wasn't how I had imagined Romania when I decided to visit. I had pictured broad expanses filled with blooming sunflower fields and desolate mountains with gloomy castles built on the edge of a cliff and occupied by bloodthirsty vampires. In short, I was completely ignorant. It's true that there are many sunflower fields in Romania, but the Carpathian Mountains that cover an extensive portion of the country were a huge surprise to me. There are never-ending forests with an abundance of water, flowers, and animals; azure lakes; narrow, winding roads that ascend and descend in waves; villagers trying to sell wedges of homemade cheese to passersby in the middle of nowhere. More than once, when I opened my eyes, I was certain that I was in Switzerland or Austria.

The steam engine train passed by a small village. My family and I glanced at the old houses and tried to guess when they were built. After a while, we gave up. We had no way of knowing whether they were two hundred years old or a month old. The village residents could easily have been dressed in the same way that their ancestors had. The impression we received was that in this region, time had stood still. About half an hour after our journey began, I found myself in a state of complete serenity – a state that allowed me to think about the five days that I had just spent in this part of the world.

The Maramures region in northwestern Romania is considered an area where advancement trickles in very slowly. In the village of Oncesti, where we stayed, farmers often work without any mechanical tools. We saw many farmers making their way out to the fields sitting on old wooden wagons hitched to horses. They harvested the fodder with a scythe, stacked it in piles, and left it in the sun to dry. On an evening stroll through the village, we saw old women spinning wool with spindles. We visited wooden monasteries from the Middle Ages and colorful cemeteries, and we saw carpets being laundered on the banks of the local stream. Not much has changed here over the past century. And yet, one thing was missing – the Jews.

In the Maramures region and in Transylvania, which are included in Romania's borders today, many Jews lived for hundreds of years. They lived alongside the local Romanian and Ukrainian population, and their standard of living was no different from that of their neighbors in this forlorn corner of the world. Essentially, in all of Romania, there were just under 800,000 Jews in the year Tzipporah Friedman was born. It was the third largest community in Europe. Today, there are no Jewish communities in northern Romania at all. Anyone interested in Judaism must go south to the cities of Brasov and Bucharest or must suffice, as in many other places in Europe, with the silent relics of the cultural and human abundance that was obliterated in the Holocaust. Yet there are a few Jewish sites that are definitely worth visiting. One of them is the childhood home of Eli Wiesel in the city of Sighet, not far from the Ukrainian border.

Before my visit, I reread the opening chapters of *Night*, which Wiesel wrote after the war. I have read this book many times in my life, and I focused primarily on the author's horrifying experiences at Auschwitz and during the death march. Planning my trip to Romania, I made sure to include a visit to Wiesel's home. If I was already in the neighborhood, I thought, it was worth dedicating an hour of my time in appreciation of the author, a Nobel Peace Prize laureate.

Sighet, where Wiesel was born, is no different than other Romanian cities in the area. Traffic is minimal, the streets are clean, and the public parks testify to the local municipality's significant efforts to improve the quality of life of its residents. The Mămăligă we ate at the local restaurant was amazing, the best I had tasted in Romania. I was sorry that I couldn't thank the chef for the wonderful meal, because not a person in the restaurant spoke English.

Wiesel's childhood home turned out to be a small museum whose very existence is its most important part. The exhibits at the site definitely need refreshing and rethinking. I cannot say that I was disappointed by my visit to the site, because the very statement that the local Jewish culture that was destroyed during the war by the Nazis and the Hungarian fascists is something to be proud of is very meaningful to me. The local pride in the famous Jewish resident of Sighet made me happy. After passing through the different rooms of the museum, I stepped outside and waited for the rest of my family to join me. Suddenly, I noticed a well in the front yard of the house. I walked over and examined it up close. It had a simple water-drawing device made of wood and a system of wheels, to which a rope and a bucket were tied. A well just like the other wells I had seen in the neighboring villages. A well that provided the Wiesel family with water to drink and for washing.

For a reason unknown to me, I was drawn to that well of water. I peered into its depths and thought to myself that perhaps I hadn't correctly understood the museum when I visited it, or the significance of a trip to the Maramures region and nearby Transylvania. The realization hit me that when I (and honestly, many others too) think of Eastern Europe, I instantly conjure up in my mind the Holocaust and the destruction that it brought upon the Jewish communities there. The prism of the Holocaust casts a shadow over any other other possible thought. I had never before thought of Eli Wiesel as a child who drew water from a well and munched on a juicy plum from the tree in his yard.

The memories from our visit to the Wiesel home and the five days I spent in this region of northwestern Romania monopolized my thoughts at that moment of contemplation in the steam engine car in the heart of the Carpathian Mountains. I slowly began to internalize the great gift that these days in a region where time had stood still had given to me. For the first time in my life, I succeeded in seeing with my own eyes, without filters, how Jewish life had looked in Eastern Europe before the Holocaust – everyday life itself, not a restoration like those featured in many museums. The old steam engine, the traditional villages, the ancient practices, and the well in the Wiesel family's yard are no less than a captivating lesson in the history of the Jewish nation. A lesson in looking at the reality of Jewish life without the prism of the Holocaust. Today, several years after this trip, I can testify that this insight changed the way I understand Jewish history and literature set in this part of the world. Things that I was unable to deeply comprehend, such as the description of the life of Tzipporah Freidman née Hager, became palpable and colorful in my mind's eye. For me, the visit to Romania was like looking into the mirror of a lost world.

Austria

9. A Jewish Waltz – Vienna
Local Personality: Sigrid Massenbauer
Hillel Meyer

Exchanging memories, decorating the past
There, they were all princes, and this is what is left
There was a piano in every room, horse stables in the yard
Every word is truth, truth – more or less…

(From the song "Sharlia," by Chava Alberstein)

I stand opposite building number 10 on Krummbaumgasse, opposite Karmlitemarkt, Vienna's colorful farmers' market. The aroma of the pastries and the sight of the cheeses and fruits, which would have caused me to take out my Euro coins on a regular day, serve as a backdrop for the hesitation that I feel. "Are you sure this is the place?" I ask Sigi, the local guide accompanying me. "Yes, this is the address that you requested, the address of your grandparents' home."

I gaze at the low, four-story building that has recently undergone renovation and at the restaurant at the entrance, which, based on the pictures on its display window, serves typical Austrian cuisine: schnitzel, goulash, potato salad, and apple strudel. I smile to myself and tell Sigi, "My grandmother tended to exaggerate and find the good in everything. According to her descriptions, Vienna was a kingdom, and she lived in a palace."

As a child, I drank up these stories eagerly – stories about a city with luxurious fashions, gorgeous gardens, classical music, European culture, strudel, and cream cakes. The film *The Sound of Music*, about the Von Trapp family, and impressions from the Salzburg Festival of music only amplified the voice of my grandmother Peppy a few decibels. She didn't speak of the war, only of the life that she had in Vienna.

In 1938, the Nazis invaded Vienna. Essentially, it was more of a royal entrance than an invasion. Austria was part of the group of German states and the only one that was not annexed to Germany after World War I. The annexation of Austria, known as the Anschluss, together with the annexation of the Czech Sudetenland, symbolized the conclusion of the creation of a greater Germany. The world's response was an expression of hope that this would satisfy Hitler (a hope that was later proven false).

Grandpa Yaakov was born in Bukovina, which was part of the Austrian Empire. Like many Jews from the villages and towns, he moved to Vienna with his wife Peppy in order to advance economically and develop his business. It was there that their son Isidor was born. They lived in a small apartment in the center of the Jewish quarter, participated in Jewish community life, and attended the Orthodox synagogue.

They watched as the Nazi army convoy, led by Hitler, drove through the main streets of Vienna. The newspaper headlines of the days beforehand did not predict good news, but they never expected the change to be so staggering. Masses of excited crowds raised their arms in salute and greeted the convoy with flowers and cries of joy. Peppy and Yaakov returned to their home and hoped that the storm would pass; unfortunately, it did not.

The next day, when Yaakov went to open his fabric store, he encountered a pair of soldiers waiting for him at the entrance with a can of white paint and a brush. They commanded that he paint the word *Jude* (Jew) onto his display window and then pushed him into a crowd of Jews who stood nearby. In the crowd, he recognized his neighbors – the respectable doctor's wife with her fur coat, the rabbi from the nearby synagogue, and a few other acquaintances. The soldiers ordered that they all take rags and begin scrubbing the street, as pedestrians stood by and cheered, including his neighbors and people he knew.

While scrubbing and getting kicked by the soldiers, Grandpa Yaakov formulated their escape plan from Vienna in his mind. Kristallnacht, which took place November 8–10, 1938, and during which hundreds of synagogues, Jewish businesses, and homes were burned and vandalized, was the last straw. On November 11, Grandma, Grandpa, and their young son Isidor, together with a few relatives, escaped Vienna hastily and left all their memories behind.

The state had always been fickle toward the Jews throughout the seven hundred years they lived in Vienna, where they served as court Jews and detested money changers. But in the mid-nineteenth century, Vienna was a safe place for Jews to settle down, and they became a significant part of the city's economic and cultural scene. In 1849, Emperor Franz Joseph publicly recognized the "Jewish Israelite community" of Vienna, and a few years later, the Jews were granted full civil rights.

Despite the anti-Semitism that existed in Vienna, Jews held key positions in the empire. Gustav Mahler, who was of Jewish descent, served as the director of the Vienna State Opera; Sigmond Freud revolutionized the field of psychology; and Theodor Herzl used the respected, prestigious *Neue Freie Presse* newspaper as a platform to publish his opinion and critical columns. This was also the newspaper that sent him to cover the Dreyfus affair in Paris, which was the turning point at which Herzl abandoned his positive attitude toward Jewish assimilation in favor of founding a national home for the Jews.

"Memories can be sneaky, escaping when we want to lay hand on them. Like little fish, like curls of waves on the beach that tickle your feet and melt into foam. Often, memory is an abstract knowledge of what once was. Memory piles up over memory, a shadow of a shadow, until one does not know which is the pure memory and which is the memory of the memory..." wrote Judith Rotem in her book *I Loved So Much* (*Ahavti Kol Kach*, Yedioth Ahronoth, 2000).

I stand at the entrance to the building and ask Sigi to take my picture, so I can show my parents that I was here. Coming closer to the entrance, I check the names of the tenants, looking for some proof or hint that my grandparents once lived here. I hope to at least find a *Stolperstein* – one of the thousands of stones of remembrance created by German artist Gunter Demnig. These shiny stones can be found all over Europe; the vast majority are at the entrances of homes that were once owned by Jews murdered in the Holocaust, with a few in front of former Jewish institutions.

"Grandma and Grandpa weren't murdered in the Holocaust," I tell myself. "They don't meet the criteria for that type of commemoration." After a few photos, I ask myself, "What now? Do I want to move on to the next stage, ring the intercom, and knock on the door? But wait, I don't know their apartment number! And how could I suddenly surprise the tenants in the building now? What would I say to them? *Hello, I'm Hillel from Israel, my grandparents lived here eighty years ago, fled from the Nazis, left you this apartment for free, and now I want to see it?* No, I didn't come to ask for it back, just to try to see it. But what's there to see? It's not the same apartment anymore. There's an intercom at the front door, the building has been painted, and I'm pretty sure there will be electrical appliances, furniture, maybe a different division of the rooms. Different from what? I don't even know what the original apartment looked like. The memory is my birthright but is not mine. It is a story atop a story, an interpretation of what my grandmother used to tell me, my imagination, movies I watched, books I read. Why is it so important to preserve a memory? Especially when the memory itself didn't end well. Maybe I should just leave."

Sigi seems to read my thoughts and suggests that we continue touring the Jewish quarter. "We can always come back here – it's not far." We walk out of the marketplace back into the city that is sparkling clean. We cross the bridge over the Danube Canal, an arm of the famous river for which Johann Strauss composed the *Blue Danube Waltz*. We walk between buildings representing Viennese architecture, influenced by Rome, the Renaissance, and Gothic and Ottoman styles. The wide boulevards, gardens, cathedral steeples, and bridges are all gorgeous. In the background, we can see Schönbrunn Palace and the opera building. We stop at Hotel Sacher, famous for the *Sachertorte* concocted in its kitchen and for the fact that the emperor himself ate there. Vienna's beauty, aside from its cleanliness and opulence, is special in an indescribable way, like a painting and a photograph combined. Every corner and every stone in a building seems to have been drawn out purposefully. The urban planning is also carefully arranged, built as rings: the further you enter into the rings, the further back you go in time, to the city's history. At the peak of the Jewish community's glory, it comprised 40 percent of the city's residents, inside the innermost ring.

We cross a busy street and enter the Jewish quarter. At the heart of a quiet street stands the Stadttempel (city synagogue). It is a regal building that is two hundred years old. Due to the imperial order prohibiting the construction of non-Christian houses of prayer with a decorated front, it was constructed between the houses on a residential street, and this is what saved it from being destroyed on Kristallnacht, for fear that the fire would spread to the nearby homes. Another reason for its preservation was that the building housed the archive of the Jews of Vienna, including registers of the population and properties, which was an invaluable asset for the Nazis. From there, we continued to the Judenplatz, the town square from medieval times, and we looked at the ruins of the ancient synagogue buried under the ground, the Holocaust monument shaped as a library, symbolizing the cultural influence of Austria's Jews, and the list of cities and towns where Jews once lived prior to the Holocaust.

The small Jewish museum is housed in one of the homes in the square, and a sculpture of the famous Austrian playwright Gotthold Ephraim Lessing looks out over it all. He wrote the play *Nathan the Wise*, in which he preaches religious tolerance, including toward Jews. I wander around, and my thoughts travel back several decades, to Grandma and Grandpa and the lives they had here. The commemoration for the Jews of Vienna is cold and symbolic, presenting the history of the Jews in Austria in a very sterile, clean manner. I would say that aside from being impressive-looking, it is also disappointing. Where are the authentic elements, such as Shabbat candles? The people dressed in their finest on the way to synagogue? The weddings? The concerts in the parks? Where are Grandma's stories? Did they even take place in this part of the city? "Your grandparents almost definitely did not walk around here," the local guide tells me. "This is only a small part that does not represent the glorious Jewish world that existed here before the war." They were there, on the other side, where the Ostjuden (Eastern European Jews) were.

Commemoration is a complicated thing. On the one hand, life goes on and leads us to create new memories, and on the other hand, we still try to preserve and hold onto the past – the smells, colors, sounds, people. In my profession as a tour guide, I often meet tourists who come in search of their roots. They are equipped with a photo, a testimony, an address written on a piece of paper. I drive with them to the towns and villages of Poland and Central Europe together with a local guide. In the end, we stand opposite a new building constructed atop the ruins of the old one, and we attempt to envision the life that was once there decades earlier. We try to find an organized register in the municipality building, a tombstone at the neglected Jewish cemetery... we hold on to every tiny piece of information, looking for former neighbors and for the old man who will say, "Yes! I remember them. You see this tree? I climbed it with their little son; his name was Jozeph."

The Israeli poet Nathan Zach wrote, "When everyone remembers, I forget. And when everyone forgets, I remember. And it hurts so much that I need to try to work hard to collect the shards, so that I don't forget that I must remember."

Before I left Vienna, I went back to Grandma and Grandpa's house. This time I came alone, to say goodbye, and I braced myself not to feel anything. I asked the taxi driver to wait across from the house, and I got out. The marketplace was already closed, dusk had begun to fall, and it was just me. I stood there and shut my eyes. In my mind, I saw Grandma and Grandpa, the Ostjuden who came from the east to Western Europe to build a new life. I smelled Grandma's lokshen kugel, with the noodles, eggs, pepper, and oil. I heard Grandpa singing "Kol Mekadesh Shevii" in the familiar Vizhnitz tune, and the scent of the restaurant's strudel mixed with the aroma of Grandma's almond cookies. I imagined her walking out of the house wearing a fur coat and pearls, holding Grandpa's arm as he wore his smoking jacket and matching cap on their way to the opera. Maybe it was a pleasant evening and they walked there on foot; maybe they rode in a horse-drawn carriage driven by a gloved groom. They had left their son at home with the nurse, who sung him to sleep with German lullabies. In my imagination, that was Grandma's Vienna.

I try to ignore the memories of what followed. The escape from Vienna, the trudging through the snow with a small child, the hiding in the home of a righteous gentile in a Belgian village. The move to Canada and settling down in a village of Quebec as destitute immigrants, where Grandma milked cows and Grandpa sold apples at the marketplace. There, my mother Leah was born. In my memory, I jump forward a few years to their move to Montreal, where Grandpa reopened his fabric business with his son Isidor (my uncle) and became successful, where my mother married my father David, and where my siblings and

I were born. A descendant of a magnificent family that traces back to Rabbi Moshe Yagid, author of the scholarly work *Machatzit Hashekel*.

I went back to Vienna to find myself there. Grandma and Grandpa never went back to Vienna. Maybe because of the crimes of the Nazis and their helpers. Maybe they were afraid of the memories. And maybe, just maybe, they wanted to leave Vienna a sweet memory. Sweet as the *Sachertorte* from Hotel Sacher.

> Somewhere deep within us
> Voices and memories are buried
> Many sights that we have forgotten
> Stories of wonders and melodies.
>
> All the memories from days gone by
> The first dreams
> And every word of father and mother
> Spoken years ago.
>
> And sometimes, the hint of a familiar scent or sound,
> or a bit of a word
> Brings back a flowering garden
> Brings you back to the starting line...
> ("Cherished Dreams," by Ehud Manor)

Russia and the Former Soviet Union

Russia

10. On Both Sides of the Iron Curtain – Moscow
Local Personality: Marina Zilberman
Lana Zilberman Soloway

The year was 1990. The Berlin Wall had already fallen, the Iron Curtain was slowly disintegrating, and the Soviet Union was about to fall apart. I was eight years old. My mother Marina, my father Daniel, and I finally received visas to immigrate to Israel.

Jews who were permitted to leave the Soviet Union were forced to pay large sums of money to the Soviet authorities to renounce their citizenship. My parents, who had been refuseniks and waited eleven years for this moment, paid everything they had, left their entire lives behind them – their apartment, property, family, and friends – and immigrated to the Promised Land, to Israel, the Jewish state.

My childhood memories from Moscow are sparse. I vividly remember the apartment we lived in, my elementary school, and the neighborhood I grew up in. I remember a lot of snow, ice skating, and sledding. I remember visiting the Kremlin during the New Year's celebrations in second grade, and I remember museums, theaters, and the music conservatory where I studied. I also remember the intense anti-Semitism that was directed at my parents and myself.

Twenty years later, in June 2010, I took a trip with my mother to visit our motherland. I had a burning desire to see the large city where I was born and spent the first years of my life. Around my neck was a thin necklace with a small Star of David, which I wore all over the world and never took off. My mother, plagued with anti-Semitic memories on the one hand and fear mixed with anxiety on the other, asked me to take off the necklace. I refused. We made our way from Sheremetyevo International Airport to Pushkin Street, in the center of Moscow, on the metro. It felt like the longest and deepest train in the world, and in fact, it is just that. With 241 stations and 14 different lines, its total length reaches 257 miles. This train is also very deep under the ground. The escalators are never-ending, taking you deeper and deeper into the earth. The stations themselves are decorated with impressive, museum-quality artwork. People from all over the world come to Moscow specifically to enjoy the phenomenon called the Moscow Metro, which has been operating for over eighty-five years, since its establishment in 1935.

When we reached our stop, we started to climb up the escalators toward street level. Suddenly, I saw a woman in front of me wearing a hat with a large Star of David pin on it. I pulled on my mother's sleeve, like a little girl, so that she could see it too. My incredulous mother could not believe that in this city where she grew up and suffered so much because of her Judaism, a woman was walking around in public with a Star of David pin on her head.

My mother, the eldest of two girls, was born in 1951 in Moscow. She grew up in a very Russian home, but their Jewish identity was always present, especially around Jewish holidays and culinary traditions. On Purim, my grandmother would bake hamantaschen filled with poppy seeds; on Passover, they ate matzah if they managed to find some on the underground market. On Rosh Hashanah, there was festive honey cake. Of course, in addition to the Jewish holidays, the national holidays were also celebrated, with the most important date being May 9, the date of the Soviet victory in World War II; Revolution Day in November; New Year's Day on January 1; and International Women's Day on March 8.

My mother didn't look outwardly Jewish. She was (and still is) a tall, beautiful woman with silky red hair, green eyes, and an upturned nose. Her appearance and her "Russian" last name never disclosed her identity, but every time she handed someone her identity card or filled out a government form, section five always had a line for "nationality," and my mother had to write "Jewish." This section prevented my mother from realizing many opportunities in life and held her back quite significantly for example, during the four consecutive years when she tried to get into university to study languages. She passed all her exams successfully, but when it was her turn to be interviewed by the admissions committee, the interview would be over as soon as the examiners reached section five on the form.

From the metro, we continued to a nearby building on Pushkin Street. There, in a friend's apartment, we spent our week in Moscow. A small childhood memory is connected to this very building, where the first McDonald's opened in Moscow at the end of 1990, about a month before we left. I remember that we stood in line at McDonald's for an entire day, most of the time outside on the cold street, and when our turn arrived, I received a tiny paper bag with about ten French fries in it. I thought it was the best thing I'd ever tasted, and I was so sorry when I finished them. That same McDonald's is still open in the building, with a rich and diverse menu similar to other McDonald's restaurants around the world. They don't serve French fries in small paper bags anymore.

We reached our friend's apartment on a Friday at around six in the evening, and I really wanted to go to synagogue for Kabbalat Shabbat service. During all the years that the Communist regime controlled the Soviet Union, there was a single synagogue that remained open in Moscow: the Moscow Choral Synagogue, then on Arkhipova Street. After the fall of the Soviet Union, the street names were changed, and today, the street is called Kitai-Gorod, freely translated from Russian "the city of China."

Construction of the Choral Synagogue in Moscow began in the beginning of the nineteenth century, and the building was opened to the public in 1905. It faithfully served the new, developing Jewish community of the capital city (Jews were only permitted to come to Moscow after the 1905 revolution). In September 1948 (Tishrei 5708), as the War of Independence raged in the State of Israel, Golda Meir was sent to Moscow to try to win the empathy and perhaps even the support of the Soviet government. Golda landed in the capital of the Soviet Union on Rosh Hashanah eve, and upon hearing that there was one active synagogue in the city, requested to visit it.

On her way there, Golda discovered that Ilya Ehrenburg, a Jewish historian and journalist, had written about her upcoming visit to Moscow in the daily newspaper and had demanded that no one come to greet her. Despite her sad feelings, Golda continued on her way, certain that she would be alone in the synagogue and that no one would show up. In her autobiography, *My Life*, she wrote of her memories from that night and shared that when the car stopped at the entrance to the synagogue, she couldn't even open the door or set foot on the sidewalk because tens of thousands of Jews from Moscow and the surrounding areas had arrived to celebrate the Jewish New Year in the synagogue and to meet Golda Meir, the woman from Palestine. Among the masses of people at the synagogue that night was my paternal grandfather Shimon Zilberman, of blessed memory. Two years later, in 1950, my grandfather Shimon would stand with his bride, my grandmother Zoya, on the bimah of that same synagogue, under their wedding canopy. Their ketubah (Jewish marriage contract), handwritten on a lined piece of notebook paper and signed by the couple – my grandparents – and their witnesses on that special occasion is still in my possession to this day.

In September 1965, Golda Meir again visited the Soviet capital, this time with the objective of forging diplomatic relationships between the two countries. Since the memory from that Rosh Hashanah at the Moscow Choral Synagogue was still so vivid after all those years, she asked to visit the site again and see its condition. Her request was honored, and when she entered the prayer sanctuary, she saw a thirteen-year-old boy standing next to the Torah on the bimah and reading from it in fluent Hebrew. That bar mitzvah boy was my father, of blessed memory, Daniel Zilberman, Shimon's son. Golda waited patiently until the prayer services were over and then approached the boy to congratulate him and gift him with a kippah. My father proudly wore this kippah his entire life, and I still have it today – an eternal testament to this story and to our family. In January 1982, when I was born, my father Daniel and grandfather Shimon hurried to the synagogue and marked my joining the Jewish nation by giving me my Hebrew name, Shifra, after my great-grandmother, who had just passed away.

Back to 2010. The Choral Synagogue was two metro stops away from Pushkin Street, but we were too tired to start traveling again. However, I still wanted to participate in Kabbalat Shabbat services, so I started searching the internet. I found that there was a synagogue right around the corner, on Malaya Bronnaya Street. When we arrived, we discovered that the synagogue had also been built at the end of the nineteenth century, but it was abandoned in the twentieth century and only renovated again in recent years. It was no wonder my mother didn't know it existed. It really didn't "exist" the entire time she lived in the city. The time was 7:30 p.m., and it was summer, so it was still light outside. Only the gabbai of the synagogue welcomed us. He greeted us very warmly and then told us that today, the synagogue is run by Chabad, and since sundown is very late in Moscow, Kabbalat Shabbat would only be in two hours, after the sun set. My mother was tired, but I insisted on waiting.

We crossed the street and sat down at a café; it was a wonderful opportunity to do a small anthropological study of the city. I'll begin by saying that the prices on the menu were sky-high. If I remember correctly, we paid close to seventy dollars for two cups of coffee and two slices of cake. In addition, the people around us were dressed according to the newest fashions in New York or Milan, in very beautiful and expensive clothing. Lastly, the cars parked outside were all well-polished luxury cars. I didn't spot a single "simple" car. The landscape was colorful and light-years away from the gray Moscow of the nineties, the one that I remembered, and from the Moscow that my mother had told me about my entire life. It was clear that during the twenty years since the fall of the Soviet Union, when we no longer lived here, life had changed in the city dramatically. It is important to note that the café was in the center of town, which is wrapped in a glittering, luminous aura, but 650 feet from there, in any direction, the real city was still there – the gloomy one with its crumbling buildings. Twenty years ago, most people had nothing, and all the shops were empty too. Now, store shelves were full of merchandise, but the socioeconomic gap between the rich and the poor was astronomical. The wealthy oligarchs drove luxury cars while everyone else struggled along on the metro.

We sat in the café waiting for the sun to set and absorbed the atmosphere around us. About two hours later, we crossed the street again and headed back to the synagogue. On the way, we saw a few dozen young men, wearing festive clothing and kippot on their heads, also walking in the same direction as us. A sight so natural and trivial elicited the same shock in my mother as seeing the woman with the Star of David pin.

On Passover eve in 2019, after living in Israel for twenty-eight years, I came again to Moscow on a quick trip, and this time, I visited the Choral Synagogue, which happened to be celebrating one hundred years since its establishment. I was a first-year rabbinical student, and it was important to me to pray at my family's synagogue. I came early for the morning Shacharit prayers on Thursday and ascended to the women's section on the second floor. I picked up a local prayer book, with the Hebrew prayers alongside a Russian translation, and immediately sunk into nostalgia. I tried to envision my grandparents' wedding and my father's bar mitzvah, and even myself as a baby. I thought about Golda Meir and the kippah, and suddenly, lifting my eyes from the prayer book, I looked down below and was astounded to see over a hundred men praying Shacharit in the large synagogue, on a regular weekday. Even my synagogue in Israel doesn't have such a minyan on a weekday morning.

Today, the Choral Synagogue is just one of the many active synagogues in Moscow, and not even the main one, but still, over a hundred people came to pray Shacharit there on an ordinary weekday.

In contrast with all the years when Russia was controlled by the Communist party and Judaism was not considered a religion, but rather a persecuted nationality, the status of Moscow's Jews today is especially "prestigious." Jews outwardly display and express their Judaism in public and view it as a source of pride. They walk the streets of the Russian capital wearing large, obvious Jewish symbols (kippah, tzitzit, a Star of David) and no longer hide their identities in shame. There is a wide range of synagogues and prayer minyans in Moscow, including even a Reform community with a number of branches in the city, as well as kosher restaurants, a wonderful Jewish museum called the Jewish Museum and Tolerance Center, a memorial complex featuring a synagogue alongside a church and a mosque, as monuments to World War II, *Stolpersteins* on the sidewalks, traditional Jewish dishes in Russian restaurants, community centers, a Jewish theater, a Jewish studies faculty at one of the large universities, Jewish schools, and even a rabbinical seminary – all of these and more are part of the Jewish Russian reality of modern Moscow in the twenty-first century. Being a Jew and visiting Jewish institutions is considered cool, interesting, and special. Belonging to a Jewish community gives members a "prestigious" status. Beyond that, being a Jew opens the possibility of immigrating to Israel and receiving a passport from a Western country, which constitutes an exit ticket to the rest of the world. Anyone who can obtain a foreign passport today does so eagerly. There is no doubt that for Russia's Jews, this option exists and is important.

In November 2019, half a year after I prayed Shacharit at the Choral Synagogue, I returned to Moscow to lead a tour for a large congregation from North America. The Jews from that community were very moved by the trip, not only because they were interested in the history, art, and culture of one of the most important capital cities in the world, but because many of them had been actively involved in the struggle to free the Jews of the Soviet Union in the seventies and eighties, until the fall of the Iron Curtain. For them, visiting Moscow today, in the twenty-first century, reflects the success of their struggle, which freed the Soviet Jews, including those who decided to run for their lives and immigrate to Israel, Germany, or the United States. It also facilitated the development of the unbelievable Jewish renaissance that has been taking place in the city over the past thirty years.

It is important for me to emphasize the complexity of the story. During that trip, we stayed at the Four Seasons Hotel for almost a week, which is in in the famous Red Square next to the Kremlin, Moscow's most famous landmark.

For an entire week, I sat with my friend Mike every morning at breakfast in the hotel restaurant, overlooking the red brick wall of the Kremlin. Mike's heart filled with wonder at the sight of the beauty all around us, the rich history, and the possibility of being free Jews who can visit the city, stay at this luxurious hotel for a whole week, and gaze out at all the glory in front of our eyes. I, on the other hand, didn't see the beauty and was not amazed at the sight of the historical monuments. I thought about my maternal grandfather, Anatoly, who worked as a barber in this very hotel in the seventies and eighties, when it was called Moscow Hotel. A Jew working in such a respectable establishment was no small feat, and it was thanks to this job that he managed to "organize" many things for his family, from food in times of famine to admission into a university. While it wasn't the school my mother tried to get accepted to for four years, at least it was an academic institution. I also thought about the KGB basements, located nearby, where my mother was "invited" endless times for interrogation, every time she finished guiding a group of tourists (in the eighties), and about other painful, hostile moments in the life of my own family and in the lives of all of Moscow's Jews behind the Iron Curtain.

Moscow is a complicated city, glittering on one side and rotting on the other. Its streets are clean, but its identity is a point of conflict. Thirty years after the collapse of the Soviet Union, Russia's capital is advancing and developing educationally, culturally, scientifically, and even Jewishly, but on the other hand, it is not democratic or liberal and is not really like the Western world. Moscow's Jews have, without a doubt, undergone a renaissance. From being considered a nationality, it has become a religion, culture, identity, and community. From being persecuted, it has become prestigious. The hidden Jews have become people who express their Judaism freely and colorfully. Jewish community life is thriving, and immigration to Israel is a goal for only a few. At the same time, however, the Jewish past in the city, with all its pain and bloodshed, has not been forgotten for even one moment. It continues to live on in the hearts of Moscow's Jews, primarily the older ones, and to remind them how fragile the Russian reality is and how it could change from one extreme to the other at any moment.

My dear mother started to guide tours of Moscow again after many years, this time guiding groups of Israelis, truly coming full circle. On the one hand, she is extremely familiar with the city – she was born there, studied there, worked there, suffered there, and got married and gave birth there too. It's her city. On the other hand, she comes as a free person, with citizenship from a different country, and most importantly – at the end of every tour she leads, she can leave with ease and return home. To Israel.

No stranger can comprehend it. Moscow is much more than can be read about in a typical guidebook. I hope that this essay will arouse your curiosity and desire to visit, while simultaneously shedding light on the complexity of this city. On your visit, it is worth having a good guide, and I recommend a Jewish one at least some of the time.

(Note: this chapter predates the 2022 invasion of Ukraine by Russia.)

Ukraine

11. Finding Our Way Back Home – Ukraine
Local Personality: The Local Jewish Authors of Ukraine
Ya'acov Fried

When I was a child, my grandfather would lead me to the bookstore in the center of Jerusalem while telling me stories about Odessa, the Ukrainian port city where he stayed with his family during the process of their immigration to Israel in the early twentieth century. He often said to me, "No other city in the world at that time could boast such an illustrious group of Jewish authors. Odessa was the city of Hebrew culture. Everybody was there, often sitting at Café Fanconi for long discussions into the night. It was there that I witnessed the birth of Zionist leadership, and especially how new Hebrew literature was created."

In the bookcase of my childhood home, the writings of Sholem Aleichem had a place of honor. As a child, I remember my father's intense dedication to reading these books out loud to me, having arrived in Israel after the Holocaust. This was primarily to instill in me the experience of the shtetl, from which the Germans had expelled him and his family. By the age of six, I had already encountered Tevye the Jewish milkman, who navigated his way between tradition, faith, modernism, and pogroms. Tevye's character overflows with humor despite the challenges of his life, representing the Jewish spirit in Ukraine prior to World Wars I and II, as expressed so poignantly in the famous musical *Fiddler on the Roof*.

The first time I visited Odessa, I felt I was retracing the steps of Bialik, Tchernichovsky, Jabotinsky, Ahad Ha'am, Pinsker, and Sholem Aleichem, who lived and created in this city during different periods. To me, visiting the city was a journey in the footsteps of these thinkers and the Zionist leaders who simultaneously led the Zionist movement and the revival of Hebrew culture in the Land of Israel.

From Odessa, I flew to Kiev, Ukraine's capital city. After visiting the childhood home of Golda Meir, Israel's prime minister, I traveled to Babi Yar, the ravine where over 135,000 people were massacred during the Holocaust, of whom about 50,000 were Jews. I discovered that throughout the valley of this ravine of death, right where the appalling massacre took place and where a monument stands commemorating the atrocities, many residential neighborhoods were built. The local guide who accompanied me even happened to meet his daughter and granddaughter, who were strolling through the pathways of Babi Yar. Mixed feelings coursed through me during the visit a sense of pride and identification with the history and the abundance of Jewish creativity that developed on Ukrainian soil alongside the terrible pain of the community's destruction, as well as feelings of animosity and even imaginary revenge toward those Ukrainian residents who didn't lift a finger and cooperated with the Nazis during the horrendous massacre. The words of Rabbi Nachman of Breslov, whose character hovers above the soil of Ukraine even today, express my feelings perfectly: "You are where your thoughts are. Make sure that your thoughts are where you want to be."

The history books tell the story of how, in the mid-1830s, a movement that changed the face of Judaism sprouted on this cold, green soil – Chassidism. Here, in this rural landscape, where time stands still, the founder of Chassidism, Israel ben Eliezer, the Ba'al Shem Tov, and his great-grandson, Rabbi Nachman of Breslov, were born. Here, the first Chassidic courts were formed, and it was from here that the movement spread to other countries in Eastern Europe, to the Land of Israel, and later to the United States.

With the rise of Communism to power in 1918, anti-Semitism was outlawed. The Communist government established a special department designed to bring Communism to the Jewish masses. In turn, Soviet Jewish activists, empowered by the state to create a Soviet Jewish national culture, cultivated Yiddish as a way to express their identity in new secular terms. Official discussions in 160 local councils were held in Yiddish. Jewish culture flourished. In 1929, the government sponsored the publishing of 800,000 copies of Yiddish books. When Stalin's Great Purge began, the brief golden age of Yiddish culture was cut short. The final blow to Ukrainian Jewry was the murder of over one million Jews, most of the country's Jewish population, in the Holocaust. Today, there are only tens of thousands of Jews left throughout Ukraine.

What really is Ukraine? Is it the land of the elegant young people on the streets of Kiev, or of the farmers' wives with the kerchiefs tied under their chins and the shapely women teetering in stiletto heels on broken sidewalks in forlorn towns? To me, Ukraine is a Jewish heritage site, and the way to connect to it is through a Jewish literary journey.

Let's begin our journey between Kosiv and Kuty, next to the forests where the founder of Chassidism, the Ba'al Shem Tov, would go to meditate in seclusion and listen to the birds chirp. Medzhybizh, where Hershele of Ostropol was a prankster in the court of Rabbi Baruch, still exists, as does Zhytomyr, the home of Bialik's grandfather, which inspired much of his poetry. The landscapes and the names are there. Only the main part is missing, the people, as a result of the Holocaust and mass emigration in the nineties. A Jewish Ukraine-born educator accompanying our group said to me, as we stood in drizzling rain in the town of Brody, the city of Yudil Chassid from Shai Agnon's book *The Bridal Canopy*: "The set is perfect; the actors are missing."

Ukrainian towns suffer from faulty infrastructure and an extremely sparse selection of stores. Yet each town is distinct with its own stamp. In Wasilków, next to Kiev, a beautiful synagogue was preserved; next to it are train tracks that seem to lead nowhere. Wasilków features in the old song mentioned in I.L. Peretz's *Migration of a Melody*.

Southward is Uman, the burial place of Rabbi Nachman of Breslov. The Breslov Chassidic movement is a "dead" Chassidic group in the sense that its leader left no successor. Rabbi Nachman was one of the most original thinkers in the Chassidic movement, and he did not tend to write down his teachings. His students listened to his stories and explanations and wrote them down. Breslov Chassidism has a mystical element to it. It developed unique and original practices, including the custom of personal meditation in the heart of nature. Perhaps this is one of the reasons it attracts many newly religious Jews. The tomb of Rabbi Nachman is found in the corner of a huge structure, and the tombstone is covered with white marble slabs, without any inscription. In contrast with the old tombstones of the Ba'al Shem Tov, Rabbi Levi Yitzchak of Berditchev, and many other righteous figures, there is nothing ancient-looking here.

About two hundred kilometers to the west, in Galicia, is Buchach, the city of Shai Agnon. Even beautiful Paris seems plain when viewed from a tower, but in Buchach, the opposite is true – for it to look beautiful, it must be viewed from the hill that towers above it. Only the crushed sidewalks dim the impression left by the Strypa River and the famous municipality building (in Agnon's writings – "the large council building in our city, for which all Polish cities envied us"). Standing there, I couldn't help but remember how excited my grandfather and I felt when Shmuel Yosef Agnon of Jerusalem, who immigrated from Ukraine and continued writing about experiences from his birthplace throughout his life, received the Nobel Prize in Literature.

Going back to the east, to Kamianets-Podilskyi, the capital of the Podolia region, there is a river surrounded by a huge canyon, an impressive fortress, and an important Catholic church. In 1757, at this church, the cruel bishop Dembowski forced rabbis to participate in a public disputation with their enemies, Jews from the cult of Jacob Frank. The Frankists, influenced by the Sabbatean movement, believed that their greedy leader was the Messiah and were fond of group licentious behavior. The rabbis persecuted them, and in response, Frank's followers spoke out against the Talmud, slandered their brothers to the Catholics, and eventually converted to Christianity. After remembering this chapter of history and seeing the low, isolated homes in the surrounding towns, one can imagine that Frank and his followers probably conducted their orgies in dismal homes such as these.

But the biggest attractions in Jewish Ukraine are the old cemeteries. Sholem Aleichem already discerned this back in 1901, when the towns themselves were still bustling with life. In the story "The Town of the Little People," he wrote: "Nowhere else is the weeping so good and so sweet like in the cemetery of Kasrilevka. They weep pretty well in the synagogue too, but how can that compare to the graves of ancestors?"

Indeed, a visit to the cemeteries evokes an emotional and aesthetic experience. This is true in Buchach, and even more so in Kuty, as well as in Berditchev, with the strange headstones shaped like boots, and the graves of the Karaites in Halych or the wonderful garden in Ostroh. In almost every cemetery, visitors must trudge their way through the long grass that surrounds the tombstones. A number of tourist groups that we brought to visit chose to spend half a day or even a full day cutting the grass and cleaning the cemetery, out of a deep feeling that they too were a link in this chain of generations. They felt that their contribution would enable others to visit the grave sites and experience the cemetery in an accessible, more inviting manner.

Hundreds of Jewish cemeteries are scattered across Eastern Europe. Historians and educators who lead Jewish trips to these sites emphasize the fact that the literary landscape included not only

Sholem Aleichem or Agnon, but also other Jewish thinkers, including many Orthodox Jews, who researched, wrote, marveled, and shared the experiences of these Jewish communities. They all had a common goal – a burning desire to revive and share the Jewish life and culture that existed in the shtetl.

Visiting Ukraine – as in Poland, Thessaloniki, Morocco, and other places where there are barely any Jews living today – is a journey back into Jewish history. These trips are a journey of Jewish introspection, helping us decipher and understand ourselves in a deeper way. What is this chain of generations? What did the Jewish world once encapsulate, and what was the culture that emerged in these towns? How did the colorful Jewish world develop, and who influenced it? How is it that the Jewish culture that developed out of the tension between tradition and enlightenment still influences and even perhaps dominates Jewish culture today?

Touring the villages and towns of Ukraine, through the green fields and flowing rivers, and encountering the wonderful Jewish world that once was and is no longer, we enter a "laboratory" where we can clarify the answers to these questions. I remember when a tour participant quoted Rabbi Nachman of Breslov, who said: "There is nothing that brings wholeness in life more than a sigh emitted from the depths of the heart." As he said this, he demonstrated with a big, heartfelt sigh, in an attempt to share the depths of his emotional experience with the group.

Visiting Ukraine is a journey through a vanishing world. Memorial plaques in the yards of the homes, commemoration statues on street corners of villages trapped as if in a time capsule, crumbling tombstones in what remains of cemeteries, old and new Jewish houses of prayer that barely round up a prayer quorum, and mass graves. An abandoned world that enchants me, as if God took a handful of geniuses and scattered them in this land: Shai Agnon, Bialik, Mendele Mocher Sforim, Sholem Aleichem, Isaac Babel, Simon Dubnow, Ze'ev

Jabotinsky, Rabbi Nachman of Breslov, the Ba'al Shem Tov, Bruno Schulz, Maurycy Gottlieb, Itzik Manger, Rabbi Israel Friedman of Ruzhyn, Meir Dizengoff, and Golda Meir. It is a real wonder that here, on the soil of Ukraine, the geography of Jewish genius was born. How is it that from such a forlorn place, generations of great thinkers emerged? This is still an unsolved question in my mind. The works of these geniuses are our guides on the Jewish journey through Ukraine. The tourist does not choose to travel to Ukraine in search of aesthetic experiences, shopping, good food, and more. The Jewish journey to Ukraine is one of Jewish research, study, and intellectual, emotional, and spiritual discovery.

During my last visit to Buchach, where Sholem Aleichem was born, I told the members of our group that I always take a rock as a souvenir when I visit countries where there was once a flourishing Jewish community that no longer exists. The rock is a physical symbol that testifies to the Jewish creativity that sprouted on Ukrainian soil and is embedded in our consciousness. Our families left the shtetl, whether it was in Ukraine, Poland, Russia, or Morocco. Although I was born in Israel, I feel like I am a villager who left but doesn't want to come back. Yet the shtetl and the culture born in it are still an intrinsic part of our identities as Jews. A trip to Ukraine can therefore be seen as a literary pilgrimage. The physical trip to Ukraine allows you go back in time to the texts where you can find your home and your heart.

Lithuania

12. My Private Genius – Vilna
Local Personality: Yulik Gurevich
Nimrod Shafran

"Palaces of the mind were built here," the famous Rabbi Abraham Joshua Heschel wrote of Lithuanian Jewry. That, and the fact that Lithuania is a small country that had been united with Poland for centuries, was more or less all I knew about Lithuania when I arrived in Kaunas, the second-largest city in the country, in August 2017. As part of my role as Senior Vice President of Sales for Da'at Educational Expeditions, I visited multiple Jewish world destinations in order to be able to plan future trips. This particular trip centered around the Baltics: Lithuania, Latvia, and Estonia. I was excited; visiting new destinations and getting to explore Jewish history and the Jewish community today was by far the best thing about my job.

Leaving the airport terminal, I knew that a local guide named Yulik Gurevich would be waiting for me and my colleague, but I didn't really know anything about him.

"Are you Nimrod?" An older man, dignified-looking with glasses and a beard, surprised me in fluent Hebrew. I definitely hadn't expected Yulik's Hebrew to be fluent! I've never encountered a local guide (who wasn't born or raised in Israel) with such good Hebrew. Yulik explained that he was born in 1946, right at the end of the war, in Lithuania, which was then part of the Soviet Union. In 1988, when Communism was already on its last leg and the winds of liberalism began to blow in the Soviet Union, a representative of the Jewish Agency opened a Hebrew ulpan in Vilnius, and Yulik started learning the language. His knack for languages was so good that one year later, he was asked to teach Hebrew at the ulpan. Aside from Hebrew, Yulik speaks Russian as his mother tongue, Yiddish (because that was what his parents spoke at home), Lithuanian as a second language, and English as a foreign language. He masters all of them.

Yulik took us to the center of town. In my mind, I had expected Lithuania to look and feel very similar to Poland – and it did. The town was picturesque, charming, and inviting, and I enjoyed the amazing cool August weather, a welcome respite from the Middle East. In Jewish history, Kaunas is known as a city of languages, and we passed by Ludwik Zamenhof Street, named after the inventor of the Esperanto language; Abraham Mapu Street, named after the famous Hebrew novelist; and the childhood home of the famous Hebrew poet Lea Goldberg. All of them lived in Kaunas for a period of their lives.

Next, we continued to the neighborhood Vilijampolė (popularly known in Lithuania as *Slabotkė*), a poor neighborhood which became the Kovno ghetto during the Holocaust. This was where Yulik's father, Benzion, was born and raised. Yulik shared that his father had been born and raised in an impoverished home, joined the Communist movement, and loved classical music, to the extent that he went to great lengths to obtain records that were unavailable in Lithuania. Yulik was nine years old when his father bought a gramophone, and he inherited his father's love of classical music. As Yulik spoke about his father, I thought about the similarities between his story and my own – my Romanian grandfather also grew up in a poor home and also joined the Communist movement. My grandfather also loved classical music dearly, and he passed that love down to my father. My bar mitzvah present from my grandfather was an annual membership shared by me and him to the philharmonic orchestra in Tel Aviv.

We then visited the Ninth Fort, one of a series of fortresses built at the end of the nineteenth century around the city of Kaunas. Before World War II, the Ninth Fort, like other fortresses around Kaunas, was used as a prison. It was here that most of the Jews of Kaunas were murdered during the Holocaust. Yulik told us about the first mass murder in Kaunas, on October 28, 1941: 9,200 Jews, 4,000 of whom were children, were murdered that day in the shooting fields of the Ninth Fort. Yulik also had a personal story to share here. His father Benzion was recruited to the Red Army, which ultimately saved his life. He was part of Division 16, which was known for having so many Jewish soldiers that the orders were given in Yiddish! Benzion was wounded in battle in 1943 and released from the army. When he returned to Kaunas, he discovered that his entire family had been murdered, apparently in the Ninth Fort. Yulik noted that the Holocaust story of Lithuanian Jewry is very different from that of the Jews of Poland – when the Wannsee Conference convened in 1942 to discuss the Final Solution, 70 percent of the Jews of Lithuania had already been murdered, most of them shot in mass murder fields like the Ninth Fort.

From Kaunas, we continued to Vilnius, the capital city of Lithuania and one of the most beautiful cities in the Baltic region. Vilnius has a population of over half a million residents, yet it looks and feels like a sleepy town, which perhaps is part of its charm. The city's beauty surprised me – I thought I would find a typical Eastern European city with relics of Communism everywhere. But the opposite was true. Vilnius actually reminded me of Scandinavia. On the one hand, history – colorful churches and antiquities, and the prevailing Baroque style of the Old City that had won it the coveted title of UNESCO World Heritage Site. But on the other hand, Vilnius featured lively pubs and bars, wonderful restaurants on every corner, unique hotels, designer clothing and stores selling high-quality handmade items, music, folklore, and cultural richness that the Lithuanians are proud of and show off, especially since their release from the strong grip of the Russian bear. It's so pleasant to stroll the streets of Vilnius during the day and at night, particularly in the spring and summer months, when the city attracts thousands of tourists.

Yulik told us that Vilnius is known as "Jerusalem of Lithuania." Why? It received this nickname in the eighteenth century thanks to the vast number of rabbis who lived in the city. There was Jewish diversity here that didn't exist anywhere else in the diaspora: the first labor leaders came from here. This was where the Bund was born. This was where the foundations were laid for a Jewish culture that included novelists, poets, sculptors, musicians, and cantors. In Vilnius, the Strashun Library was created, hosting the richest public book collection of Eastern European Jewry. It was here that a diverse Jewish educational system developed – secular, religious, Zionist, and socialist, in Hebrew, Yiddish, and Lithuanian. Yulik reminded us of the Tarbut schools, a network of Jewish schools that exist to this day around the world, founded back in 1915. The Tarbut school here was a secular Hebrew-language school, attended by famous Jews such as Abba Kovner, leader of partisans and fighters from the Vilnius ghetto; Antek Zuckerman, one of the founders of the Jewish Combat Organization in Warsaw and one of the leaders of the Warsaw ghetto uprising; and Meir Vilner, a signatory of Israel's Declaration of Independence. The nickname "Jerusalem of Lithuania" might have also been a matter of numbers: at the end of the nineteenth century, Jews made up almost half of the population in Vilnius.

During our visit to the Jewish museum in Vilnius, Yulik explained to us what Jewish life was like in the city until the Holocaust: there were four theaters, two choirs, six daily newspapers, youth movements, sports clubs, political parties, 130 active synagogues, and 240,000 Jews in Lithuania, of whom 80,000 lived in Vilnius.

What is the community like now? A small number of Holocaust survivors returned to Lithuania after the war, like Yulik's parents. But most of the Jews living in Lithuania today immigrated to the country while Lithuania was part of the Soviet Union, at the encouragement of the Soviet authorities, who were interested in introducing Russian culture and language into the Baltic states. Under the Communist regime, there was no official Jewish community life in Lithuania, but when Lithuania became an independent democratic country in 1990, the Jewish community witnessed a revival. While it is a mere shell of its pre-Holocaust glory, it is still alive and kicking.

Yulik is an active member of the community, of course, and he told us about the Jewish school in the city – the Sholom Aleichem School, named after the famous author who wrote in Yiddish, and currently attended by Yulik's grandson. There are about four thousand Jews living in Lithuania today, the vast majority of whom live in Vilnius and Kaunas. The community is active in a number of areas and pays special attention to maintaining a sense of Jewish national identity and rehabilitating religious life and Jewish cultural heritage. They organize events, lectures, and exhibitions dedicated to a range of subjects, including Israel and Jewish holidays. *Jerusalem of Lithuania,* a journal published in four languages (Yiddish, Lithuanian, English, and Russian), reports events in the community with a special emphasis on cultural aspects. In addition, there is an extensive welfare program that supports its needy members. The Jewish museum is managed by the community and features a special tribute to those non-Jewish Righteous Among the Nations who saved Jews during the years of the Nazi regime.

We continued to visit the Choral Synagogue of Vilnius, the only synagogue in the city to survive the Holocaust. It was built in 1903, and many of the economic and cultural elite of Vilnius Jewry prayed there. In its prime, there was a choir that accompanied the prayers, hence the synagogue's name. The synagogue was looted during the Holocaust, but survived because it was used as a storage area by the leaders of the Nazi occupation. During the Soviet era, the building was used as a factory for metalworks. After Lithuania regained its independence, it was renovated in 1994.

Of course, there's no such thing as community life without some tension and fights – and the synagogue is no exception; there is a constant struggle for control and honor between the non-Chassidic Orthodox Jews and the Chabad Jews. While the synagogue serves as the religious center for the Vilnius community, most of the Jews in the community do not visit it often – they define themselves as Jews culturally, but not necessarily in terms of religious observance.

Yulik didn't cease to surprise us with his extensive knowledge. He is such an impressive, courteous, and worldly man, but at the same time very introverted, modest, and simple, almost ascetic. Even when he told us his own personal story, he didn't express any emotion. He always spoke quietly and with the utmost solemnity, speaking only when he had something important to say. Perhaps his reserved personality was the result of living many years behind the Iron Curtain. In those days, any friend could very well have been a foe, an informer of the terrifying Communist regime, capable of sealing your fate with cruel torture, exile to Siberia, or even death. Therefore, you don't speak if you don't have to, even though Lithuania has been an independent country for over thirty years now.

Our next stop was at the remains of the Great Synagogue of Vilnius, which was the beating heart of the Jewish community for hundreds of years but was completely demolished during World War II. The synagogue was built in the seventeenth century in the Renaissance-Baroque style. It includes a building for the community council, twelve synagogues and study halls, ritual baths, kosher meat stalls, and the *beit midrash* of the most famous rabbi from Lithuania, Rabbi Eliyahu ben Shlomo Zalman – the Vilna Gaon. He lived in Lithuania in the eighteenth century, spoke Hebrew, studied the Jerusalem Talmud and not only the Babylonian Talmud, was proficient in the intricacies of mathematics and geometry, and encouraged his students to study general subjects, not only Jewish books.

Yulik shared with us his love of visual arts and classical music and noted that he guides art and music tours throughout Europe. We learned that guiding tours is actually his second career – he studied physics and mathematics in university and worked in computers for about twenty-five years, before he caught the travel guide bug. When I heard this, I had an epiphany: Yulik's story essentially represented the story of Lithuanian Jewry! The son of Holocaust survivors; a man who spoke Hebrew, Yiddish, Russian, Lithuanian, and English too; a learned man with an extensive knowledge of literature, Jewish history, classical music, and the arts. A diverse man, an exceptional Renaissance man, who embodies the cultural richness that existed in the Lithuanian Jewish community prior to the Holocaust. One man – a *gaon* (genius) – who represents the story of Lithuanian Jewry. It was my honor and pleasure to spend three days in Lithuania with my own private Vilna Gaon.

Azerbaijan

13. Jerusalem of the Caucasus – Krasnaya-Sloboda
Local Personality: Rabbi Yoni Yaakobi
Ya'acov Fried

Spring 2009. I landed in Baku, the capital city of Azerbaijan, to visit for a few days. During my stay in the city, I discovered a complacent nation that had been controlled by many foreign rulers. I was exposed to the rich Caucasian culture and to their religious moderation, which was apparent everywhere. Never before had I encountered Azerbaijani-style hospitality.

On the second evening of my trip, I stayed at an Azerbaijani home. At my host's suggestion, I took off my shoes, and he handed me his slippers. My host also gifted me with a beautiful painting. This was the first time that I was a guest but received a gift from my host. At a wedding that took place the next day, which I was invited to attend by my host, the guests wore fancy clothing, and most of them were wearing slippers too.

At the wedding, I understood from my hosts that anytime someone is hosted in a private home or at an event, the guest is honored with a lavish feast, regardless of the host's wealth or lack thereof. Stuffed vegetables and "mountains" of rice dishes were served on huge copper platters. While eating, my host began to share his inner musings. "In Azerbaijani culture, courage means using your discretion to know when to escape... We Azerbaijanis make do with any situation; we relinquish in fights and are opposed to belligerence. We respect history very much and the encounter between the Persian, Russian, and Turkish cultures, from which we have inherited many things. We don't even feel angry at our neighbors, some of whom have opposite interests to us. We are thankful for the discovery of black gold [oil] along the length of the Caspian Sea, which changed the face of the country and promised us many years of economic prosperity."

Indeed, Baku's skyline is similar to the oil kingdoms in the Arabian Gulf, Dubai, or Qatar. There are high-rises used as public buildings, residential housing, or luxury hotels, including broad boulevards with about ten traffic lanes. I told my host about my walk that morning along the promenade, during which I understood the source of the name Baku. According to Persian tradition, it means the place where the winds blow. I told him how much I enjoyed walking on the beach as the forceful winds hit me while they pushed the sea waves.

After drinking an ample quantity of wine, as his daughter played the *kamancheh* (a traditional string instrument), my host lamented the loss of the beaches – a consequence of the Azerbaijani oil "treasure." "The oil stains that you saw today on the sea as you enjoyed the breeze and the high waves are a reflection of the tears that drip from my eyes and my broken heart. We enjoy economic prosperity and the profits of the oil, but at the same time, it is important that we remember that we ruined the environment, especially the sea and its shores."

I visited the Old City of Baku, referred to as the inner city, which flourished between the twelfth and fifteenth centuries and is still surrounded by its ancient wall. Its mosques bustled with activity. I visited the main tourist attraction in the area, the royal Palace of the Shirvanshahs from the fifteenth century, which dominates the Old City. In the buildings that were once used as housing for the palace servants, there are now restaurants, cafés, and carpet stores.

Eighty percent of the residents of the republic of Azerbaijan are Shiite Muslims. Even after decades of secular Soviet policies, religion is still present. Most of the Azerbaijani people conduct their lifecycle events, such as births, weddings, and funerals, according to Islamic tradition. Even the more secular among them make pilgrimages to holy Muslim tombs to ask for blessings or assistance. But in contrast with their Iranian neighbors, most Azerbaijani citizens live a secular lifestyle. In the home where I stayed, alcohol was served opposite walls decorated with quotes from the Quran. In Baku, I saw for the first time what "light" Islam looks like.

I spent time with friends in modern areas of the city, where I visited authentic restaurants that served traditional dishes, international restaurants, and luxurious spas, and I walked through glittering, ultra-modern shopping centers. On my previous trips to Former Soviet Union countries, I felt that the years of Soviet governance had succeeded in making many of the cities gray and uniform, removing elements of the local culture. But this was not the case in Baku.

Two statements repeated themselves among the locals during my stay in Baku. The first: "In Azerbaijan, the Soviets were unsuccessful in their attempt to erase the local culture." The majority of Caucasian culture remained strong and authentic. The second statement was: "Baku is not Azerbaijan." Good friends suggested that I visit the fire temple, where a fire constantly burns due to the subterranean natural gas, or the fire mountain, where fire also leaps up from the ground with flames visible even from a distance. They also told me to visit the Shamakhi District, whose namesake city was one of the most important on the Silk Road, or Quba, located several hours away from Baku and known as "Jerusalem of the Caucasus."

"Travel to Quba, and you will understand these two statements you were told," they advised me.

This was my first time hearing about the Jewish community, numbering a few thousand, living near Quba, a few hours north of Baku. I learned that the community was concentrated in a town close to Quba called Krasnaya-Sloboda. This is the only town outside the State of Israel in which the majority of the residents are Jews.

I headed toward Krasnaya-Sloboda, which is also called Qirmizi Qasaba, the Red City, and Jerusalem of the Caucasus. The first sight that appeared before my eyes was a group of three hundred women wearing traditional black clothing, sitting on the floor in a tent. From my conversation with someone passing by, I understood that these were Jewish women sitting in mourning over a young Jewish man who had been killed in a car accident just a few days earlier. From the tent of mourning, I turned toward the alleyways of the old city to meet with Rabbi Yoni Yaakobi, the Chabad emissary of the town. "I moved here from Kfar Saba about fifteen years ago as an emissary of Chabad. My family originally immigrated to Israel from the Bukhara area, in the Caucasus Mountains. I am a dentist and had a successful career in Israel. But my wife and I felt an inner duty to return here with our children in order to help, preserve, and revive the Jewish community in this forlorn Jewish city in the heart of the snowy mountains.

"Jews have been here for twenty-five hundred years, even before the Second Temple period. The Jews of the region were nicknamed the 'Mountain Jews' because of their location in the Caucasus Mountains. They aren't considered Ashkenazi or Sephardic. Most of them are the descendants of Jews who began arriving from Persia in the thirteenth century. This is the reason that most of their writings are in Juhuri, an ancient language based on Farsi and mixed with some Arabic as well.

"The Jews here had no Jewish spiritual leadership for many generations, and as a result, the youth grew up without a stable Jewish heritage. The ignorance that prevailed in the mountain region left its mark, and many Jews left the path of their ancestors. The youth grew up without any Jewish tradition, and it is our job to reintroduce them to the concept of faith in God. The community here is concentrated in one area, and at its peak, numbered sixteen thousand Jews. Wherever I go, I am told that the Jews arrived here during the exile that followed the destruction of the First Temple. Most of them refused to return to the Land of Israel with Ezra and Nehemiah and remained in exile.

Throughout history, Jews were accepted here by the local rulers with open arms, due to the moderate Azerbaijani culture, and especially because they excelled in commerce and significantly contributed to the country's economy. On the border with Tajikistan and in the area of the border with Russia, there were also other Jewish communities in the mountains throughout history. Why is it that our community survived here, while others disappeared? This is a mystery to me. Perhaps it is because during the days of the Soviet regime, when Azerbaijan was part of the Soviet Union, the authorities allowed some of the religious practices in the country to continue. Mosques and synagogues remained open, under the supervision of the authorities. Nevertheless, most Jewish learning during this period took place in secret, keeping the Jewish flame burning."

After my initial conversation with Rabbi Yaakobi, I went to visit the charity center of the Joint Distribution Committee, which supports the community economically and socially. I discovered there that the vast majority of the women sitting in the tent of mourning did not know how to read or write and did not work for a living. Here, the role of the women was to tend to their homes and their children, who learned in a conservative-religious school system, while most of the husbands worked in the capital city of Baku, in Moscow, or in other distant cities. The husbands returned home several times a year for set intervals each time.

Did the Mountain Jews have cultural traditions and unique customs that more closely resembled those of their Muslim neighbors than those of other Jews? Everywhere I turned in Krasnaya-Sloboda, I discovered that the people around me were Jews who spoke in a Jewish-Persian dialect that was foreign even to the driver who accompanied me. On this visit, I was unsuccessful in uncovering the secret of the continued existence of this Jewish community.

However, over the past year, a new Jewish museum was opened in the town that preserves the traditions of the Mountain Jews. It features a silver Kiddush cup from the nineteenth century. There are worn

Soviet propaganda manifestos from the twenties, letters secretly sent from Jewish soldiers who fought the Nazis, medals from the painful war against Armenia in 1992. These are just a few of the hundreds of items on display in the museum. Of the few Judaica exhibits in the Former Soviet Union, this is one of the only ones that is not in a main city. The museum is housed in the renovated Karchogsky Synagogue, which was empty and abandoned for years. It now symbolizes Azerbaijan's efforts to preserve this isolated Jewish community. The museum's construction was sponsored by Jewish billionaire Semenovich Nisanov, vice president of the World Jewish Congress, together with two other Jews who live in Moscow but were born in the town.

Recently, I had another conversation with Rabbi Yaakobi. "The idea of the museum has been around for some time now. But we couldn't find the right place to house it. In the end, we chose the synagogue, which was partially destroyed. We renovated it and turned it into a modern, dynamic, visitor-friendly museum. We are very proud to display at the museum, among other things, ancient manuscripts of travel journals of local Jews who visited Israel in the nineteenth century."

I had a few more conversations with Rabbi Yaakobi about the singularity of this community, and he mentioned to me, "The new museum has many exhibits that show the unique characteristics of the Mountain Jews, including traditional garments and jewelry, and ceremonial items, manuscripts, and ketubot. One of the most important exhibits in the museum is the "slayed prayer book." This is a prayer book that was used by the local rabbi hundreds of years ago to protect himself from the sword of a Muslim general, after his army arrived to attack the Jews living in this region. The general tried to stab the rabbi, but when the rabbi instinctively thrust out his prayer book, it was slayed instead of him. In the town, the saying is that if your religion protects you like this, then this is a safe place for Jews to live. The prayer book was passed down from generation to generation and is now on display at the museum."

Many of the residents of Krasnaya-Sloboda immigrated to Israel or live in Russia, but Jewish life continues in this corner of the Caucasus Mountains. In contrast with Baku or other locations in the Former Soviet Union, intermarriage is rare here.

So what is the secret of the community's continued existence?

According to Rabbi Yaakobi, the key is their adherence to the laws of modesty, arranged marriages, maintaining ancient traditions, clear relationships in which the youth respect their elders, as well as a system of mutual respect between Jews and non-Jews.

Jewish life in an open world is a huge challenge in terms of maintaining Jewish identity and preserving the Jewish community. In the Orthodox sector, the more religious a community is, the more closed off and separate it tries to be. The challenge of maintaining Jewish life in North America or Western Europe is especially difficult, because most of these communities are located within modern cities with a wide range of temptations.

The Krasnaya-Sloboda community, on the other hand, enjoys a religious, conservative lifestyle alongside the benefits of being far from a large, modern city. The men conduct modern lives, in contrast with the women. The women maintain the Jewish home according to the traditions of the past, and as a result, the community's character has been preserved for generations. Will the Krasnaya-Sloboda community continue to exist in this format, with the uneducated women responsible for raising the children and preserving the family, while the husbands live in both worlds?

As long as female empowerment, equal rights between men and women, and especially self-fulfillment for women aren't on the agenda, it seems that this format will be preserved. The isolated city, its perfect weather, the uplifting panoramic views, and the feeling that the residents aren't lacking anything are apparently a unique recipe for preserving this Jewish community.

Western Europe and the Mediterranean

France

14. Like a Bridge Over Troubled Water – Paris
Local Personality: Dr. Marc Cohen
Yishay Shavit

"The Jews of France can choose to live anywhere in the world. Those who have stayed are doing so because they love France and their lives there." These words were said to me by Dr. Marc Cohen when we met in the heart of Jerusalem's Katamon neighborhood, at the home of Daniele Tzoukerman-Melzer. Daniele, herself a native of France who immigrated to Israel in 1982, was among those who chose otherwise. She left France for Zionist reasons, making Jerusalem her home and living her life as an Israeli. Naturally, many of her acquaintances are from the French Jewish community. This is how she met Dr. Marc Cohen, a Parisian geriatric specialist, about twenty-five years ago while he was visiting Israel. Dr. Cohen is an enthusiastic member of the city's Jewish community and a man whose French and Jewish identities are intertwined. Daniele thought that Dr. Cohen and I shared many areas of interest and that we would enjoy each other's company, so she invited us to her apartment one sweltering Jerusalem afternoon in August to sip French vanilla tea together.

Marc turned out to be a very impressive and pleasant person. He captured my heart from the first moment with his modest smile and the way he spoke fluent, confident Hebrew with a heavy French accent. He was born in Casablanca, Morocco, and his family immigrated to France in 1964 when he was twelve years old. His father, who was a rabbi in Morocco, had connections in France and was invited to serve as a kashrut supervisor in Paris, an honorable position. Comparing the Cohen family's story to other immigration stories from the same period, it sounds like they started out with a solid foundation. But through the eyes of young Marc, things looked different. The transition from his familiar environment in Morocco to the modern city of Paris shook his world. Naturally, he was worried what the future would bring. But it was the Jewish community that came to the family's assistance during its first days in France. To this day, Marc remembers the words of the community representative who told them that they would receive everything they needed – and only pay for it once they had enough money. This welcome was what caused Marc to later dedicate his life to the Jewish community in Paris.

Being a Jewish teenager in Paris after the Six-Day War was a momentous experience for Marc. During those years, the State of Israel's reputation was at its peak, and he, like many other Parisian Jews, felt immensely proud. I can just imagine him walking around with his Jewish Scouts uniform in the Marais district, down Rue de Rosiers where many Jews lived. He probably stopped to eat lunch at the famous Chez Jo Goldenberg restaurant, sitting next to Holocaust survivors and French Resistance fighters, and then headed toward the Agoudas Hakehilos Synagogue. I'm pretty sure he did not stop to pray there. As a Sephardic Jew born in Morocco, he probably wouldn't have felt comfortable participating in the ultra-Orthodox Ashkenazi prayer services. While the Sephardic Jews who arrived from Algeria, Tunis, and Morocco became the majority during those years in the Parisian Jewish community, and their relationship with the original Ashkenazi community was excellent, the differences in the prayer texts and customs caused the Jewish immigrants from North Africa to prefer their own synagogues, which they established upon arriving in Paris.

At the age of nineteen, after a short period of living in Israel and encountering a Jewish lifestyle different from his own, Marc began to study medicine in Paris. In 1978, he was certified as a physician, and six years later, he completed his residency in geriatrics. Marc started to work as a geriatric physician at a Jewish organization called OSE (Œuvre de secours aux enfants). This organization was and still is one of the flagship organizations of the Jewish community in France. Established in 1912, it was dedicated to the health of the most vulnerable members of society – children, the elderly, the disabled, and immigrants. The organization's most significant period was in World War II, during which its members saved about five thousand Jews from the hands of the Nazis. The OSE's philosophy that anyone in need of medical care is entitled to receive it even if they are unable to pay for it resonated with Marc. Essentially, as a geriatric physician, he placed special emphasis on the connection between medicine and social work. Treating patients' medical ailments, Marc believes, is inseparable from concern for their overall well-being. While it is possible throughout history to find similar ideas in various societies, not only Jewish ones, in many ways I believe that Marc's outlook is rooted in the traditional Jewish value that the community must support its members in every possible way. As Chazal (the Jewish sages) would say, *"Kol Yisrael areivim zeh la'zeh"* (All Jews are responsible for each other).

Paris of the mid-eighties was completely different from Paris of the late sixties. The Marais district was transformed and became one of the most tourist-oriented squares in the city. Sites such as Centre Pompidou were built there by top French architects and began attracting large numbers of visitors. Many shops upgraded themselves, and the Hôtel de Saint-Aignan building underwent a face lift before becoming the Museum of the Art and History of Judaism. But something else also changed in Paris during the eighties: the attitude toward Israel, and consequently toward Jews.

For over a century, many academic scholars have been trying to define the term *anti-Semitism* and its various appearances in French society. There are scholars, such as the famous sociologist Michel

Wieviorka, who identify three stages in the development of Jew hatred in France. During the first historical stage, the hatred was directed toward the Jewish religion and those who observe it, while during the second stage, it evolved into hatred of the Jews as a race. The event that signifies the transition between these two stages in France was the Dreyfus affair. The third stage, many believe, is the stage of hatred toward Zionism and the State of Israel. This hatred was directed at Jews based on the popular prejudice that all Jews support Israel. It does not matter that there are many Jews who do not define themselves as Zionists, or others who even define themselves as outright anti-Zionists. In general, hatred of Zionism is directed at all Jews. This does not mean that classic anti-Semitism ceased to exist, but it definitely changed. There are those who point to the Chez Jo Goldenberg restaurant, in the heart of the Marais district, as the place where the transition between the second stage and the third stage occurred in France.

On August 9, 1982, while Israel was immersed in the first Lebanon War, which was criticized by many in France, two armed Palestinian terrorists from the Abu Nidal Organization burst into Chez Jo Goldenberg and started shooting. After the terrorists left and got into their escape vehicle, it was discovered that they had murdered six diners in the restaurant. This was the heaviest toll suffered by the Jewish community in France since the end of World War II. The terrorists chose this restaurant for the exact same reason that I had imagined young Marc eating there – it was the symbol of Jewish life in Paris after World War II. As far as the terrorists were concerned, there was no difference between the State of Israel and Jews in Paris.

One of the places where the approach that fully identifies Zionism with Judaism found an attentive ear was actually the Sarcelles district. In this northern suburb of Paris, many Jewish immigrants from North Africa built a new home for themselves in the fifties and sixties. During those years, this was one of the largest concentrations of Jews in France, and the Jewish community did everything in its power to help its residents establish religious institutions and schools. The OSE opened clinics, homes for the elderly, day care centers, and more, and loyal to their mission, these services were provided for a very nominal fee or even free of charge. Marc, who became one of the directors of the organization over the years, witnessed with his own eyes the changes in this neighborhood. Beginning in the late eighties, the percentage of Jews in Sarcelles began to drop, primarily due to an influx of Muslim migrant workers from North Africa to the neighborhood. After the First Intifada erupted in Israel in 1987, many of the new Muslim immigrants began to voice anti-Semitic opinions of the third type, identifying Judaism with Zionism and the State of Israel. The Jews who were still living in the neighborhood were afraid to walk down the street wearing a kippah or a Star of David necklace.

The anti-Zionist form of anti-Semitism in France increased as the years went by. It reached its peak with three bloody terror attacks between 2006 and 2015, which specifically targeted Jews (the murder of Ilan Halimi, the attack on the Jewish school in Toulouse, and the Hypercacher kosher supermarket siege in Paris). These horrific events, which were all perpetrated by Muslim immigrants or children of immigrants, shattered the sense of security that French Jews once felt. This reality of increasing anti-Semitism caused many to immigrate to the United States, Canada, or Israel. According to several estimates, about fifty thousand Jews (out of about half a million Jews living in France in 2005) left France during these years as a result of the increasing feeling of danger.

Throughout those years, the OSE continued, under the leadership of Dr. Marc Cohen, to operate geriatric centers in Sarcelles and other suburbs of Paris. While the organization was and remains Jewish, the population using its services changed. Most of the patients at the geriatric clinic in Sarcelles are Muslims from North Africa who came to France as migrant workers. Naturally, a large percentage of the employees, physicians, and nurses are also Muslims originally from North Africa. Marc shares that there was one man who refused to participate in a continuing education course at the OSE geriatric center, claiming that he was not prepared to cooperate with a Jewish center, but throughout Marc's entire career, this was a one-time occurrence. For most of the Muslims on the professional staff at the OSE geriatric center in Sarcelles, this is their first encounter with the Jewish world. There, they get to know Jews on a personal level, and this contributes significantly to breaking anti-Semitic stereotypes.

It is difficult to speak in the name of all of the quarter of a million Jews living in Paris, but it seems reasonable to say that most of them are concerned by the rise in anti-Semitism in general, but do not feel it on a day-to-day basis. The truth is that the danger involved in walking down the street wearing prominent Jewish items actually caused many Jews to band together around the Jewish community and reinforce it. Over the past few years, more and more Jews have chosen to leave the neighborhoods where they live and where they have encountered displays of anti-Semitism. However, most of these Jews do not leave Paris; they move to different neighborhoods where the Jewish community is stronger.

Another element that contributes to the sense of safety of the Jews of Paris is the warm political embrace that they receive from the French public. Over the past few years, hundreds of thousands of French citizens have filled the streets protesting the hostility toward France's Jews, and they have held very impressive solidarity rallies with the community. Anti-Semitism, which was definitely present in French politics in the past, is frowned upon today as a worldview that must be criticized and opposed. Even parties that toyed with such ideas in the not-so-distant past have put an end to that attitude. Let us not forget, France is the only country other than Israel that has had six prime ministers with Jewish roots. The public sentiment that anti-Semitism must be fought has led to a number of interfaith collaborations in recent years, in which Jewish, Christian, and Muslim religious figures have organized projects encouraging religious tolerance.

Sitting in Daniele's home in the Katamon neighborhood of Jerusalem, I again envision Dr. Marc Cohen walking down the streets of the Marais district, in the third and fourth arrondissements of Paris. What goes through his mind as he walks on Rue des Rosiers? What does he think of the Hebrew bookstores found on one of the most expensive streets in Paris? Can he still imagine Louis de Funes in the role of Rabbi Yaakov, dancing in Chassidic garb at the street corner, where fashion boutiques stand today? What does he think about the wonderful Musée d'Art et d'Histoire du Judaïsme (Museum of Jewish Art and History) that was finally opened to visitors in 1998? Does he see all of these as signs that the Jews are part of the French people, or as a monument to the Jewish life in Paris that will one day disappear?

These musings bring me back to the beginning of my encounter with Marc and his statement that the Jews who still live in France are there because they love the country and their lives there. When we visit Paris and walk down the streets of the Marais district, or in any other neighborhood of this gorgeous city, it's easy to see what he means. How could you leave Paris? But on the other hand, how can you imagine this city without its Jewish population? I have no doubt that the situation of the Jews in Paris specifically, and in France as a whole, is complex. The community is going through trying times, but Marc's optimism and the strong stance of the French nation against displays of anti-Semitism arouse a spark of hope within me. I know that on my next trip to Paris, I will make sure to visit one of the OSE's clinics, where the traditional values of the Jewish community align with those of their neighbors, building bridges over troubled water.

Germany

15. The City Where Everything Is Possible – Berlin
Local Personality: Rabbi Regina Jonas
Rabbi Lana Zilberman Soloway

I arrived in Berlin in the autumn of 2008. It was a long visit that lasted two full months, and I fell in love with the city. I ended up returning to it dozens of times – as a tourist, a musician, and as a tour educator and leader of educational trips. Now, I feel at home in Berlin, but that only happened after an extended process of deep searching and clarification of my identity.

During my teenage years, I was privileged to sing and train with the Moran Choir, and we traveled and performed in countries around the world. While I had visited Germany several times, I had never been to Berlin. My memories of those visits to Germany were always clouded by a sense of alienation, because of the foreign language, the culture, and the coldness that the people radiated. So in the summer of 2008, at age twenty-six, when I received a letter notifying me that I had received a scholarship to study German at Goethe-Institute in Berlin, I was hesitant. I wasn't sure it was the right fit for me. Luckily, many of my Israeli musician friends told me, "Berlin is not Germany, just like New York is not the United States. Go and discover this city of endless possibilities for yourself." I listened to them and went, and they were right.

I vividly remember my first days in the city, walking around Friedrichstraße, stopping for coffee at the squares and at verdant hidden spots. I felt like I was walking down Fifth Avenue in Manhattan, only that everything was much smaller and more compact, and instead of English, German was the language that filled the air. I encountered a first-rate cosmopolitan city, replete with history, culture, music, tourists from all over the world, lovely shops, bars, clubs, restaurants, cafés, concert halls, opera houses, museums of worldwide renown, galleries, Bikram Yoga studios, and bicycle paths. There was accessible public transportation, and the travel times were reasonable, making everything within reach. Even the Germans in Berlin looked different to me.

During those two months, the center of my life revolved around East Germany. (While the physical Berlin Wall fell thirty years ago, the differences between east and west are still significant and noticeable to this day.) I rented an apartment in a neighborhood called Prenzlauer Berg. It is a young neighborhood with a great night life, colorful art exhibitions, a famous restaurant and bar scene, and many green parks.

I spent my mornings in the adjacent neighborhood, Mitte, which is true to its name – "the center." Every morning, I would take the no. 5 tram to Alexander Platz, home to the city's famous television tower, or to the vibrant marketplace, Hackescher Markt, and then walk to Goethe-Institute, right in the heart of the center of the Mitte neighborhood.

After my courses, I would wander the area for hours, eating lunch at one of the wonderful restaurants (in Berlin, you can find every type of international cuisine, according to your preference). My afternoons were spent at one of the many museums or galleries in the city, and in the evening, I usually enjoyed a concert at one of the opera houses or jazz clubs. All in all, it was a wonderful bourgeois lifestyle, filled with that European flavor of culture, art, music, and color.

While I came to Berlin as a musician with a scholarship to study German, I did not forget my original identity as a Jew, an Israeli, born in the Former Soviet Union, with grandfathers who fought in the Red

Army. One of them was even in Berlin when the war ended (he was on the front lines of the Red Army in Berlin at the end of the war), while my other grandfather lost his entire family in the Holocaust, in Belarus (White Russia).

I never thought I would study German, until that year of my master's degree in vocal coaching for opera singers. Yet despite being three generations removed from the Holocaust, its memory was still very much fresh in my mind. Studying German in Berlin was a very strange experience for me. Doing so specifically in the eastern half of the city made it even stranger. East Berlin is very Jewish. The memory of the Jewish life that once existed there is everywhere: the street names, the *Stolperstein* stones (those shiny memorial plaques all over the sidewalks bearing the names of Jewish men and women who once lived there and were sent to their deaths), the ancient Jewish cemetery and the Jewish high school right next to it (which still operates to this day), and more.

On one of my walks, I discovered a sign affixed to the entrance of a residential building on Krausnickstraße 6, bearing the inscription "The home where Regina Jonas, the first female rabbi, was born." I assumed that it was referring to someone who had lived in this house before World War II, and the words "female rabbi" really aroused my curiosity.

I did some research and discovered that this woman had been ordained as a rabbi in Berlin before the war, in 1935. Due to the tragic circumstances of her life, Regina was forgotten and left off the pages of history. I couldn't forget her, though, and I continued to search for more information.

I found that Rabbi Regina Jonas was born in Berlin in 1902 into an underprivileged Orthodox Jewish family. She received a Jewish education, including in the subjects of Talmud and Jewish law. At the age of twenty-two, she received a teaching certificate from a school for girls, but she continued her studies at Chochmat Yisrael, the Higher

Institute for Jewish Studies in Berlin. While Regina was not the only woman at the school, she was the only one who was set on becoming a rabbi, a position she did not think was unusual given the general atmosphere of emancipation that was prevalent at the time, giving Jews full equal rights. Regina believed that the time had come for female emancipation as well. She based her extensive thesis on the subject of "The Rabbinate and Women: Can Women Serve as Rabbis?" and used references from Jewish law and examples from the classic sources as proof. But finding a Talmud expert who was willing to ordain her proved a challenge. Professor Hanoch Albeck, one of the main teachers at the institute where Regina studied, refused to ordain a woman as a rabbi, and Rabbi Dr. Leo Baeck, the spiritual leader of liberal Judaism in Germany as well as a teacher at the institute, hesitated to comply with her request, as well. At the end of her studies, she was only awarded a diploma as an "Academic Teacher of Religion" and a special document signed by Leo Baeck expressing his support for her. For five years, Regina searched for a rabbi who would agree to test her and ordain her as a rabbi. In the end, on December 27, 1935, after Regina successfully passed the oral examination in Talmud, Rabbi Dr. Max Dienemann (rabbi of the Offenbach am Main community and head of the Conference of Liberal Rabbis) granted her rabbinical ordination. He wrote, "I testify that she can answer questions of Jewish law and that she is worthy of serving on the rabbinate." Thus, Regina became the first Jewish woman in the world ordained for a rabbinical position.

Despite her ordination, Jonas was not officially recognized as a community rabbi. Throughout her life, she maintained a Jewish lifestyle that was faithful to Jewish law, and she fought for her right to serve as a rabbi in the Jewish communities in Germany, to deliver sermons, and to teach Judaism. Jonas eventually managed to advance in the rabbinate and in preaching following the pogrom of Kristallnacht in November 1938. Following the difficult events, many communities were left bereft of their rabbis due to the many arrests, transports, and emigration. At first, they agreed to accept her as a rabbi at synagogues located in homes for the elderly and in institutes for the blind. But by 1941, she had already replaced rabbis in Frankfurt, Bremen, and the main community of Berlin (Die Neue Synagogue). Even after she was assigned to forced labor at the Afiko cardboard factory, she continued with her rabbinical work and relief efforts. On November 6, 1942, she was deported with her mother and many other elderly Jews to Theresienstadt ghetto. Before she left, Regina left her writings in the archive of the Jewish community of Berlin. At the concentration camp, she joined the "self-help organization" founded by psychologist Viktor Frankl. She would greet the Jews as they first arrived at the ghetto, encourage them, and help them deal with the initial shock and the cruel reality. She tried to give them hope and worked as a rabbi and a therapist, dedicating her energy and her soul to sanctifying life even during the Holocaust and maintaining Jewish existence and identity. She continued to deliver sermons and lectures in the ghetto until October 12, 1944, when at the age of forty-two, she was sent to Auschwitz-Birkenau, where she was murdered.

There is no doubt that Rabbi Regina Jonas was ahead of her time, but if not for the fertile soil on which she was educated in Berlin of the Weimar Republic, during the late twenties and early thirties, when the air of Berlin was filled with liberalism, success, new possibilities, and entry into the modern world, her rabbinical dreams may not have been realized at all. The Berlin where Rabbi Jonas was active was the same Berlin of Moses Mendelssohn, father of the Jewish Enlightenment movement, of Rabbi Abraham Geiger, father of the Reform movement, and the city of Rabbi Leo Baeck, who, although he did not agree to ordain her, supported her from a distance. By the time Regina was finally ordained in 1935, it was already two years after the Nazi regime came to power. Perhaps an initial understanding of the changing times helped push the Jews of Germany toward such a grandiose decision.

Regina grew up in an Orthodox Jewish family and strictly adhered to Jewish law. I am sure that she considered herself an Orthodox rabbi and would have probably vehemently opposed being defined as a Reform rabbi. Looking back at history, however, it is clear to us that being a female rabbi in the Orthodox world was impossible, and only progressive Judaism could have accepted her. It is no coincidence that she was forgotten in the pages of history until the end of the twentieth century, despite the fact that both psychologist Viktor Frankl and Rabbi Leo Baeck, two very famous Jews, were at the same ghetto in Theresienstadt and survived the war. They never spoke of her, not even mentioning her slightly. This is strange in and of itself. It took thirty-seven more years until the second Jewish woman was ordained as a rabbi. In 1972, in the United States, Sally Priesand was ordained by the Reform movement. It took about two more decades for the Berlin Wall to fall (1989), which finally gave access to the archives of the Jewish community of Berlin, where Rabbi Jonas's memory was buried.

The Reform movement was founded and established in Germany in the mid-nineteenth century. Toward the end of the century, as many German Jews immigrated to the United States, the Reform movement also immigrated and developed significantly, but in more liberal directions. Looking at the state of Judaism worldwide, it is evident that among American Jews, over the years, the Reform movement became dominant, while in Germany, it is a small, reserved minority.

In modern-day Berlin, there are a very small number of Reform synagogues, the most famous of which is located at Pestalozzistraße. This is a beautiful, two-story synagogue with lovely decorations and a pipe organ that is played at every prayer service. However, the men pray on the first floor, while the women are in a separate section on the second floor. Of course, the Reform Abraham Geiger College is also worth mentioning, where male and female rabbis and cantors have been trained and ordained from 1872 to this day, except for during the years when the Nazi regime was in power.

I wonder what Regina Jonas would have thought of Judaism in Berlin in the twenty-first century. Alongside the historical Jewish quarter, in Mitte, in addition to everything I mentioned, one can visit the impressive building of the Neue Synagogue on Oranienburger Straße. The building was erected at the beginning of the twentieth century, and despite being severely damaged during Kristallnacht, it survived the war. On the entry floor, there is a small museum that depicts Jewish life in Berlin throughout the generations and includes a photograph of Rabbi Jonas on the day of her ordination. This is the only existing photo of her. On Jewish holidays, one can ascend the stairs to the top floor and enjoy an egalitarian service by the Masorti community of Berlin, led by a female rabbi – Rabbi Gesa Ederberg. To me, that is very symbolic. Rabbi Jonas was the first pioneer who paved the way for many other women who chose to pursue the path of the rabbinate and leadership in the Jewish community. I am fortunate to be one of them; following in her footsteps as well, I have chosen to study Judaism in depth and become a rabbi. When I have a chance to attend prayers at the Neue Synagogue when visiting Berlin, I always encounter Rabbi Jonas's photo at the entry. As I ascend the stairs to the prayer sanctuary and step inside, into the vibrant holy space to welcome the Sabbath with a woman leading the service, I think of everything that Rabbi Jonas could have accomplished if not for the war.

From the synagogue, it's a short walk to the Jewish Museum, located in the nearby Kreuzberg neighborhood, as well as to the memorial for the Jews of Europe who were murdered in the Holocaust, which is located close to Brandenburg Gate and the Reichstag.

The Jewish Museum Berlin was designed by Jewish architect Daniel Libeskind and inaugurated in 2001. The museum building integrates elements from classic Baroque architecture with modern motifs, and its exhibition rooms share the history of the Jewish community of Berlin from its start until the new age. One of the powerful wings of the museum features a memorial pillar for the Holocaust.

The large memorial next to Brandenburg Gate, erected in 2005, was planned by architect Peter Eisenman and is dedicated to the memories of the Jews murdered in the Holocaust. The location and size of the monument were carefully planned. It cannot be missed and is impossible to pass without noticing it. It is composed of 2,711 (the total number of Talmud pages) black cement blocks of varying sizes; those who walk between them are enveloped by a sense of uncertainty and confusion, like in a maze. It is interesting that while the architect decided not to install an explanation plaque next to the memorial, everyone who sees it knows exactly what it is meant to express.

There are about thirty thousand Jews living in Berlin today, many of whom are Israeli. There are dozens of active synagogues of various denominations. There are kosher restaurants, extensive student activities, and a vibrant and diverse Jewish scene (albeit small in numbers).

Today, it is easy to be a Jew in Berlin; it is even welcomed. The city where everything is possible, and anyone can rediscover themselves without encountering criticism or receiving reprimanding looks. The freedom to be what you want, to do what you please, to wear whatever you want, and to choose whatever spiritual or religious path that your soul feels, makes Berlin what it is – an international microcosm filled with opportunities. I think that Regina Jonas would have loved modern Berlin, where everything is truly possible.

16. Beating Serendipity on the Rhine – Speyer, Worms, and Mainz
Local Personality: Rashi
Muki Jankelowitz

The first question I ask almost every group I guide is: Where is Ashkenaz? I always get the same answer – Eastern Europe. In fact, as a young man, I remember my deep surprise the moment I discovered that my Lithuanian-born, Yiddish-speaking grandfather, while certainly Ashkenazi, was not from Ashkenaz. It was then that I also learned that in fact Ashkenaz was not Eastern Europe at all. That moment of discovery ignited my deep desire to delve into the origins of Ashkenazi Jews.

Whatever I have learned about Ashkenaz since then has sadly involved waves of persecutions and expulsions, but happily also constant rebirth, periods of prosperity, and especially a great scholarly tradition. Central to the story of Ashkenaz were the ShUM cities, ShUM being an acronym for the Rhineland Jewish communities of Speyer, Worms, and Mainz (named collectively for the first letters of their Hebrew names Schpira, Warmaisa, and Magenza). The three cities were centers of Jewish scholarship and were of great importance to Ashkenazi Judaism.

Nothing in the dry reading of the word *Rhineland* can quite prepare one for the grand scale and beauty of the Rhine. A cruise along the Rhine reveals the stuff of fairy tales – a landscape of castles and churches, forests and mountains, villages and cities. However, it was not this beauty that attracted the first Jewish settlers to the area, but rather the opportunity to earn a decent living, engaging in trade along the busy Rhine waterway. Although there were already traces of a Jewish presence in the Rhineland from as early as Roman times, the community began to grow significantly in the tenth century.

At the outset, the small number of Jewish inhabitants of Ashkenaz had to grapple with the new reality of no longer living under a more tolerant Muslim rule. Instead, the Jewish inhabitants of medieval Ashkenaz had to function in the complex and frequently challenging Christian context. It was here that they had to create their communities and develop their internal leadership while learning to navigate their delicate relationship with the dominant and often antagonistic surrounding Christian neighbors.

In time, the community in Ashkenaz came to be dominated by learned scholars, and despite Europe being largely illiterate, literacy and learning were highly prized in the Jewish community. The ShUM cities came to be home to great yeshivot and generations of great rabbis. Of the many important rabbinic personalities, Rashi, an acronym for Rabbi Shlomo Yitzchaki, is the most prominent.

I had "met" Rashi long before I knew of Ashkenaz. His commentary appeared on every page of my Bible growing up, and his insights and interpretations had informed my understanding, as they did for other Bible students who studied in traditional Jewish frameworks. I didn't always agree with Rashi, but I knew my teachers thought he was important.

I vividly remember learning Rashi's explanation of the second line of Genesis, "*V'ha'aretz haitah tohu va'vohu*" (והארץ היתה תהו ובהו), usually translated as "the earth was desolate and void." Rashi translates the word *vohu* to mean "emptiness," while the word *tohu* signifies astonishment and amazement, for a person would have been astonished and amazed at its emptiness. In this way, Rashi added layers and layers of meaning to individual words.

The son of a scholar in Troyes, then an important market town in Champagne in northern France, Rashi was educated there by his father. After his father's death, seventeen-year-old Rashi married and departed to learn with the great rabbis in Worms. Later he moved to Mainz, where he continued his studies. From his teachers, he accessed the collective learning of the great rabbis of Ashkenaz who had preceded him.

An exceptional student, Rashi was aware that his family commitments would sooner or later require his return to Troyes. As a result, he sought to understand the logic of the Talmud and the oral traditions used to explain it. He took copious notes of all that he learned and developed a system of concisely explaining both the Bible and the Talmud, integrating midrashim (ancient commentary on part of the Hebrew scripture, attached to the biblical text) with geographic, botanical, and linguistic explanations. He took these notes back with him, when after six years of study he was obliged to return to Troyes. Here in 1070, he established a yeshiva, which attracted many students, who were taught Bible and Talmud, based on the commentaries he had written down, refining his notes as he taught to help him in his explanations.

In 1096, the Crusades passed through the Rhineland, devastating the ShUM communities physically, intellectually, and spiritually. Among the many murdered in Worms were three of Rashi's relatives, sons of his teacher Rabbi Isaac ben Eliezer Halevi. There was not only physical destruction; generations of accumulated learning in the Rhineland scholarship were almost completely destroyed.

Since it was not in the path of the Crusades, Troyes was physically unaffected. Although the Jews of Troyes, Rashi among them, were deeply shaken by the news of the destruction, they were not physically harmed. Rashi's comprehensive knowledge survived the Crusader catastrophe, and his commentaries soon came to be recognized as the most significant. So significant that his commentaries on the Bible and the Talmud were among the first Hebrew books to be published. Indeed, since it was first printed, the standard format of the Talmud contains Rashi's commentary. In traditional Jewish circles, the Bible is always published and taught with Rashi's commentaries.

I have visited the modern ShUM communities twice. All three communities, each of which are relatively small in size, can be visited in one day and provide different ways of remembering and preserving its past.

Ruins and Artifacts in Speyer

In Speyer, a small Jewish museum is housed on the site of the partial remains of a twelfth-century synagogue and the oldest intact mikveh (a bath in which certain Jewish ritual purifications are performed) in Europe. The site lies in the shadow of an impressive twelfth-century cathedral.

The synagogue fell out of use when Jews were expelled from the area in the early sixteenth century; after being used by the city as an armory, it was later destroyed. The modern city-run museum preserves these partial remains and a few artifacts of a Jewish life now completely gone. Speyer offers a glimpse of a Jewish life that once was but is no more, telling the story through ruins and artifacts.

Reconstructed Glory in Worms

Worms preserves its Jewish heritage in a different way, with two sites of Jewish significance. One is the Heiliger Sand, the oldest surviving Jewish cemetery in Europe. The tombstones tell the story of nine hundred years of Jewish life in Germany and reveal the pity of it all.

The other site is the rebuilt medieval synagogue known as the Rashi shul. It was named in honor of its most prominent student when it was rebuilt after the earlier synagogue was destroyed by the Crusaders. This medieval structure was maintained and repaired and continued to be used until it was, with the exception of the mikveh, totally destroyed on Kristallnacht in 1938.

In 1961, at the initiative of the city, the building was carefully reconstructed, using as many original stones as possible. The completely rebuilt synagogue was built to look exactly as it did on the eve of the destruction and today functions as both a museum and houses a small active congregation.

Worms tells the Jewish story through recreating the physical building to look as it did on the eve of its destruction. The reconstruction is meant to evoke the past glory of Jewish life.

Futurism in Mainz

The medieval synagogues did not remain standing in Mainz. But until Kristallnacht, there were several functioning synagogues, which were all obliterated by the Nazis.

In 1999, an architectural competition was held to design a new synagogue and community center on the site of a synagogue destroyed by the Nazis. The state-funded building is a prize-winning architectural masterpiece, built in the shape of the Hebrew word *kedushah* (holiness) and filled with lots of Jewish symbolism integrated into the architecture. It functions today as a synagogue, educational center, and community center.

Although it does house a modest community, the futuristic synagogue in Mainz seems almost out of place, the bombastic building filled with symbolism out of sync with the humble reality of the community.

The Scholarly Monument of Rashi

There was no central planning regarding the commemoration of Jewish life in the cities of ShUM, but serendipity provided three different models of relating to the rich Jewish world that once was. Each of the models offers a different way of thinking about Jewish life in Ashkenaz. It strikes me, however, that despite their variety, all three models offer just a sad glimpse of the essence of Ashkenaz, the layers of destruction presenting too much of an impediment to allow one to really see what once stood there.

Rashi witnessed the destruction of the ShUM cities by the Crusaders. Fate ensured that he was not injured and the layers of knowledge that he had gathered were not lost in this catastrophe. The Jews of ShUM who survived the Crusades, along with Ashkenazi Jews of other communities, gradually rebuilt their lives, until many of them, including my grandfather's ancestors, headed east into the Slavic lands to reestablish their lives there.

But this too was serendipity. Some stayed and rebuilt. Some left to build their lives in the east. Later, some others made longer journeys to the New World or the Land of Israel. Wherever they went, they took Rashi with them. His revolution in explanation, combining concise detail and broad scope, is the essence of the Ashkenaz tradition.

I feel a deep and powerful connection to the sites of Jewish interest in the ShUM cities. Yet the sum of all the parts falls far short of the whole. While one can see glimmers and glimpses of a richness vastly depleted, there is a deep astonishment and amazement in imagining what once was.

And then I remember Rashi. Throughout all the destructions, exiles, and rebirths, his commentaries have survived. His commentaries offer insights into the canonical texts of the Jewish people that also preserve the essence of the scholarly tradition of Ashkenaz. Not an archaeological remain, nor a reconstruction, and definitely not a futuristic building, his work is the real fitting monument to the world of medieval Ashkenaz.

Portugal

17. Unveiling the Mask – Belmonte
Local Personality: Samuel Schwarz
Ya'acov Fried

During each of my three visits to Portugal, I experienced amazing weather, vibrant ancient cities, wonderfully restored castles and monasteries, breathtaking gardens, thick forests, dreamy beaches, picturesque fishing villages, and an inspiring cuisine.

Lisbon and Porto, the main cities, would have been enough of a vacation destination alone, but the best way to really get to know Portugal is a trip that involves exploring the heart of the country. My first trip started off in Óbidos, a charming fortified town north of Lisbon where each reigning king left a lasting impression. I then visited Nazaré, the Silver Coast city at the foot of the cliffsides on the coast of the Atlantic Ocean, followed by a trip to Porto, a romantic city featuring a collection of Art Nouveau buildings that were declared a UNESCO World Heritage Site. From there, I traveled westward toward Douro Valley, one of the oldest wine regions in the world, and to the converso towns of Belmonte and Coimbra. My trip culminated with a visit to the town of Sintra with its many castles, which made me feel as if I were vacationing with the kings of Portugal in the colorful summer palace, painted in so many different colors that it seemed to have jumped out of the pages of a fairy tale.

As I stood in line to buy an entry ticket to visit the palace, a young man turned to me and asked if I was from Israel. Could he have noticed my accent? I answered that I was, and with the excitement of someone who had just discovered his long-lost brother, he shared that he had returned from a trip to Israel with the Birthright program the previous week, along with a group of young Jews from Portugal. "My family is originally from the area of Belmonte. I returned to Judaism after discovering that my grandmother and mother, who always carefully cleaned our house on Fridays and lit candles next to the door, were descendants of converso families."

Jews first arrived in Portugal in the second century CE. The Jewish community grew in the twelfth century with the establishment of Portugal as an independent state and due to immigration from Spain. After every violent wave of rioting, Spanish Jews would find a safe haven in the neighboring country. Immigration from Spain to Portugal peaked in 1492, the year the Jews were expelled from Spain. During those years, the entire population of Portugal numbered about one million, and a quarter of them were Jews.

For the Jews of Belmonte, every day was essentially Purim, as of the fifteenth century. At home, they behaved as Jews, but outside, they dressed up as Christians for fear of the Inquisition. A trip to the towns of Belmonte, Coimbra, and Tomar is a journey back in time to areas where a few Jews finally removed their masks and exposed their Jewish identities.

On my first visit to the converso towns, I wondered how I would have reacted to a world in which it was forbidden to express my Jewish identity. A world where one cannot celebrate Passover, perform circumcisions, celebrate bar mitzvahs, eat kosher food, sing Jewish songs, or speak Hebrew. A world where there are no synagogues and no Jewish institutions. This is exactly how the Jews of Belmonte, in northeastern Portugal, lived from the sixteenth century until the twentieth century, covertly preserving the heritage of their ancestors for about four hundred years. In contrast with the Jews of Spain, who had to choose between converting to Christianity or expulsion in 1492, the

Jews of Portugal were ordered by King Manuel I to choose between Christianity or being burned alive at the stake. Many Jews chose life and accepted the yoke of the Catholic Church. They pretended to be "New Christians" and lived as Anusim, or Marranos, which is a derogatory nickname meaning "swine" in Spanish. They performed the Christian customs, celebrated Christmas, baptized their children, and wore Catholic garb, but inside, they preserved the Jewish spark.

Samuel Schwarz (1880–1953), a Jewish mining engineer from Poland, was invited about a century ago to Belmonte with a delegation of engineers on a work assignment and discovered the town's Anusim. A Christian businessman warned Schwarz and his friends against working with his competitor, Baltasar Pereira de Sousa, "because he is a Jew." Until that point, the world had no idea that there were still Portuguese Jews left. Schwarz became very curious and decided to locate those hidden Jews in Belmonte. He asked questions, researched, and finally found the community, which included about two hundred families at the time. But they refused to admit any connection to Judaism. Schwarz discovered that their customs, liturgy, and blessings were similar to those practiced by other Jews, but they were different from the versions he was familiar with in Poland and throughout Europe. After a while, Schwarz managed to earn the trust of some of these "New Christians" and began to collect information about them, but he was unsuccessful in penetrating the secret community. During his searches, one of the elderly women of the community was brought before him, and she asked him to prove his Judaism by quoting a Jewish prayer or blessing. When Schwarz started reciting the Shema Yisrael and reached the word *Adonai*, the old woman recognized it, because this was one of the few words preserved by the community. She turned to the others and said decisively, "He said *Adonai*. He is one of us."

"Be a Jew at home and a Christian when you go out" is the sentence that Schwarz heard often during his research. Schwarz also learned that the figure who made sure to secretly transmit Jewish tradition to the children and to future generations was the mother. She received this tradition orally from her own mother and grandmother. Eventually, in 1925, Schwarz wrote his book *Os cristãos novos em Portugal no século XX* (The New Christians in Portugal in the twentieth century), which shared the story of the discovery of the lost Jews of Portugal and essentially exposed their secret to the public eye. The Jews of Portugal continued to live in hiding and only came out of the religious closet in 1970, after the dictator Salazar was removed from office.

At first glance, Belmonte looks like a small, pleasant tourist spot that adorns the Serra da Estrela ridge in Portugal. The town is renowned by the Portuguese and the rest of the world primarily because of the explorer Pedro Álvares Cabral, who was born there and is credited with discovering Brazil in 1500. This is the reason that the Museu dos Descobrimentos was founded here; to the residents of Belmonte, this is where the discovery of the New World began.

During my visits, I realized that the residents of Belmonte are proud to mention in their tourist pamphlets not only the museum in honor of the discovery of Brazil, but also the Jewish museum that was opened in the town in 2005. The museum features items and paintings from the life of the Anusim in the town, including a secret device made of a pair of roofing tiles that was used to bake matzah, a pocket mezuzah that the Anusim used to take with them, and other items from the world of Jewish tradition. One of the most interesting items is actually an ancient stone safeguarded from the ancient synagogue that was destroyed in the town, dating back to 1297 CE, upon which the following words were etched: "But the LORD is in His holy temple; let all the earth keep silence before Him" (Habakkuk 2:20). In 1996, the Beit Eliahu Synagogue was inaugurated in the town and put on the list of attractions that Belmonte markets to tourists. Every time I have visited this town, I have made sure to pray at the synagogue on Friday night.

Wandering the alleyways of Belmonte is a walk through a time tunnel of Jewish memories. As I strolled between the small homes and tiny shops, I noticed many doorposts with holes carved into them to insert a mezuzah, which was no longer there. The Anusim would often carve a cross into these mezuzah slots to note their "new religion," so that the Inquisition would skip over their homes.

The Inquisition fought against practicing Jewish tradition, which the Anusim continued to do in secret. The Inquisition authorities operating on behalf of the church in Portugal between 1536 and 1821 acted as police, judge, and executioner. Anyone suspected of not being a good Christian was faced with interrogations, torture, and of course, "purification of their sinful souls" by means of an auto-da-fé, which means "act of faith" in Portuguese. This entailed burning the New Christians alive if they were suspected of continuing to practice Jewish commandments and celebrate Jewish holidays, especially the two symbolic holidays of Passover and Purim. Passover, because of the exodus from slavery to freedom for which they yearned, and Purim, because of Queen Esther, who behaved just like them, a Jew in her heart and a non-Jew in the palace of Ahasuerus.

The Anusim were forced to adapt to a lifestyle that was designed to trick the inquisitors, who were constantly trying to catch them and often visited their homes. For example, they baked matzah in their basements on the third day of Passover, instead of in advance. They would convene to pray on Yom Kippur under the guise of a card game; they lit Sabbath candles and pretended that they were candles in honor of Jesus. They even built sukkahs inside their homes.

It was difficult to continue pretending for years, and many of those who were interrogated confessed under unbearable torture and exposed the secret traditions that continued to take place. It is estimated that the number of victims of the Inquisition throughout the three hundred years that it dominated Portugal exceeded forty thousand people, 1,175 of whom were burned alive at the stake.

Over time, the Anusim forgot their traditions in a world where there was no Judaism, no holy books, and no Jewish leadership to guide them. Christian customs became an inseparable part of their daily lives; even Queen Esther became a Catholic saint called Santa Esther. The Fast of Esther, a fast day observed on the Jewish calendar right before Purim, became a holiday on which mothers would teach their daughters the secrets of keeping a Jewish home and holding a festive meal (this may have been a relic of the famous Purim feast). When the Inquisition was finally over in 1821, a Christian lifestyle and practices had almost completely taken over the lives of the Anusim. They continued to live dual lives, keeping whatever was left of their Jewish heritage in secret, until 1917.

Schwarz is a celebrity in Belmonte, and while he can't compete with Cabral's discovery of Brazil, he most certainly has a place of honor at the Jewish museum in the town and in the country's converso literature. Openness to the Jewish story has recently made headlines in Portugal, both because it's the right thing for a democratic nation and member of the European Union to do, and also because the Portuguese realize the lucrative potential of attracting Jewish tourism to Portugal. A handful of the descendants of Anusim have started to ask questions about their past, and they have made it their goal to teach the Portuguese an important lesson in the lesser-known history of their nation. This group has started to buy homes that were built as synagogues, primarily in the fourteenth and fifteenth centuries. They are restoring them and turning them into Jewish museums, in towns such as Castelo De Vide, Tomar, and Belmonte, where the small community returned to practicing Judaism, undergoing an Orthodox Jewish conversion process. These have become tourist attractions and important sites on the Portuguese tourism map. In addition, the fact that the Jews of Belmonte went public encouraged other Anusim to bring ancient pieces of Judaica out of their basements, items that had been secretly handed down in their families for generations.

Sometimes, Torah scrolls or ritual baths were discovered, such as the one found in Coimbra.

I have visited the Jewish community of Belmonte three times and participated in the Friday night services at their synagogue, as I do every time I visit a Jewish community over the weekend. On my last visit, I was saddened to notice a significant change. During my first visit, there were about 150 Anusim at the Sabbath services at the synagogue; this time, there were only about a third of that number. Based on discussions with the congregants, I understood that the community is gradually dying out due to immigration to Israel, the elderly members passing away, and because, after all, the return of the Anusim to Judaism is complicated and challenging.

At the entrance of the synagogue in Belmonte, a sign hangs on a memorial stone: "Here in this spot, the chain was not broken... Here in the town of Belmonte, in this home and in the neighboring homes, the heart of the Jewish area, full and rich Jewish life existed since early times. Following decrees from the authorities, the Jewish residents of the town, like the other Jews throughout Spain and Portugal, were forced to convert, but they preserved their Judaism at home. Here, the candle was never snuffed out... Here, the Jewish soul was not lost... Here, the Jewish soul remains forever... and from out of the past, the future will grow. From the darkness and gloom of the Middle Ages, the light of the synagogue and spiritual center will shine." I wonder, will this sign withstand the test of time?

Not only are the members of the Belmonte community gradually waning, their customs and traditions are disappearing too. On Friday night during my most recent visit to the synagogue, the prayers were no longer held in the Portuguese style and language. It was Israeli-style, led by a rabbi originally from Brazil and conducted in Hebrew. The few worshippers did not really take part in the prayers or in the Sabbath experience that was completely led by the rabbi.

During the Kiddush after prayers, I wondered how complicated and multifaceted the process of removing the masks of those Anusim who returned to their Judaism must have been and continues to be. We usually put on a mask as a wistful dream of an alternate reality, at carnivals, festivals, during ritual acts, or at parties. We dress up in a costume of our own free will, so that we can experience a different reality. The mask enables us to use different identities, even when they are strange or contradictory. A mask is always put on out of free will and for a short period of time. The Anusim put on Christian masks for hundreds of years, and essentially, they slowly began to identify with their costumes. The Jewish spark and the Jewish traditions dwindled and shrunk. Life under the mask, which did not allow for meaningful practice of the traditions of their forefathers nor preservation of the ethos of the Jewish tribe, also prevented the transmission of family customs and of a living culture, aromas, flavors, and music that combine to create our deep internal experiences. A sense of belonging, identification, and sharing are created through involvement and discussion, but even these elements could not exist among the converso community. In the end, the mask was not removed; rather, it sunk in. Perhaps, the physical mask was removed, but the behavioral patterns to which they had become so accustomed were stronger among most of the Anusim.

The return of the Anusim to Judaism was conducted through an Orthodox Jewish conversion process. The rabbi sent to the community tried to build a religious and spiritual framework according to the fairly rigid Orthodox way. The prayers that he taught were foreign to them in their language and didn't draw from ancient Portuguese culture at all. In Porto and Lisbon, as well as in neighboring Spain, there are currently very small Jewish communities from other denominations as well, such as Reform and Conservative. I wonder: Would the pluralistic option, which is more open and attentive to people, have allowed more Anusim to return and remain part of the Jewish community in Belmonte, or in general?

It is important that the miracle of the continued existence of the Anusim for five hundred years not disappear. Its preservation requires the utmost sensitivity, inclusion, and endless openness to their process of returning to Judaism. Flexibility in areas such as conversion, intermarriage, and more could help us successfully deal with the challenge of preserving and connecting with additional Jewish communities all over the world.

Italy

18. A Tale of Two Piazzas – Rome
Local Personalities: Shmuel Alatri and Enrico
Gilad Peled

I always believed that the best way to get to know a city is through your feet. I spend my first day in any new city aimlessly wandering the streets with no specific destination in mind, listening to the city's unique soundtrack and trying to feel its pace. In Rome, somewhat like in Jerusalem, I continued to do this long after I had already become familiar with every street and every corner of the center of town. Next to the bustling Piazza Venezia, there is a maze of small, quiet streets. A constant chill is always in the air because sunlight can barely penetrate the narrow sliver of heaven above the tall homes with their crumbling walls. Walking through them requires extreme vigilance lest you slip on one of the smooth, round cobblestones and so you don't lose your way. Mildew covers the corners of the houses, and the smell of a different era hangs in the air.

American author Anatole Broyard once said that Rome is a poem pressed into service as a city. Rome is a city of surprises – you never know what will be found around the corner: a small piazza adorned by climbing vines, a Baroque-style fountain, the ornate façade of a Renaissance church, or a small, dusty family store selling kitchen utensils or textiles. Next to the center of town is a small piazza featuring a turtle-decorated fountain, from which there extends a narrow and intimate alleyway, echoing your footsteps. At the end of the alley is my favorite street corner in the city. From the shadows of the alley, you step out into the wide square of the Jewish ghetto of Rome, and you are always greeted by the vibrant mayhem of activity. It's a bit like entering the kibbutz dining room or the neighborhood synagogue sanctuary. At that corner, I would always shed the anonymity that accompanied me through the city's alleyways and immediately become a member of the community. For better or for worse, I was now "Gilad, the *shaliach* from Israel." A noisy rabble of children whom I guided would come out of the school. The community's security guards, with whom I worked on a regular basis, stood in strategic locations and peered warily at the passersby. Friends and acquaintances waved to me, and I greeted parents and colleagues. Over time, I learned about the family stories of the passersby and about the community history that was hidden in the space among the living.

There are very few examples of a Jewish community that defines itself so clearly by its physical location the way that the Jews of Rome identify with the ghetto. Even today, a Roman Jew's level of involvement in the community is measured by the frequency with which he visits the ghetto, and the community members assess the extent to which other members belong to the Jewish community with remarks such as, "I've never seen him at the piazza," or "Who's his father?" The ghetto is home to the community's offices and many of its institutions, the main synagogue, Rome's Jewish school, and a few kosher restaurants.

In one of the corners of the ghetto, half-hidden to the eye, is Pasticceria Boccione. Behind the modest façade of this kosher bakery hides one of the wonders of the Jewish kitchen of Rome. On dented shelves covered in crumbs sit traditional baked goods such as ricotta and sour cherry cake, which is cut with a large knife and melts in your mouth, or Jewish pizza – a sweet almond pastry filled with dried fruit, nuts, and other surprises, which is always scorched just a bit too much, comes out hard as a rock, and is grabbed off the large pans the moment it comes out of the oven. The five older sisters who run the aromatic bakery aren't known for their outstandingly courteous service, but patiently standing in the tiny bakery's line is worth the wait.

A nearby alley houses another culinary site. The small Sora Margherita restaurant will host you at homely tables and serve you a selection of traditional Roman dishes. Waiters and diners hurriedly pushing their way between the tables will brush your shoulders due to the crowding, as you munch on leaves of "Jewish artichoke" (Carcciofo alla Giudia) that just came out of the bubbling oil. Fried artichoke is a Roman Jewish dish rooted in the ghetto – invented out of scarcity and hunger by the poor families who lived here – which is sold today at a steep price by restaurants throughout the city.

The reality of the ghetto life that existed for about three hundred years in this very place is barely discernible now. At the end of the eighteenth century, development of the modern city led to the demolition of the narrow alleyways, where basic hygiene and sanitation were impossible. They were replaced by sunny streets and aesthetic blocks of residential buildings that were considered modern at the time. But the Jewish community, which scattered throughout the city, remained loyal to the site. The wide street at the center of the ghetto was closed off to vehicles and became a public square bustling with Jewish life. The Jews of the community refer to it simply as "the piazza," and the "Jews of the piazza" are the Jews whose social lives revolve around the community. The piazza is a social cultural space as much as a physical location, and belonging to it is more important than the level of a person's religious observance. Essentially, the Jewish community in Rome is not a religious community at all; it's an ethnic-national community. Therefore, it is open to accepting a wide range of Jewish identities – as long as they are connected to the piazza in some way.

"The Jews of the piazza," the core of the community, are usually traditional in their religious practice, conservative in their social-political opinions, and Zionist in their national opinions. It has been said about the Jews of Rome that they live like Reform Jews, practice like Conservatives, and have Orthodox leaders: they keep kosher but don't wear a kippah in public; they don't drive on the Sabbath but use their mobile phones; they pray according to an ancient text unique to Roman Jews but attend synagogue mostly on holidays. Many of them earn a living from retail stores. Some trace their family's roots in the city to Jews expelled from Spain who arrived at the end of the fifteenth century, and some can even trace their roots back to the Jewish slaves who reached the city after the Temple was destroyed in Jerusalem two thousand years ago. The Jewish community of Rome has a place of honor in the story of Rome, and many local residents view the Jews as the real Romans, the ones who were always here and didn't arrive in later waves of immigration.

As a result, the Jewish community of Rome, despite the Catholic church's efforts over the years to suppress Jewish practice, does not apologize for its existence, its location, or its way of life.

Yet in addition to the sense of uniqueness, the Jewish community of Rome is deeply involved in the urban scene. Symbolically, one can say that the history of the Jews in the city revolves around a triangle of three squares that had a decisive impact on the life of the Jews during the past few centuries. The first is the piazza of the ghetto, the square of Jewish life. Two additional squares also constitute not only a physical location, but a cultural and social space of Jewish existence. One is St. Peter's Square in the Vatican. It represents more than anything else the religious oppression led by the church throughout history. The more its influence increased, the more fearful the Jews became of expressing their Judaism in public, outside of the ghetto. The second square is Piazza Venezia (Venice Square), around which are the ruins of ancient Rome's former glory and many cultural and governmental institutions of the modern Italian republic. This is the square that represents the hope, equality, and normalcy that the modern Italian state offered to the Jews. The more its influence increases, the more comfortable the Jews feel expressing their Judaism in public.

These last two squares define the degree of visibility of Jews in the public sphere. For many hundreds of years, the lives of the Jews were shaped by the popes from St. Peter's Square and were limited to the physical and mental space of the Jewish ghetto. Over the past 150 years, Piazza Venezia has been the more influential square when it comes to Jewish existence. St. Peter's Square and Piazza Venezia are two poles pulling in different directions, which determine how far the Jews are from the piazza of the ghetto. The degree of influence that each of these poles has on the city's Jews is expressed through the lifestyle that they choose for themselves and the degree of closeness that each Roman Jew feels toward the Jewish community. Jews who feel threatened get closer to the ghetto; those who feel hopeful can distance themselves from it. However, the nucleus around which Jewish life has always revolved is the community located at the piazza of the ghetto.

I would like to mention two people whose lives define the struggle for Jewish existence in between these three squares.

For most of the nineteenth century, Shmuel Alatri led Rome's Jewish community. I never met him, of course, since he passed away 120 years before I first stepped on Roman soil. In all my years in the city, I never heard of him either – there are no streets named for him, books do not laud his work, and the Jews of Rome do not boast his name. Only recently, a tiny public park was dedicated to him. Shmuel Alatri was apparently the most important Jewish leader in Rome – whom no one remembers. Unlike most of the prominent Jewish leaders who were active in the city, he was also born in Rome. When I first encountered his name in a short footnote while I was writing my master's thesis, I envisioned a thick-bearded Jew with a heavy step, walking through the ghetto streets. He is wearing black and has a wide-brimmed hat on his head as he's making his way to the synagogue. While attempting to sidestep the sewage flowing through the streets, he exchanges greetings with the underprivileged Jews he grew up with, Jews whose fate rests on his shoulders.

The material found about Alatri online is scarce and scattered, but it is enough to provide a captivating glimpse into the life of a person who was anything but the way I imagined him. Alatri divided his time between the troubles of the dilapidated ghetto in Rome and the halls of the most wealthy and influential people in Europe and in Italy. He was probably one of the first Jews in town whose life was shaped by the increase of the symbolic influence of Piazza Venezia and Italian nationalism. He led the Jewish community for about sixty years, longer than any other Jewish leader over the past hundreds of years. Shmuel Alatri was the person who succeeded in carrying the weight of the Jewish community on his shoulders through the transition from the aggressive reign of the Vatican to the Italian nation-state and was thus awarded the title "father of the ghetto." For many decades, his very presence represented Jewish existence in the city, yet although he represented the traditional Jews of the ghetto, he was not religiously observant himself. In the only surviving photo of him, he is bareheaded, has a white moustache, and is wearing modern clothing.

As head of the community, Alatri was in direct, constant contact with the two forces that influenced the lives of the Jews at that time – the popes and national Italian forces. As a young man, Pope Gregory XVI, who was especially fond of him, nicknamed him "our young Cicero" for his outstanding diplomatic skills. In Rome, Alatri was known for his ingenuity and his financial talents, and he won himself many friends from among the most prominent figures in politics and economy. He was one of three Jews who served on the city council of Rome during the short national uprising at the end of the 1840s. This did not prevent the pope from inviting him, after reinstating his power, to serve as a member of the board of directors of the papal bank, where he played a central role in saving the bank from a dramatic financial collapse.

Alongside the trust that he earned from the Vatican, Alatri also won the faith of the city's citizens fighting for national independence. When they historically voted in favor of joining the Italian republic, Alatri was among the public representatives who submitted the results of the public referendum to King Victor Emanuel II. He was elected as treasurer of the free city and was a member of the Italian parliament. In one of the only stories that survived about his life, it is told that during a tempestuous meeting of the city council, a proposal was made to take down the cross hanging on the wall of the council's meeting room. This was an expression of the increasing secular tendency in the city during those years. But it was actually Shmuel Alatri, the Jew, who was most vehemently opposed to the idea. Instead of removing the cross, he suggested, a Star of David should be added to it. In reaction, as the story goes, the pope himself said that "Alatri is the most Christian of all of the members of Rome's city council." During all those years of public activity at the Vatican and in the institutions of the Italian republic, Alatri was the leader of the Jewish community and fought for its rights. In his old age, he was even the one who fought for its reorganization as part of the new Italian state, and the person behind the plans to demolish the ancient ghetto and improve the Jews' quality of life.

Shmuel Alatri was an exceptional phenomenon in the world he grew up in. He broke boundaries and consensuses without leaving the ghetto, and with his sharp senses, he knew how to adapt himself to the rules of the game in several parallel worlds. In the ghetto, he was a proud Italian, and outside of it he was proud of his Judaism. He used his public influence for the benefit of the community and represented it in the finest halls of Italy without any feelings of inferiority. However, no less than his story testifies to his greatness, his life testifies to the community's ability to accept him.

Indeed, the piazza of Rome knows how to accept a range of diverse Jewish lifestyles to this day, without compromising on its principles. I believe that the story of Enrico, another Roman Jew, is one of the best examples of the way that magic can exist in places that facilitate it, and of the power that the community has to create such magic.

Enrico was the first person I saw when I landed in Italy for the first time. He came to meet me at the airport and made sure that I safely reached Rome. Over the next years, we shared many moments of intensive work, meaningful talks, educational concerns, and good food. Enrico was and still is one of the most impressive young people I have ever met. He is the perfect balance of a classic intellectual and a great conversationalist; he is blessed with high emotional intelligence together with a sense of deep responsibility, and the ability to integrate a good joke with a quote in fluent Latin.

Enrico's family is Catholic on both sides. His father, a revolutionary personality in his youth, decided to convert to Judaism. He did so with the seriousness reserved for spiritual people who fall in love with a philosophical idea and then encounter its physical expression in reality. He fell in love with the idea of a nation without a homeland, a nation whose essence is an ancient tradition, who have survived for thousands of years with willpower and faith, and he decided to join them. Enrico's mother converted after him and for him, but never fully internalized the fact that she became a Jew. While Enrico's father lived as an Orthodox Jew, due to the differences in background, culture, and personality he never became a full member of the Jewish piazza. He lived his life as a Modern Orthodox Jew even after he became one of the leading sociologists in Italy, and despite being detached from Jewish community life, he was more careful about religious observance than most of the piazza Jews.

On Friday night, Enrico's father would sit with him and teach him fundamental Jewish ideas and a bit of Hebrew. There was no coercion at home regarding observing the commandments; rather, Enrico's father would provide explanations about their inner meaning along with deep conversations about Jewish philosophy. However, Enrico's parents enrolled him at a public school and not at the piazza's Jewish school. Thus, he grew up as the only Jew in his surroundings, without a connection to the Jewish community. With a Jewish father, atheist mother, large extended Catholic family, and no community, Enrico struggled for years to explain to himself and to those around him exactly who he was.

Until one day, he fell in love. It was immediate, complete, and total love, and it shook him to his core. Not of a romantic nature, Enrico's new love was sparked by question marks. At the age of fourteen, he joined a Jewish Zionist youth movement. "There," he later told me, "I was asked the right questions for the first time in my life." These were questions about identity, belonging, and purpose. For the first time in his life, he was in an environment that accepted him the way he was – with a unique story, but not an impossible one. For the first time, he belonged to a community that sparked his mind and allowed him to freely express who he was. He was fully drawn into the move-ment and developed a completely different Jewish identity than that of his father, a secular identity based on culture, history, and national-ity. "Over the years, I realized," Enrico told me, "that this community of people is what connected me to Judaism." His father found Judaism through faith but did not find a community for himself; Enrico found his Judaism through community, even without the faith.

Through the movement, for the first time, he met children who grew up in the piazza. It was love at first sight – he opened up new intellectual horizons for them, and they in turn introduced him for the first time to the secret of organic Jewish existence, the kind based on family Sabbath meals, the gaggle of uncles and cousins around the Sabbath table, and visits to the piazza. It wasn't just intellectual study anymore. "A regular Jew is born in a community and searches for his own path outside of it," Enrico said to me. "I was born outside the community, and all I wanted was to find a path into it." The community that he found through the movement gave him the freedom to talk about his unique background in Jewish settings and the power to be proud of his Judaism in non-Jewish ones. In this way, Enrico is a clear result of the symbolic power of Piazza Venezia, which enables Jews to feel comfortable with their Judaism anywhere.

As in Alatri's case, Enrico's life was also shaped by the willingness of the Jewish community to accept a range of Jewish identities, as long as they maintain some form of connection with the piazza. Alatri was born into the community and searched for his way out; Enrico was born outside the community and searched for a way in. He became active in other communal educational frameworks, broadening his familiarity with his inner world and allowing the community to broaden its familiarity with him. Many of the choices that he made in his life, he confessed, were spurred by his fear of losing this connection, the concern that "everything would suddenly be over," and the desire to continue to strengthen the Jewish aspect of his life.

In contrast with many cities in the world, if you're a Jewish traveler in Rome, you won't need to search for the Jewish community for very long. It's always there, in the piazza of the ghetto. Between your visit to Piazza Venezia and your visit to the Vatican, find the time to sit on a shaded bench next to Boccione bakery, and remember to ask yourselves whether you are looking from within your community outward, or looking at your community from the outside.

Greece

19. Journey to Freedom – Lesbos, Athens, Thessaloniki
Local Personality: Rabbi Ammiel Hirsch and the IsraAID Organization
Ya'acov Fried

I have known Rabbi Ammiel Hirsch, the senior rabbi of Stephen Wise Free Synagogue in New York, for close to thirty years. Over the years, I became familiar with Rabbi Hirsch's philosophy, which focuses primarily on promoting social justice in Israel and around the world based on the Jewish value of *tikkun olam*, repairing the world. This philosophy is also a central value in the community that he leads and defines his perception of Jewish identity in the twenty-first century.

At the beginning of 2017, Rabbi Hirsch contacted me and requested that I organize an educational tour of Greece for leaders in his community. His primary objective was to get a firsthand look at the plight of the refugees who arrived in Greece and subsequently flooded Central and Western Europe. He was also interested in introducing his group to the Jewish communities in Thessaloniki and Athens, and in the little time that remained, they wanted to enjoy a few pearls of Greek culture.

In his telephone call and in the email that he sent, Rabbi Hirsch provided a detailed explanation of the reasons behind the trip:

> We should create a connection with the refugees in Europe, we should pay more attention, we should be more involved, we

should mobilize our congregation, we should have been jolted out of our moral complacency long ago.

It was the President of the United States who lit the fires of our simmering moral indignation. His actions, his words about not allowing refugees to the United States pushed me to respond. If only to preserve our synagogue's dignity and to soften the coarseness and make more gentle the callousness of our national discourse.

I am all for pursuing American interests. But I am also for Torah: "Do not sit idly by while your neighbors bleed. You shall not wrong a stranger or oppress him, for you were strangers in the land of Egypt. You know the soul of a foreigner, for you were foreigners in the Land of Egypt."

We have a job. We are not politicians. We have an obligation to remind politicians of our moral imperatives. We see the world from our religious obligations, not from political calculations. We are driven not by what is popular, but by what is right. We are driven not by the words of pollsters but by the words of God: "Love the foreigner. Defend the orphan and the widow."

This is the "extreme vetting" that the Bible demands.

Jews have a special obligation to protect the weak. History has cast us into the role of perpetual wanderers: the wandering Jews. We are a refugee people. We know what it feels like. We are, or should be, especially sensitive to the well-off turning their backs on human suffering, unwilling to stare it in the face, or only pretending to care.

Guided by Rabbi Hirsch's words, we crafted a trip for his group of community leaders. Upon arrival in Greece, we reached the island of Lesbos, one of Greece's tourist treasures, to meet the refugees. The island's beaches are the first soil that the refugees set foot upon at the end of their journeys from Syria, Afghanistan, Iraq, and North Africa and were from their perspective the gateway to freedom in Europe.

Members of the Israeli humanitarian aid organization IsraAID, which works to save the refugees, welcomed us. Naama Gorodischer, the organization's program director; Dr. Tali Shaltiel, a physician; and Orly Unger, a social worker, moved to Lesbos in order to greet the refugees the moment they reached the shore, but some of them found themselves acting as physical rescuers: a few months before, on Rosh Hashanah eve, IsraAID members noticed a sinking boat with fifty Syrian refugees on board, at a distance from the shore. Women, children, and babies were falling into the water, and many of them did not know how to swim. The IsraAID members jumped into the water and rescued them.

IsraAID provides humanitarian aid at crisis points all over the world, including Lesbos. The aid centers for the refugees on the Greek islands are operated, to a great extent, by Israelis who are sometimes accompanied by Jewish volunteers from the United States. All of them are driven by a sense of mission, justice, and *tikkun olam*.

Khaled, who came from a refugee camp in the city of Halab (Aleppo) in northwestern Syria, shared: "Throughout my entire life, since I was a child, I was taught in the Syrian educational system that Israelis and Jews are the enemy. The first thing I saw when I approached the Greek coast was the Star of David on the volunteers' shirts, as they extended their arms and pulled me out of the water." According to data from the United Nations High Commissioner for Refugees, Khaled is one of fourteen thousand refugees living on islands around Greece, and one of sixty thousand Syrian refugees living in all of Greece. He fled from the civil war in Syria without any of his family members and has no information regarding their fate today. After living in Turkey for two years, he decided, like hundreds of thousands of other refugees, to try his luck and escape to Europe.

In Lesbos, IsraAID established the School of Peace, which has classrooms in different languages: Arabic, Dari (a dialect of Persian spoken in Afghanistan), Kurdish, and English. All the teachers at the school are refugees themselves, and there is also a Greek coordinator who connects the school to the Greek educational system and teaches the language as well.

At the school, the Israeli and Jewish demon slowly dissipates. "How can I continue to say that you are the enemy?" says Waleed, one of the students. A coordinator at the school who is an Iraqi refugee, Nasrin, adds: "I was only exposed to Israelis on television, which repeatedly told us that Israel was the Satan. But the reality tells the truth. We are cousins. It even says so in the Koran."

The islands struggle to deal with the influx of refugees, which is even more burdensome on the mainland, where Greece as a country is dealing with a deep economic crisis and surging unemployment. IsraAID's dozens of volunteers help refugees with the absorption process and stay in the country for several months. They are educators, social workers, psychologists, and physicians who have left their regular jobs to dedicate their time to helping the refugees.

In a joint discussion between the group members from the United States and the local teachers and volunteers, Rabbi Hirsch shared his feelings:

> Look where we stand, across the sea, only fourteen miles away. Lesbos is Europe, Lesbos is freedom, Lesbos is never having to worry about chemical attacks again and never having to face religious persecution.
>
> I could not help but think of our own people who stood on slavery shores, behind them persecution and oppression. In front of them – the sea. On the horizon was freedom: the last goal of the long, cruel journey to escape from slavery.
>
> Jewish tradition tells us that these refugees were stranded on the shore. They could not go back; Pharaoh's army would slaughter them. They could not go forward; there was an ocean in front of them. Finally, the Midrash tells us, one man, Nachshon the son

of Aminadav, took the first step. Nothing would have happened,
had not the Israelite taken that one step forward and then the
seas split, and waters parted. They just had to take the leap. We
are here to follow.

His words provoked a moving conversation among the participants
about the personal obligation of each Jew to save, help, and support
the refugees. Everyone present felt that stepping out of your everyday
comfort zone does wonders both for the recipient of the assistance
and for the person helping. The amazing work of the charity organizations in Greece, and especially IsraAID, elicited in me a sense of pride
as a Jew and as an Israeli. This reality, in which both the group members and the IsraAID volunteers had set aside their daily routines and
made time for others, enhanced my sense of pride in belonging to the
"Jewish tribe."

After the visit to Lesbos, I traveled with the group to visit Athens.
I shared my memories from my first trip to Greece with some of the
group members. Then, I had seen Greece in all its beauty, with its abundance of nature sites, and the country immediately beckoned me to go
on hikes, rafting trips, and jeep tours through the verdant mountains.
I recalled being struck by the sight of the gorgeous beaches, the azure
lakes between the hills, the cascading waterfalls, and the copious and
lush national parks. I retraced the footsteps of Greek ancient history
of thousands of years, the cradle of Western civilization as we know
it today and the basis of democracy. At every archaeological site I visited, I felt as if the thoughts of the great Greek philosophers Socrates,
Plato, and Aristotle were accompanying me.

I told them that I had noticed that Greek culture is composed of
different layers – ancient (classic) Greece, the Hellenistic period, and
the Roman, Byzantine, and Ottoman Empires. Elements from all these
layers can be found in every corner of the country, from the museums, theaters, and music to the historical and architectural sites, the

world heritage sites, and the many festivals that take place in Greece throughout the year.

When we went to eat our first dinner at a typical Greek restaurant, as a Greek ensemble played in the background, we paid attention to the freshness of the Greek kitchen, the abundance of *mezethes* (Greek little dishes), and ouzo, the national drink. The heads of the Jewish community, who were present at the meal, spoke to the members of the group about the complex reality in Greece and the huge challenges the community faces. Against the backdrop of the ensemble's music, they spoke of the central role that food and music play in Greek culture and lifestyle. Greeks listen to music nonstop and visit taverns where food and song go hand in hand. It is no surprise that even the words *melody* and *harmony* have Greek origins.

On all my trips to Greece, I loved wandering outside in Athens, Greece's bustling capital city, and taking part in the festivals and the upbeat music performances that penetrate the heart. A visit to Athens in the winter months, when the city is not overflowing with tourists, allowed me to discover lesser-known artists and musical talents and to feel the intensity of the local sounds. Even though I didn't understand the words of the songs, Greek music slowly became a significant part of the musical repertoire in my life. As a result, I discovered artists and composers such as Mikis Theodorakis, Maria Farantouri, and Eleni Vitali.

We continued on our journey to northern Greece and Thessaloniki, the second-largest city in Greece and a center of industry and commerce. The Jewish community in Thessaloniki, nicknamed "Jerusalem of the Balkans," existed for about two thousand years, and during certain periods, it was one of the largest communities in the world. Jews were dominant players in city life, and at points were even the majority there. During certain years, the Jewish presence was so significant that the city's port, which was its primary source of income, was closed on Shabbat. During our visit, we met with the community leaders and visited the synagogue, but most of the visit was a journey through memories of the community, which was decimated in the Holocaust. Only a few thousand Jews are left in the city today. I shared with the members of the group that from my perspective, a visit to Thessaloniki is an encounter with the music of Israeli singer and songwriter Yehuda Poliker, whose family lived in the city for generations and many of whom perished. In his work, Poliker emphasizes the rich Greek musical culture as well as the personal, family, and community loss suffered in the Holocaust.

In the winter after the visit to Lesbos, I also traveled to Athens for a few days, as is my custom every year. I enjoy the large variety of Greek music. But the music that penetrated the depths of my heart and soul was that written by Mikis Theodorakis to the texts of Iakovos Kambanellis, sung by Maria Farantouri. None of these three artists are Jewish, but they share the memory of the Holocaust with us. During the sixties, Mikis Theodorakis composed the music for *The Ballad of Mauthausen* based on four poems written by the Greek poet Iakovos Kambanellis, a native of the island of Naxos who was imprisoned at the Mauthausen concentration camp during World War II. The part of the ballad called "Song of Songs" conjures up an open wound that has not yet healed. The first time I heard Maria Farantouri sing it, in her deep and fragile voice, the tears rolled down my cheeks incessantly, despite the fact that I did not understand a word. Beyond the barrier of nationality, I feel that with these three, I am in a place common to all human beings. A place where we all share the beauty and the pain, and weave hope for a better world. All human beings were born equal, and so they will one day be united by love.

I watched Mikis Theodorakis conducting with hand motions that resembled butterflies lighting up the dark. In my opinion, this is one of the greatest works, designated to illuminate the darkness of human actions with compassion and kindness. The music reminds me, time and time again, that when no one else is behaving like a human being, we must stand up and be human. A human being searching for his love, for love itself, for humanity... when I listen to the song, I become a free man in the simplest and fullest sense of the word. I become aware of the fact that the light created by Mikis Theodorakis and Kambanellis in contrast to the immense darkness of Mauthausen is appropriate and relevant to the darkness of our times as well. "Song of Songs" by Theodorakis and Kambanellis softly shines light on the darkness of the abyss.

Theodorakis brought me back to the experience of the group's visit to Greece and helped me understand that in addition to the Jewish commitment to championing social justice, such a commitment also existed among the Greek nation. During World War II, the Greek population treated the Jewish community in different ways. Some of them even cooperated with the Nazis by informing on Jews and deporting them to death camps. However, among the Righteous Among the Nations those people who were not members of the Jewish tribe yet risked their lives to save Jews during the Holocaust there are several dozen Greeks. It can be assumed that there were more who acted in the same way, although their actions were not documented or awarded by Yad Vashem. Therefore, as we focus on Jewish social justice, it is also appropriate to take a closer look at the Greek nation and recognize the good deeds that some of them performed in the past and in the future.

As organizers of the trip, did we emphasize the role that the Greek nation itself is playing in the refugee saga, by opening its arms to millions of refugees? Is it possible that we did not give the Greeks themselves an opportunity to share and expose us to their feelings, their motivation, and their willingness to behave in such a noble and inspirational manner? It is true that the Jewish tribe is actively involved in assistance and lifesaving efforts disproportionate to the norm around the world. But our commitment is so strong that maybe sometimes, similar efforts by others go unnoticed by us.

The Ballad of Mauthausen 1995
Poetry: Iacovos Kambanellis
Music: Mikis Theodorakis
The English version is sung by Joan Baez

How lovely is my love
in her everyday dress
with a little comb in her hair.
No-one knew how lovely she was.
Girls of Auschwitz,
girls of Dachau,
did you see my love?
We saw her on a long journey;
she wasn't wearing her everyday dress
or the little comb in her hair.
How lovely is my love
caressed by her mother,
and her brother's kisses.
Nobody knew how lovely she was.
Girls of Mauthausen
girls of Belsen
did you see my love?
We saw her in the frozen square
with a number on her white hand
with a yellow star on her heart.
How lovely is my love
caressed by her mother,
and her brother's kisses.
Nobody knew how lovely she was.

North Africa and the Middle East

Morocco

20. On the Shoulders of Giants – Marrakech
Local Personality: Yitzchak Ohayon
Yishay Shavit

I arrived in Marrakech for the first time in my life on a Friday afternoon, five hours before the Sabbath was to begin. Despite the long journey to the city and the intense heat, I couldn't bring myself to go straight to my hotel room. Something pulled me out to the city streets. Perhaps it was the strong aroma of the spices that hit my nostrils as soon as I got out of the car; maybe it was the shouts of the merchants selling dates for prices that they claimed absolutely no one could refuse. Or was it the many stories about the city that I had heard as a child – stories in which legends were intertwined with historical facts, and heroes larger than life rode to the city in camel caravans laden with goods after having crossed the Sahara Desert. I was lucky that my two friends felt the same way. Together, we set out to explore the city.

Our feet took us straight to the mellah, the historical Jewish quarter of the city. To reach it, we had to cross one of the local marketplaces. The noontime Friday prayers were just taking place at the mosques, so most of the stores in the narrow streets were closed. Yet we still found ourselves walking between a large mass of shoppers buying wedding gifts, selling sandals, begging for money, holy people wearing traditional Moroccan jalabiyas, strange people staring into space, and various pedestrians. The experience of walking through the Moroccan marketplace in the Medina, the ancient part of the city, was pure joy for me. The market that we walked through led us to a huge square, the main square of Marrakech, Jemaa al-Fnaa. Thousands of people filled the area, clustered into groups around street artists who seemed to have stepped out of *Arabian Nights*, storytellers who enchanted the audiences, snake charmers playing the flute, and dancers who amazed spectators with their movements. It is an entire cacophony of colors, scents, people, and sounds that create an inexplicable sense of harmony, drawing the visitor into the different circles with invisible strands.

It's easy to forget yourself in Jemaa al-Fnaa and spend hours in the square. After about half an hour, we managed to pull ourselves away with great effort and continue on our way, but not before promising ourselves that we would come back the next day after sunset for dinner at one of the many food stalls at the site. We returned to one of the narrow streets that branches off the square and walked down it for a few minutes. Suddenly, we found ourselves standing under the entrance gate of the mellah. This is the gate where, according to tradition, Rabbi Mordechai Ben Attar buried an amulet over five hundred years ago, in which he wrote that no enemy would cross the entrance. The stories claim that this amulet prevented many tragedies and saved the Jews of Marrakech on more than one occasion. Filled with a sense of confidence, we walked through the gate and into the mellah. After a short walk, we found ourselves in a narrow alleyway. A quick glance at the blue sign on the wall divulged that we were on a street called Talmud Torah Street. On our right, we suddenly spotted a small door, which a sign identified as the famous synagogue Slat al-Azama, the synagogue of the Jews expelled from Spain in 1492. We went inside.

On the other side of the door, we found ourselves in a *riad*, a beautiful Moroccan courtyard with a fountain, trees, and arches supporting the structure on the second floor. The strong blue color of the *zellij* tiles almost blinded me. I entered the small synagogue located in the lower part of the *riad*. Sitting down on one of the benches, I looked at the gorgeous ark. After a few minutes of prayer/rest/meditation, I got up and started to explore the other parts of the complex. It turned out that the many rooms once used as study areas for hundreds of Jewish students now housed a small museum. I studied the photographs and saw Jewish Marrakech in all its glory. Photos of rabbis, poets, cantors, rabbinical judges, and other Jews covered the walls. Testimonies that proved like a thousand witnesses that here, there was once a city with an impressive Jewish community. A city whose scholars illuminated North Africa with their teachings, whose influence is still felt to this day.

Ten minutes later, I was standing in the heart of the Jewish cemetery of Marrakech. It was well tended and preserved, and it was obvious that time and money were being invested in the maintenance of the many tombstones. Opposite the entrance, I noticed a wall with information for visitors. Reading it, I discovered that this is the largest Jewish cemetery in Morocco. Over the past few centuries, tens of thousands of members of the community were buried here, including over 660 rabbis and *dayanim* (Jewish judges), as well as famous tzaddikim (holy people) whose names were known throughout the Jewish world. A treasure trove of wisdom and learning. The relics of a glorious community. Suddenly, a thought crossed my mind that bothered me for the next few hours. Where are the next generations of these giants? Who is keeping the spark of Jewish Marrakech alive today? As an Israeli, I have met quite a few descendants of this community. I went to school with them, served in the IDF with them, studied with them in university, worked with them. Few were able to relate something about their ancestors' legacy. Many knew very little. But I wasn't thinking about them. The thought that bothered me revolved around the city of Marrakech itself. Is the Jewish community living in Marrakech today strong enough to stand in the shoes of those early giants and carry the legacy of those generations on its shoulders?

I didn't have much time left when I reached the hotel. I showered quickly and put on the nicer clothing that I had brought with me to honor the Sabbath. I set out on foot to the Beit El Synagogue located outside the Medina, not far from my hotel. There at the synagogue, I had to find Yitzchak Ohayon, a Jew living in Marrakech who was supposed to be hosting us for the Sabbath meal. Walking alone through the streets of the modern neighborhoods of Marrakech during the cool evening hours felt wonderful. I passed teenagers wearing modern clothing and eating ice cream together and saw families taking an evening stroll. It felt like walking through a European city, just with less strict traffic regulations. In the end, when I reached the synagogue, I felt a bit embarrassed – how would I find Yitzchak Ohayon among all those present?

The task turned out to be easier than I anticipated. I was ten minutes early to the services, and the only worshipper waiting there was actually Yitzchak himself. We introduced ourselves to each other quickly and sat down to pray. I am not an Orthodox Jew who prays three times a day, but I can definitely say that I have participated in many different kinds of Sabbath services. Yet nothing prepared me for the prayer experience at Beit El Synagogue that Friday night. In the modest building, about two quorums of older worshippers eventually gathered. At any given moment, a different person led the prayers, and while reading the chapter from Tractate Shabbat in the Mishnah, *Bameh Madlikin*, as customary during the Friday night service, it seemed to me as if the members of the community were conducting an internal dialogue between them. One would read a few lines and then stop, and the next would pick up from there, and so forth. Some of the customs and tunes were foreign to my ears but made me feel such a strong sense of belonging, despite me being so far from my home in Jerusalem. I shut my eyes for a moment and listened to the music of their prayers. It could not have changed much over the past several hundred years. The experience I was feeling now was the exact same experience that Jewish visitors in Marrakech felt fifty, a hundred, or two hundred years ago.

At the end of the service, Yitzchak Ohayon led me and my friends who had joined me to his home, a short distance from the synagogue.

His home turned out to be a modern Moroccan apartment building that was extremely similar to apartment buildings from the sixties or seventies in many locations across Europe. We ascended the stairwell to Yitzchak's apartment, entered, sat down in the neat living room, and started chatting. The conversation took place in modern Hebrew. Yitzchak's perfect fluency in that language took me by surprise. I decided to ask him about it. It turned out that while Yitzchak was born in Marrakech and lived in the city for most of his life, he lived in Israel for a few years during the seventies. We connected quickly and began exchanging stories from Israel and Marrakech. A bottle of *mahia*, a homemade alcoholic drink, was opened and soon emptied.

Yitzchak turned out to be a colorful personality with strong opinions on current issues, a person whose feet were firmly planted in the Jewish scene in Morocco, Israel, France, and North America. He shared lengthy stories about the opulent Jewish past of Marrakech. We heard about Rabbi Chananya Hacohen, who thwarted the plot of the king's evil advisor to expel the Jews from the city, and about the liturgist Rabbi Shlomo Abitbol, who wrote the song "Yafah v'Tamah," one of the most well-known songs among Jews of Moroccan descent to this day. Yitzchak emphasized the significance that the sages of Marrakech assigned to learning in general and to Talmud study in particular. Important local yeshivas became famous centers of Torah. He concluded by remarking, as a side note, that there were only about a hundred Jews still living in Marrakech today and that the future of the local Jewish community was uncertain.

Hearing this comment, I couldn't hold back from expressing the thoughts that had been bothering me since my visit to the cemetery. I turned to Yitzchak and said, "You live in an amazing city. A city with a place of honor in Jewish history. You own a store in the mellah, in the very same place where Jewish shop owners have worked for hundreds of years. You visit the Slat al-Azama Synagogue, where giant Torah scholars once stood. You pray in the exact same words that tens of thousands of Jews, your ancestors, prayed in this very city. Do you, Mr. Yitzchak Ohayon, feel the weight of the generations on your shoulders? Do you feel, in your everyday life, an obligation toward the extensive Jewish life that once flourished here in the past?"

"Listen," Yitzchak replied, "did you visit the Jewish cemetery?" After I replied in the affirmative, he continued, "The cemetery was completely destroyed. All the tombstones were broken; it was impossible to walk between the graves. Weeds grew tall there, and snakes slithered freely between them. For over three years, twelve workers toiled at the cemetery. Every day, they poured out forty or fifty bags of cement. Do you know how much time, effort, and money I invested in that place? You saw how beautiful it is now. All altruistically. Do you understand now?" The truth was that I wasn't sure I had fully understood his answer, but the Sabbath meal was already laid out on the table, and everyone started singing "Shalom Aleichem." We soon recited the blessings, washed our hands, and started to eat.

A Jewish Friday night meal in Marrakech. Just the salads would have been enough for an entire meal in itself. The *zaalouk*, traditional Moroccan eggplant salad, was simply divine. After the meal, we continued to talk and laugh. It wasn't the time to bring up heavy, serious topics. Only later at night, in my hotel room, did I allow myself to reflect on Yitzchak Ohayon's answer to my question about the weight of the generations and the feeling of commitment to the city's Jewish history. Why did Yitzchak bring up the cemetery? What caused him to visit the site every single day for years and spend an entire hour there between eight and nine in the morning? Something didn't make sense to me. Renovating the cemetery couldn't be the heart of it all. Yes, it was an important act, even a very important one, but it was meant to reflect a greater truth. After pondering some more, a thought occurred to me. Perhaps everything that I had seen today connected to Yitzchak's answer. The beautiful Slat al-Azama Synagogue, the Shabbat prayers in the local tunes, Yitzchak's insistence on living in Marrakech and not in Casablanca, Israel, France, or anywhere else where temperatures don't reach 45 degrees Celsius in the summer, and yes, the story of the cemetery renovation too. All of these facets, together, were the answer to my question. The sense of commitment to past generations was in fact what motivated Yitzchak and the other Jews in this small community in Marrakech.

I believe that Yitzchak's efforts stem from a deep familiarity with the Moroccan Jewish heritage and a commitment to it. Two thousand years of history of the largest Jewish community in North Africa would disappear if people like Yitzchak Ohayon didn't insist on continuing to live in the geographic and cultural locations where the glory of the past was born. I believe that preserving Jewish heritage, in Marrakech and in other places, including the original buildings and culture, allows us to honor those who preceded us and simultaneously advances our ability to connect to ancient roots and formulate a more complete Jewish identity. To achieve this, people sensitive to the historical significance and a deep understanding of the practical ways of the world are imperative. To achieve this, the Jewish people need more people like Yitzchak Ohayon.

21. When the Jewish Saints Come Marching In – Fez
Local Personality: Lalla Soulika
Michal Granot

Tight alleyways, small shops offering their wares on the street, craftsmen busy dyeing hides and tapping copper – crafts that seem to have become extinct and in the background, the smells of spices and the sound of the mosque calling the worshipers for prayers. I could have made the mistake of thinking I was in Jerusalem. But this isn't Jerusalem; it's Fez, a city often referred to by Jews throughout the generations as "Jerusalem of the Maghreb." I have loved Jerusalem since I was a child, but it took me time to get to know Fez and to love it.

I arrived in Morocco for the first time as a guide in 2005. I was leading jeep tours for Israelis crazy about adventure, mountains, and the desert. The Moroccan cities felt distant to me, and Moroccan Jewry was an unknown, incomprehensible subject, which I admit I was a bit afraid to broach. That year, I wrote a booklet for tourists about Morocco, and in the summary that I wrote about Moroccan Jewry, I stated that "this column will not discuss the phenomenon of worshiping saints." Later, I definitely did reach the lauded Moroccan cities, and everything that was unknown and incomprehensible about Moroccan Jewry suddenly captivated me.

It was then that I studied and researched the subject, and today, I know that it is impossible to write about Moroccan Jewry without mentioning the phenomenon of veneration of saints. I can just imagine the question mark that pops into the mind of the Western reader at the sight of the words "veneration of saints." Let me mention that although Morocco was referred to as Maghreb, meaning "west" in Arabic, due to its geographic location at the western edge of the old world, there is a large culture gap between today's Western visitors and the Maghreb culture they will encounter. It is specifically this gap that encapsulates the magic that has attracted so many Western visitors to Morocco. Each person and the gap that they discover – for me, the veneration of righteous people by Jews, a phenomenon that brings together the poor and the rich, the mountain man and the city folk, the northern Spanish residents and the southern desert residents, and men and women – was the gap that I sought to understand. Today, I know that wherever Jews lived in Morocco, I will find tombs of men and women who were venerated by members of the local Jewish community, to which they make pilgrimages even today. One such location is the Jewish cemetery of Fez, which I make sure to visit every time I am there.

The city of Fez was established toward the end of the eight century CE by Idris II, the son of Idris I, founder of the first Moroccan royal dynasty and considered a descendant of the prophet Muhammad. Immediately after it was established, Fez became the first imperial capital of Morocco. They say that Idris II wanted to give the city an economic push and invited Jews to settle in the area. Fez became a large, vibrant city known as a center of Muslim and Jewish scholarship. Among the famous Jewish scholars who lived in this city are Dunash ben Labrat, who lived in the tenth century and whose influence on Hebrew grammar is still felt today, and the Rif – Rabbi Yitzchak ben Yaakov Alfassi, whose work on the Talmud was one of the three sources used by the Rambam (Maimonides) in his work of Jewish law *Mishneh Torah*. The Rambam himself lived in Fez for a short period and studied in the city. There were also famous dynasties of rabbinic families from Fez, such as the Tzarfati family and Ibn Danan.

Old Fez is special because it has two parts. Fez el-Bali is the old city, founded in the eighth century, which grew and was surrounded by various walls throughout history. A new city was added to it in the fourteenth century that was referred to as Fez el-Jdid (New Fez), which is also considered part of the ancient area of the city today. In the twentieth century, the French built the Ville Nouvelle, which is the new, modern city of Fez.

The sultans of the Marinid Dynasty, who built Fez el-Jdid, decided to move the Jews of the city to the new region that they built, and thus, right next to the king's palace, the Jewish neighborhood known as the mellah was built. Did they do so to protect the Jews of the city? Or to make it easier for them to collect taxes from them? Or perhaps they hoped that during times of political unrest, the raging masses would first encounter the Jews before they reached the king's palace? It seems that the answer is all of the above. The mellah of Fez, built in 1468, became the first in a series of mellahs that would later be formed in all Moroccan cities.

The veteran Jewish community living in the mellah was joined at the end of the fifteenth century by many thousands of Jews who had been expelled from Spain. Many of them did not wander very far, crossing the Mediterranean Sea and settling down among the Jewish communities that already existed in Morocco. These Jews were named and identify themselves, from the fifteenth century to this day, as the Megorashim (meaning "the expelled"). The merging of these two communities was not easy, and tensions arose between the Vatikim (meaning "veterans"), the local Jews of Morocco who lived there prior to the fifteenth century, and the Megorashim. The Megorashim influenced all areas of local life – the language, the customs, the clothing style – and their impact can still be felt today in the architecture of the neighborhood. Although the Spanish exiles had a strong impact on the Jews of Morocco, one area was not influenced by them – the custom of veneration of saints.

I will never forget the day I stood with a group in the cemetery of Fez on one of my first trips to the city and spoke about the righteous people buried there. One of the women, a sharp attorney from the United States whose family was originally from Morocco, shared that throughout her entire childhood, she slept with a picture of her family's esteemed saint under her pillow, and how meaningful it is for her to make the pilgrimage now to his tomb and connect to her family's long-time tradition. I admit that I was shocked. Until that day, I associated veneration of saints with religious people who belong to an older generation, whose lifestyles are not very similar to mine. But here was a woman my age, and although we didn't grow up in the same country, at first glance, we both seemed to belong to the same Western culture – watching the same shows and listening to the same music. However, during the years that I was dreaming of fairies, princesses, Bilbi (the Israeli version of Pippi Longstocking), and a few other superheroes who watched over me, she also had her own private saint right under her pillow who safeguarded her.

I realized that I didn't understand a thing about what those righteous figures or saints meant to the Jews of Morocco. When I returned to Israel after that trip to Morocco, I went to the large cemetery on Har Hamenuchot in Jerusalem to see if here too, people were lighting candles and making pilgrimages to the tombs. To my surprise, there were many people who had come to the cemetery to visit the gravesites of honored Ashkenazi rabbis. I discovered more and more pilgrimage sites, such as the tomb of Rachel the Matriarch, the tomb of the Rambam in Tiberias, or of the Arizal in Tzfat, and I realized that even in America, many Jews visit the Ohel, the site of the tomb of the Lubavitcher Rebbe, as one American tourist told me. The subject became a research topic, and today I know that in all religions, even monotheistic ones in which God is a lofty entity that handles matters of the utmost importance, human beings feel the need to find an intermediary figure who helps them deal with their daily lives and earthly problems. As a result, in all religions and in every country, there are sites where people made pilgrimages and performed various customs that made them into saints. Often, those locations that became holy are tombs of people who, whether because of their healing powers, religious scholarship, exceptional asceticism, or spirituality, were considered closer to God even during their lifetimes. It is amazing to discover that in all religions, the same universal customs can be found of making a pilgrimage to the tomb, praying, and using candles as part of the worship.

Settling next to Muslims and living among them influenced Moroccan Jewry in this context of veneration of saints as well, since maraboutism was a central motif in Moroccan Islam. A marabout is a holy man or scholar. Muslim marabouts possessed *baraka*, a blessing power, whether as sharifs (people of noble lineage), descendants of the prophet Muhammad from his daughter Fatima, or as descendants of other marabouts who received the *baraka* in other ways. Yet a significant difference is the fact that most of the Muslim saints were honored during their lifetimes, while most of the Jewish righteous people became saints after their deaths and were often venerated by the local Muslims as well.

So what is a Jewish saint, and what does veneration of saints really mean?

There are six ways that a person can become a saint: personal example, performing miracles, revelations related to death or the grave, a connection to the Land of Israel, descending from righteous lineage, or revelations in a dream.

During my first visit to the mellah of Fez, I visited the impressive, restored Ibn Danan Synagogue. I knew that right behind it was the Jewish cemetery of the local community, but that knowledge didn't prepare me for what I saw. The area where the cemetery is located is huge, and its round-shaped graves make it look different from Jewish cemeteries in Europe or North America. More than anything else, I was shocked by the white color of the graves, in stark contrast with the blue sky above them, creating a colorful image that arouses a sense of liveliness. It is a place of life, not of death.

Despite the blinding white of the graves, a few different-shaped tombs stand out in the cemetery. Some are family plots, and some are the tombs of those venerated saints.

Many saints are buried in the Fez cemetery, and each has many merits. Various Jews will prefer to visit the gravesite of a specific saint, but it seems they will all stop for a moment next to the tomb of a very special female saint, the tomb of Lalla Soulika.

Many saints were rabbis who influenced the community during their lifetimes, but Lalla Soulika was an unknown Jewish girl who was born in the city of Tangir in 1817 and named Sol Hachuel. When Sol was seventeen, her Muslim neighbor fell in love with her and wanted to marry her. Sol refused because she was a Jew, and it seems that her offended neighbor wanted to get revenge and spread a rumor that Sol had converted to Islam but then retracted it – a deed punishable in

Morocco during those years by death. Sol was brought to trial before the ruler of the city, who offered her a pleasant life married to a local noble, protection, and grandeur, but Sol refused to convert. The angry ruler threatened to execute her. The Jewish community turned to the Spanish consul, who intervened and arranged for Sol to be brought before the sultan in Fez for trial. When Sol arrived in Fez, everyone was shocked by her beauty, and the sultan's son offered her a royal life alongside him if she would only convert. Sol stood by her refusal, claiming that no life of luxury could compensate for losing her faith. She was sentenced to death.

The story relates that the community's rabbis, who feared for the fate of the entire Jewish community, also turned to Sol and asked that she consider changing her answer, but Sol clung to her faith. Sol was executed in 1834 at the age of seventeen, and thus joined the long chain of saints who perished in order to sanctify God's name throughout the generations. Sol's death shook the Jews of Morocco. Sol was buried in Fez, and her gravesite became a pilgrimage site, in respect for the personal example that she set, as well as her unwavering faith and her courage. The Jewish community of Fez adopted her, and Sol later became a preferred saint by women looking for a righteous female figure to venerate. Today, she is known by the name Lalla (meaning princess) Soulika, and her story is one of the most well known of the saints of Morocco.

The story of Moroccan Jewry is incomplete without understanding this connection to stories about saints. If, in the past, I had difficulty connecting with this form of worship, today I understand how meaningful it is to so many people. Even in today's modern world with its endless technologies incorporated into every aspect of our lives, at the end of the day, people are still human. We all deal with challenges in our lives and with existential problems that shake our world. The very belief that lighting candles next to the gravesite of Lalla Soulika in the Fez cemetery is a protective ritual can ease the tension of life a bit. Perhaps if each of us had a picture of a righteous person under our pillows, we would have another way dealing with the trials and tribulations of our daily lives.

Since the nineties, when relations between Israel and Morocco softened, many Israeli Jews have traveled to the country and enjoyed its culture and landscapes. Some of those visitors are Israelis from families who immigrated from Morocco or were even born in the country and are now coming back to visit their place of birth. Among these visitors, some are vocal about their desire to transfer the bones of Jewish saints such as Lalla Soulika for burial in Israel. It is interesting to note that the king of Morocco is vehemently opposed to this proposal. I am sure that while visiting Morocco, you will hear about the significance of Jewish emigration from Morocco in terms of the social and economic ramifications. But as far as the king sees it today, even in the twenty-first century, if the saints leave, the *baraka* will leave with them – and to that, he cannot agree.

22. One Step Away from the Sahara – Atlas Mountains
Local Personality: Rabbi Shlomo Bel Hens
Eran Shlomi

"Let's travel to Morocco," my good friend Shai said to me a few years ago.

"Morocco? But that's an Arab country, and we're Israeli Jews."

"It'll be fine," Shai said. "We just won't stand out. No one will know."

We flew. One week into our trip, and none of the locals had asked any complicated questions. We felt safe, but we were always cautious, because after all, how safe can Israelis really be in an Arab country? After a few days in Marrakech, it was time to climb the High Atlas mountain range. We planned a two-night, three-day hike, laced our hiking boots, took water and supplies, caught a bus to the starting point deep in the mountains, and started climbing. As the sun began to set, we walked toward a small village. We found the only house that featured the word *hostel* on it in French, asked politely for a room and a meal, and went to shower. That night, we sat in the empty dining room, just Shai and me. Suddenly, we heard a foreign language in the background; it was an Austrian couple who had arrived at the hostel a bit after us. We introduced ourselves and started chatting and telling stories from our trip. The next day, the four of us set out to continue climbing.

The landscape was breathtaking. We hiked across valleys and up snow-covered mountain passes, and at times I felt as if I were in the Alps or the Andes. As we crossed villages, the residents waved to us. They looked to me like the natives I had seen on my trips through the mountains of eastern Asia or South America. Before it became dark, the four of us entered a village and looked for a place to stay. From one of the paths emerged a mustached man wearing a djellaba (traditional Moroccan robe). "Welcome, I am Mohammed. Where are you from?"

Shai and I were silent. We let the Austrian couple introduce themselves and hoped that he would think that we were with them and that we were all Austrians.

"Austria, welcome," Mohammed said to the couple and shook their hands. "And where are you from?" he turned to us.

"Israel," I replied, almost in a whisper. "Israel?! Welcome!" he said with a huge smile, outstretching his arms to hug us. "Do you know Shuka? He comes here every year." We followed him into the yard as he continued to tell us endless stories about past Israeli guests while he showed us around his home. I felt bad for the Austrian couple, to whom he was no longer paying any attention.

From that evening onward, until our stay in Morocco was over, we made sure to introduce ourselves as Israelis, and we received only love and warmth from the locals. But the hospitality of Mohammed the Berber, man of the Atlas, I will never forget. Since then, every time I return to this area of the High Atlas mountain range, the Berber hospitality and their kind attitude toward Jews always warms my heart.

But what is the High Atlas, who are the natives of the Atlas, and what is the reason for their warm attitude toward Jews?

A visit to the Atlas Mountains is undoubtedly one of the highlights of any trip to Morocco. The grand mountain range stretches across fifteen hundred miles and crosses three countries: Morocco, Algeria, and Tunisia. The High Atlas range, which separates between the plain where Marrakech is located and the huge Sahara Desert, is the most impressive part in the eyes of many. For those coming from the direction of Marrakech during the spring and winter seasons, a breathtaking panoramic view is visible: tall mountains with snowcapped peaks whose slopes are carpeted with green flora, reddish-brown rocky outcrops, and streams of melted snow. This beauty is dotted by the homes of the villagers, built of red mud bricks and usually surrounded by green plants.

The residents of the Atlas are mainly tribes known as Berbers, populations that preserve ancient traditions and lifestyles to this day. They call themselves Imazighen (free men) and live in small villages or towns, some of which are very isolated. They primarily engage in agriculture, shepherding, trade, and tourism. Once upon a time, trips to the Atlas Mountains were very difficult and dangerous, and the area of the Berbers was mostly cut off from civilization. Today, thanks to a modern system of roads, the Atlas and its Berber residents are opening their gates to visitors.

Driving up the Atlas inclines or across one of its valleys – the Ourika Valley is the most popular – it is impossible not to notice the rich Berber culture that meets the eye. Many eateries show off steaming tagines in which chicken or meat dishes with cooked vegetables simmer. Cafés along the way serve tea made of aromatic leaves on lovely porches.

On traditional woven carpets, artists spread out a selection of unique jewelry made of gold, silver, or copper, as well as beautiful pottery pieces made of the rich muds of the mountains. Cooperatives of farmers invite visitors to try rubbing a bit of argan tree oil, which is famous for its unique beneficial qualities, on their skin. Thus, a trip through the Atlas Mountains is an experience that stimulates all your senses.

It is difficult to find Jewish heritage in the Atlas Mountains today. According to tradition, Jews reached the Atlas Mountains following the destruction of the First Temple, in their search for a safe refuge. Throughout the generations, they enjoyed good neighborly relations with the Berbers and maintained their traditional Jewish lifestyle, while adopting many elements of Berber culture as well. Until the mid-twentieth century, Jews in the Atlas Mountains in Morocco maintained their traditional practices almost completely. Thousands of Jews were scattered across dozens of mellahs next to the Muslim Berber villages, but with mutual involvement. In other words, they were significantly involved in village life despite belonging to a separate religious community. The Jews were mostly craftsmen shoemakers, saddle makers, tailors, silversmiths, and blacksmiths and they provided their services to the Muslim farmers and shepherds in the Atlas. As opposed to the rest of the Jews in Morocco, the Jews of the Atlas spoke the language of the Berbers with its three different dialects and adopted many elements of their culture, from various spiritual and mystical customs such as ceremonies and amulets against the evil eye and magic spells to jewelry design traditions with unique Berber elements. During the nineteenth century, and even more so after the establishment of the French protectorate in 1912, many of the Jews of the Atlas immigrated to the big cities, such as Casablanca and Rabat, in search of modern jobs. Only the Jews who lived more traditional lifestyles remained in the Atlas Mountains.

Where are they today?

When I first started guiding tours in Morocco, I happened upon a video from the sixties about the immigration of the Jews of the Atlas to the State of Israel, while searching for information about Jewish life in Morocco. The video focused on a village called Agouim, located at an altitude of 5,800 feet – in the middle of the route that crosses the High Atlas, hours away from the winding road from Marrakech. In the village's mellah, there were a few Jewish families. The men had beards, walked in sandals and with walking sticks, and the women drew water from the well. It all seemed like a picture frozen in time from the days of the Bible. This pastoral biblical setting shown in the video was suddenly interrupted one morning when a group of young men wearing suits and ties showed up in the village. They were representatives of the Jewish Agency from Israel, who sought to speak with the elders of the community and organize the immigration of the Jews of Agouim to Israel. The Jews packed up their belongings, removed their mezuzot from their doorposts, took their Torah scrolls, parted with the local *tzaddik* (holy man) buried in their cemetery, and boarded a small bus that took them toward the port in Casablanca.

According to the film's narrator, the video was part of a campaign to raise money for the United Jewish Appeal (UJA), the Jewish American philanthropic organization, in 1964. It was entitled *The Jews of Morocco: An Account of the Last Days of an Ancient Jewish Community.* The film was accompanied by explanations by Herbert A. Friedman, a Reform rabbi who later became president of the UJA. In the film, Friedman warns American viewers, who are potential donors, of what lies ahead. Now that Morocco has become an independent Arab country, he says, the Jews can expect danger, as has happened in other Arab countries that won their independence. On the other hand, the gates of immigration to Israel have opened, so "Donate to the UJA," Friedman requests at the end of the segment, "and support the exodus of the Jews of Morocco to the Promised Land, where they can live in peace, each under their grapevine and under their fig tree."

I am very familiar with the narrative presented by Rabbi Friedman. My father's family was expelled from Cairo, Egypt, in 1956, after Gamal

Abdel Nasser rose to power. They had to flee after violent riots broke out against the Jews in various locations in Cairo and Alexandria, and their neighbors told them that they might be next in line. When their fear was too much to bear, the family – my grandfather, grandmother, father, and his two older sisters – packed everything that would fit into their suitcases and made their way to the port in Alexandria. Together with many other Jewish refugees, they boarded a ship that sailed to Athens and then continued to Haifa. They left behind a house filled with furniture and expensive belongings, which was immediately looted as soon as they left. The looters were waiting in the stairwell for them to leave, my father recalled.

We do not see any of that in the film about the Jews of the Atlas – no rioters and no looters. I watched the video many times, and every time I see those biblical villagers folding up their lives into a suitcase, I have a better understanding of the story of Moroccan Jewry – the largest Jewish community in an Arab country, which numbered a quarter of a million members at its peak, of which only about twenty-five hundred remain in Morocco today. Their story is more complex than the stories of Jews in other Arab countries, and definitely different from my father's experience. Most of them didn't leave Morocco because of distress. They left because they wanted to live in the new Jewish country. Most of the Muslim Berbers could not understand why their Jewish neighbors left.

What remains of the ancient rich Jewish heritage in the Atlas Mountains today? Travelers passing through Ourika Valley can't miss the tomb of the righteous Rabbi Shlomo Ba'al Hanachash – or as he is known locally, Rabbi Shlomo Bel Hensh. Rabbi Shlomo was a rabbinical emissary who traveled in the sixteenth century to collection donations from Jewish communities throughout the diaspora on behalf of the Jews living in the Land of Israel. According to the legend, the rabbi entered Ourika Valley on Sabbath eve while sitting in his wagon, but then died suddenly at the entrance to one of the villages. His two horses bearing the sacks with the donation money that he had collected remained driverless. The local qadi (Muslim judge) sent his men to steal the money, when suddenly a miracle happened. The reins on the horses turned into snakes. The qadi's men fled and left the money behind, to the joy of the Jews in the village. Bel Hensh's name is still remembered by Moroccan families to this day, and his tomb became a must-see site for Jewish and non-Jewish tourists alike visiting the Ourika Valley. Until recently, it was possible to find the Alfassi couple there, who protected the site for decades as part of their family's tradition. The two had no children, and they adopted a Muslim girl named Fatima. Since the couple's death and to this day, their adopted daughter has been safeguarding the tomb.

On my last visit to the tomb of Rabbi Shlomo Ba'al Hanachash, I had the good fortune of talking to Fatima for a few minutes. She told me what I already knew about the many Jewish visitors who come to the righteous man's tomb. But what surprised me were her stories of the Muslim Berbers who seek the rabbi's blessing. I got the impression that for the local residents, who believe in God, it doesn't really matter that this holy man happened to be Jewish. To me, the story of the tomb of Rabbi Shlomo Bel Hensh represents the overall relationships between Jews and Muslims in this part of the world – communities who lived alongside each other, together and separately, in mutual respect, for thousands of years. This type of connection leaves a tradition that cannot be erased by the few decades since the Jews left Morocco. This tradition, I realized at the foot of the shrine, is the clearest explanation for Mohammed's hospitality, which left such a lasting impression on me.

On the eastern side of the High Atlas mountain range, on the seam between the mountains and the desert, is the Todgha Valley. At the center, there is an expansive palm grove, and next to it lies the village of Tinghir. Most tourists who come to this region stop in Tinghir to rest on their way to the Sahara Desert. Almost all of them visit the steep Todgha Gorge or enter one of the famous carpet shops. But few of them are familiar with the mellah of Tinghir or the song that was inspired by the life of the Jews in this village.

The song "Here in the Village of Todgha" (referring to the village of Tinghir in the Todgha Valley) was written by Israeli screenwriter Yehoshua Sobol in the seventies based on interviews he held with Jews who immigrated from the village of Tinghir to Israel. The song describes the traditional festival that was held by Jewish families before bringing their five-year-old sons to the Jewish school for the first time, where they would begin to learn the Hebrew alphabet. They would crown the child with a wreath of flowers, and as he walked through the streets to the synagogue, everyone would cheer for him. He was brought into the synagogue, "...and they would write on a wooden board / in honey from *alef* to *tav* / all of the letters in honey / and say to him: *habibi* [my dear], lick! / And the Torah in his mouth / would be as sweet as honey / here in Todgha / in the heart of the Atlas Mountains." The words of the song are framed and featured in the small Jewish museum in the Slat-al Azama Synagogue in Marrakech, but the best place to listen to this beautiful song is while traveling the winding road through the heart of the Todgha Valley, approaching the village of Tinghir.

Even if there isn't much Jewish heritage left to see today in the Atlas, it is definitely still possible to feel the Jewish past. This is true of the Atlas and of Morocco in general. I believe that this is because of the way that Moroccans in general, and especially the Berbers, view the Jewish past: Moroccans miss the Jews. This is expressed in various ways: through the amendment to the constitution of the Kingdom of Morocco, which states that Jews are part of Moroccan heritage; through the government funding for renovating synagogues and cemeteries; through sponsorship of the Jewish museum in Casablanca – the only Jewish museum in the entire Arab world; through learning about the Holocaust in local schools; through establishing diplomatic and economic relations with the State of Israel; through the warm welcome that Israeli and Jewish tourists receive; and so forth.

The Muslim Berbers and the Jews of the Atlas, I feel, miss each other a bit differently. Many of the villagers at the mountain peaks didn't understand why their Jewish neighbors suddenly picked up and left. The Jewish minority was part of the fabric of their lives. The Jews were protected by the Berber tribes, participated in joint ceremonies, spoke the Berber language, and enjoyed mutually beneficial relations. A moving example of the Jewish-Berber sentiments of yearning can be found in the film *Tinghir–Jerusalem: Echoes from the Mellah* by Kamal Hachkar, a Moroccan-French-Muslim director whose family came from Tinghir. During one of his visits to Tinghir, Hachkar discovered the Jewish past of the mellah – which has been empty of Jews for some time now – and decided to create a film that explores the memories of the Muslims and Jews from the Atlas Mountains who miss the neighborly relations and lives that they once shared. His quest to learn about the Jewish-Muslim connection led him to Israel, where he filmed interviews with Berber Jews who spoke to him in the Berber language and shed tears over the world they left behind. Many of them told him that if they were younger, perhaps they would go back.

One day, I was in Tinghir with a group of tourists from the United States. On the way there, I played the song "Here in the Village of Todgha" to them and explained the words, as I do every time. While the group was admiring the colorful Berber carpets, I took a short stroll through the open market. Suddenly, I spotted a small object that ignited the Jewish spark in my heart, lying on the table in one of the stalls. It was a small wooden board engraved with Hebrew letters. The seller, a mustached man wearing a djellaba, asked me, "You're a Jew, right? Sorry, but I don't have any honey." I smiled back at him.

Tunisia

23. The Wonder Island – Djerba
Local Personalities: Alite and Goel Sabban
Sam Amiel

The first time I met Alite and Goel Sabban in their home one warm evening in 2014, I had come on a professional mission for the JDC to learn about the Jewish community, but found myself choked to tears, overcome by a feeling that my head would combust at any moment. I had left Tel Aviv nearly twenty-four hours earlier to reach the remote island of Djerba off the eastern coastline of Tunisia. Soon after landing, I felt famished, and luckily I was invited to the Sabban home for a welcoming meal that included some of the spiciest but most innocent-looking small hot green peppers I'd ever bit into.

Alite and her husband Goel, both in their late thirties, who trace their roots back to the Land of Israel before Djerba, live on a semi-paved dusty alleyway off the main street that runs through the Hara Kebira, the largest of two historic Jewish quarters in Djerba. They are a traditional and religious Jewish family, married young by Western standards, and are proud parents to nine children.

Desperate for relief from the hot peppers wreaking havoc inside me, but careful not to make a scene nor a poor first impression on my hosts, I calmly attempted to cool my mouth with anything at hand – cold water, bubbly beer, locally made crispy matzah from the recent holiday – to no avail, nothing helped. Finally, Goel, with his sympathetic smile of understanding and his silent devilish laugh that I would soon learn to adore, handed me relief in the shape of an ice-cold shot glass filled with *boukha*, a fig-based liqueur produced more often at home than bought in liquor stores. At that point, now more calm, not so cool, but definitely more collected, I began my friendship with the Sabbans as well as my respect and admiration for this uniquely historic Jewish community of Djerba, Tunisia.

Across the Middle East, Jewish communities have been steadily vanishing over the past seventy-five years, since the establishment of the State of Israel. While before 1948, there were close to a million Jews living across the Arab world, today there are approximately forty-five hundred, mostly in Tunisia and Morocco. Tunisia's Jewish population of thirteen hundred is based in the capitol city of Tunis (two hundred) and in the southern enclaves of Djerba (a thousand) and Zarzis (a hundred), a shadow of the once-enormous Jewish population in 1940, which surpassed 100,000 in dozens of cities, towns, and villages across the North African country.

I grew up in a suburban Jewish neighborhood in Seattle with a concentration of traditional Sephardi Jews, many of whom hailed from the Ottoman Empire like my own family, but I had never witnessed anything like Djerba's Hara Kebira, an actual thriving Jewish village, sectioned off from the rest of the town and populated almost uniquely by Jewish families guarding age-old traditions in the same location for more than two millennia and counting! These remaining Jews of the once-enormous Tunisian Jewish community had no concept of an "old-country," because they have never emigrated to the "new country."

This fascinated me since, until I visited Djerba, I was only too familiar with Jewish communities that struggle to uphold their unique traditions and customs in a faraway land to which they emigrated. My own grandfather, a talented cantor and master of Jewish Ottoman music, left Edirne, Turkey, for Geneva, then Seattle, and dedicated his life to upholding and transmitting the rich musical traditions of his nascent community in a faraway diaspora Turkish Jewish community in Seattle. I grew up immersed in these traditions and customs from the "old country," but I couldn't help wonder what would have happened had our family never left Turkey. Who might I have become or what would have been the fate of these unique traditions had we stayed behind? The answers to these questions were obviously clear as only a handful of Jews remained in Edirne, Turkey, by the latter part of the twentieth century, and the great chain of Jewish Ottoman musical tradition moved into preservation mode.

Djerba's Jews are not unlike most traditional Jewish communities around the world. The Jewish leaders of this tiny minority are also concerned about assimilation, so contacts with the 150,000 Muslims on the island are limited. At home in the Hara Kebira, Jews like the Sabban family speak Arabic as well as Hebrew; only a few speak French. Relations between Jews and Muslims are complex: proper and respectful, though not especially close. Goel, like most Jewish men in Djerba, works in the jewelry business alongside Arab merchants in the local *souq* (market) and enjoys friendly ties with Muslim customers and neighbors.

With its low-lying houses and narrow, mostly unpaved, streets, the Hara Kebira is modest. While not entirely walled in, it is insular and self-contained. Jewish boys run through the streets en route to yeshiva with kippot on their heads, and women wear colorful house coats or long skirts with head scarves, as is the tradition of Orthodox Jews. Along with a half dozen rabbis, this community boasts twelve functioning synagogues, two kindergartens, several kosher butchers, a community wedding hall, ritual baths, a communal oven, two girls' schools, and a boys' yeshiva.

Although Djerba's rich Jewish life and its institutions date back centuries, things I often take for granted such as girls' education didn't always exist, and that piqued my interest as I visited the island and opened a clear path for ways in which I felt I could help this community preserve its traditions yet move boldly forward.

In the early 1950s, a pioneering part-time school for girls opened, teaching them to read and write Hebrew. Though it was only two hours a day, the school was seen as transformational and a leap toward progress. But for Alite and her sister-in-law Hannah, who also graduated from Djerba's part-time girls' school, this was no longer enough. "When a girl studies for two hours a day, what can she do with her life?" Alite explained. "We wanted to learn more; we wanted our daughters to develop academically and intellectually beyond what we had achieved." The two women bonded, not only because they married two brothers and are neighbors but also because they shared a passion and a belief that life for a Jewish girl could be better – even with the limitations of tradition and faith that run so deep in their community.

Beginning in 2014 with a study group of high-school-aged girls meeting in Alite's father's garage basement, these tenacious sisters-in-law have worked tirelessly to establish Kanfei Yonah, a new all-day educational home for more than a hundred Jewish girls situated in a brand-new building in the heart of the Hara Kebira. I've always believed that education is key to success in life, but I've come to understand just how critical it can be since I began working with this unique community. While working with Alite, Hannah, and a new generation of Djerban Jewish women to build their new school, I am constantly amazed by their ability to straddle the tenuous line between moving toward progress and respecting the past. These brave women are paving an innovative path into the future for the next generation of Djerban Jewish girls, while never losing sight of the age-old traditions and awesome history at the very heart of this twenty-six-hundred-year-old Jewish community.

And these lines of tension are everywhere. As most young girls in the community today are now educated through their high-school years, the tradition of early teen marriages has begun to fade away. However, that doesn't mean that traditional customs of matchmaking and engagement while sometimes still in the teen years have abated. Although the introduction of smartphones and access to social media have facilitated communication between boys and girls in the community, the Friday-night custom of a community-wide meet-up on the main thoroughfare remains intact and is a sight to behold. Dressed in their best, packs of boys and girls stroll the Hara Kebira's main streets laughing loudly, cracking salted sunflower seed snacks and wishing each other Shabbat Shalom while stealing curious glances whenever possible. Their parents' watchful eyes are never too far away, but they too enjoy the opportunity to socialize with friends and neighbors.

As I roam the alleyways of Djerba's ancient Jewish community, the delicate balance between progress and tradition is palatable. As boys make their way in the early morning light to their age-old yeshiva buildings, they cannot help but look in envy at the girls' school's modern building and playground. Perhaps they think about what they'll do for a living with dreams about modernizing or expanding their father's jewelry store, or maybe they dream of paving a new path for themselves in France or Israel. But no matter where they will find themselves in the future, the Jews of Djerba stay put, firmly rooted in the past, and my passion to help nurture this unique bastion of Jewish life burns like an unassuming spicy green pepper.

Egypt

24. The Jews Left Egypt but Egypt Never Left the Jews – Cairo
Local Personalities: Marcel and Magda Haroun
Ya'acov Fried

On a Thursday night in November 1977, my world stood still. All the regular television broadcasts were paused, and an announcement was made that Anwar Sadat, the president of Egypt, had accepted an invitation from Menachem Begin, Israel's prime minister at the time, to visit Israel in the coming days, possibly even within forty-eight hours.

Saturday night of that same week, the Egyptian president's plane landed in Jerusalem, and I hurried in the freezing Jerusalem night, as if in a dream, with thousands of other Jerusalemites to welcome him at the entrance to the city. Rows of thousands of pedestrians jammed the streets toward the Egyptian president's delegation and cheered in support of his brave decision.

During his visit, my mind vacillated between apprehension and fear, on the one hand, and hope and raised spirits, on the other. One of the questions that crossed my mind was whether, after so many bloody wars, the Israeli-Egyptian conflict could really end, heralding a new age of peace. Another thought that occupied me was whether I would be able to visit Egypt. Yes, visit. Not just because of the novelty of visiting an enemy country. I was mostly interested in seeing two ancient civilizations that no longer exist: the Jewish culture that developed in Egypt and the ancient Egyptian culture. I feel that both of them had a decisive influence on our identity and culture as Jews and as members of a universal world.

I remembered the prayers I recited in synagogue as a child, and my Bible studies, which both feature Egypt in so many different places. Yes, it is the same Egypt, the land that is mentioned so often in the Bible and in our prayers. The Jewish nation lived in many different exiles and countries in the Diaspora, but there is no doubt that Egypt is the most prominent of them all. Egypt is etched into the history of the Jewish nation and its collective memory as the symbol of exile and slavery. The exodus from Egypt, in contrast, is perceived as the symbol of freedom. Would the arrival of Sadat and the peace that might follow enable the transition from being enslaved by wars and bloody clashes to a period of freedom, tranquility, and fraternal relations?

Sadat's visit took me back to childhood experiences and to our ritual of my father Moshe telling me stories from a book called *Bible Stories in Pictures*. I especially remember the story of Moshe, who was born in Egypt and led the Jewish people from slavery to freedom. Despite his stutter and speech defect, Moshe led such a complex process of creating a nation with his quiet charisma. He inspires every step of my life.

During Sadat's visit in Israel, I pondered the fact that Egypt seems to be a land of opposites. The abundance of water from the mighty Nile River contrasts with the vast, arid desert, and for the Jewish nation, Egypt was the land of both slavery and redemption. Throughout history, Egypt was often a safe haven for Jews and a place where they flourished, but it also pushed them away and alienated them.

Three years after Sadat's visit to Israel, and following extensive negotiations that led to the signing of the peace accords, I reached the border crossing between Israel and Egypt at Rafah, in northern Sinai. I got off the Israeli bus and switched to an Egyptian tour bus, which drove for about seven hours through northern Sinai, heading toward Cairo. We were an Israeli group of very curious tourists who had just been permitted to visit Egypt. The desert journey was pretty monochromatic. Huge, dull sand dunes surrounded us throughout the drive. But inside, my emotions were tempestuous. The skeletons of scorched tanks dotted the landscape. I remembered that this was an enemy country where, not long ago, a series of bitter wars with Israel had taken place. I wondered whether these tanks were Israeli or Egyptian, but immediately reminded myself that in war, there are no winners; only in peace...

In the background, music by the Lebanese singer Fairuz played in Arabic. The bus driver drove us for hours, his eyes half-shut, and he seemed to be engrossed in his own meditative musical experience. The Egyptian guide sitting next to me whispered in my ear, "Welcome to Egypt. Notice the serenity of the driver, who is enjoying the music and has decided to drive extremely slowly. It's important to him to match the energy of the songs. He will accelerate once the cigarette that he currently isn't smoking burns his fingertips. It'll bring him out of his meditative state." The Egyptian guide's predictions really came true. A few minutes later, he said to me, "Welcome to Egypt! What you just experienced is an introductory lesson for understanding the national Egyptian personality: tranquility, quiet, and dissonance with the fast-paced, intense modern world."

Two people accompanied us during the eight days of this first visit to Egypt. Omar, the Egyptian guide, and Sammy Albucher, an Egyptian-born Israeli who moved to Israel in the late fifties. He studied archaeology and history, and this was his first visit back to his birthplace, where he had lived until the age of twenty-five. I was excited and moved to be part of Sammy's trip back to his birth country.

I remember Sammy's comment on the way: "The Jewish nation traveled from Egypt to the Land of Israel, the Promised Land. But there is no reason we shouldn't go in the opposite direction, like we're doing today."

It was an ecstatic week, a flurry of sights, sounds, scents, tastes, history, heritage, desert landscapes, an amazingly huge river, and human encounters. Sammy guided us in Cairo, a crowded, noisy city with impossible traffic on the roads, which nonetheless imparts a sense of security and wonder. We visited the Egyptian Museum, which displays archaeological artifacts including mummies from the days of the pharaohs; the Khan el-Khalili bazaar, where time seems to have stood still since its establishment in the fourteenth century; and the City of the Dead, where people now live between the tombs due to a lack of housing. Next to Cairo, on the west bank of the Nile, we visited the Pyramid of Giza. Visiting the famous Pyramid of Khufu gave us a chance to experience the only Wonder of the Ancient World that is still intact.

Two archaeologists, Omar the Egyptian guide and Sammy the Israeli guide, held a discussion opposite the pyramid. Omar said, "I've heard the Jewish legend claiming that the Jewish nation built the pyramids." Sammy didn't react to the insult. I sensed his admiration for those who built this architectural wonder. He said, "These pyramids were built without any technological machinery, and that magic is more important than the question of whether the Jews built the pyramids or not. Let's concentrate on the experience of ancient Egypt and the magnificent civilization that existed, using the testaments between which we are now walking. It is important that we remember that the Jewish ethos is more important to the Jewish cultural and national heritage."

We walked the short distance to the Great Sphinx, which is about sixty-six feet tall and features a figure with a human head on a lion's body. The next day, we flew to the city of Luxor and visited the most impressive open archaeological museum in the world: the Temple of Amun and the Valley of the Kings, which feature dozens of tombs of the pharaohs, including the tomb of Tutankhamun. Sammy looked at these testimonies of ancient Egyptian culture, and his face remained expressionless.

On the fifth day of our trip, Sammy boarded the bus, took the microphone, and said: "We had an opportunity to enter a historical time machine and experience ancient Egyptian culture together. But I don't know if I will be able to make it through the experience that awaits us today. Together, we are now entering the time tunnel of the history of the Jews of Cairo. For the first time, I will be going back with you today to the locations of my childhood. I feel the need to apologize in advance. If I am unable to conduct the full tour, please forgive me. The memories, and most of all, the fact that there is no longer a Jewish community in Egypt, are unbearably difficult for me."

The small alleyways of Muski, not far from the Khan el-Khalili bazaar, were crowded with people. On foot, we weaved our way between merchants pushing wagons, and we advanced through the narrow, noisy passages. These are the non-touristy marketplaces of ancient Cairo. We crossed these alleys to reach what was once the Jewish neighborhood, Harat al-Yahud. Sammy told us, "Remember that for decades, the Egyptians have been denying the fact that there was once a glorious Jewish community in the land of the Nile. The average Egyptian on the street knows nothing of the community's rich history. When I was a child, Harat al-Yahud was mostly a poor neighborhood, and it still is, but I remember it as a vibrant neighborhood where Jews comprised the majority, and it bustled with kindergartens, schools, shops, and businesses."

We turned into one of the alleys, and Sammy led us toward the wholesale market, a few dozen meters away. We looked for the synagogue named after Maimonides (Rambam). On the way, Sammy shared a story about his family, who had lived in Egypt for about 150 years. He spoke of his father, the barber, and his mother, the housewife, who took care of him and his six siblings. His family members emigrated at the beginning of the sixties to various locations, including Israel, England, Canada, and Chile. Sammy became emotional as he spoke of "Maimonides, the great man of science and spiritual giant, who worked here in Cairo and according to tradition was buried here in 1204, before his bones were moved to Tiberias." The synagogue was closed, and we attempted to find the guard, who was on his noontime break. He finally arrived, rubbing his eyes and apologizing that he had neglected his guard post.

The guard was a Muslim man who studied antiquity preservation at university and was hired by the Egyptian Supreme Council of Antiquities to guard the synagogue. He told us that he had learned a bit about Maimonides from stories told by visitors, and he understood that the Rambam's legacy is still very important in Jewish culture today. Maimonides Synagogue, bereft of its community, became dilapidated over the years, and only many years after this visit did the Egyptian government decide to renovate it and restore it to its former glory. When I visited the synagogue years later, I indeed saw that the ark, featuring a Torah scroll on display, was covered in a beautiful silver preservation box. On the wall at the back of the ark, I could see remnants of the original wall paintings. I realized the uniqueness of Maimonides; he combined the spiritual world with the world of medicine.

Sammy led us on a tour of the adjacent Jewish neighborhood. We identified the Jewish homes with the help of symbols that had been imprinted at the entrances: the remains of Stars of David, a hand with outstretched fingers, or the Jewish names of the owners and builders of the homes. We turned toward the synagogue on Maadi Street, called Sha'ar Hashamayim, which was established at the beginning of the twentieth century. Sammy noted once again that the impressive Jewish community in Egypt in general, and in Cairo particularly, had once numbered tens of thousands of Jews, of whom only a few dozen were left today. We met two elderly women who were members of the community. They were both afraid to talk to us at first, since we were Israelis, and they avoided mentioning the conflict that was only newly over. Sammy could not hide his deep sorrow and said, "My pain is not at the fact that my family's life in Egypt was cut off, but rather that the chain of Jewish generations in Egypt that was thousands of years old was severed. The loss of a vibrant, flourishing Jewish community fills me with pain that I simply cannot bear." Immediately afterward, he asked to return to the hotel.

One of the women shared the history of the community. When she spoke of the days of Jeremiah the prophet, the Roman and Ottoman Empires, the immigration of European Jews to Egypt in the eighteenth and nineteenth centuries, I felt as if she had been present during each of these periods. It seemed that she was the "eternal flame" of the community. She barely spoke of oppression or the problems experienced by the Jews beginning in 1948, when the State of Israel was founded, or the persecution that was furthered by Egyptian president Gamal Abdel Nasser. "I accept the fact that a few dozen Jews still live here. The historical circumstances caused me to choose to stay in Cairo. The synagogues are not being preserved for prayer, but rather as a testament to our Egyptian Jewish heritage."

The peace that exists between Israel and Egypt is not a warm peace, but it prevents bloodshed, and it has also enabled me to visit the time tunnel of ancient Egypt several times. About four years ago, I completed my visit with a trip to the Jewish quarter and the other synagogues in Cairo. I returned to the Sha'ar Hashamayim Synagogue and met two women, a mother and daughter. I recognized Marcel because of her shining eyes, and I remembered that she was the woman who had touched my heart during the visit to the synagogue in Egypt. Magda, the other woman, Marcel's daughter, had become the head of the community over the past year. "There was once a flourishing Jewish community in Egypt. But now, there are only twelve Jews left in the most densely populated Arab country in the world. They are primarily older women who hope to preserve their heritage. There are twelve synagogues left in Egypt, and they are in need of renovation, in contrast with the other historical heritage sites in Egypt." Magda

opened the ark and carefully took out the Torah scroll. "The synagogue is usually empty. I still remember the days when the benches
were filled with worshipers, including my late father. Now, I am the
head of the Jewish community of Cairo, whose members are older
women like my mother and myself. We are trying to preserve the local
Jewish tradition, which is hundreds of years old. It is my duty to future
generations."

Her mother was too frail to take part in the conversation. Magda
added, "My mother Marcel is ninety-one, and she cries when people
talk to her about the community's past. They say that Jews lived in
Egypt since the days of the pharaohs. We cannot allow hundreds and
thousands of years of history to simply disappear. Until the middle of
the twentieth century, there were about 120,000 Jews living in Egypt.
But with the establishment of the State of Israel, the Jewish community began to fall apart, and many left or were expelled by Gamal Abdel
Nasser. Today, there are only a few Jews living in Cairo and Alexandria.
We don't have the money to renovate the synagogues. My dream is
for the works of the Jews to be presented to the public in the Egyptian
cultural museum that is going to be founded. The Antiquities Authority
promised me that it would represent all of the populations in Egypt."

Magda spoke of the construction of the Grand Egyptian Museum
that is underway next to the pyramids and will feature a concentration
and documentation of the largest collection of ancient Egyptian cultural artifacts. It will be the largest history museum in the world and
will focus on the ancient culture that disappeared, facilitating research
and connections between ancient Egyptian heritage and the modern
world. She related that next to this museum, the Egyptian authorities
promised to build another museum that will concentrate on the different cultures and religions in Egypt, and she claimed that she was promised that the Jewish culture, which developed in Egypt for thousands
of years, would be featured in an exhibit at the museum. Over the past
two years, the Egyptian government also started to contribute funds

to renovate the synagogues, which has enabled Magda to lead a project to renovate the ancient Jewish cemetery, located inside the City of the Dead in Cairo.

These trips led me to a deep and powerful realization. The Jews may have disappeared from Egypt, but Egypt did not vanish from the Jewish heart. Ancient Egypt was the glory of Egyptian culture for generations. The Ben Ezra Synagogue and the large national Egyptian museum that will be opened soon next to the pyramids are the steam engines for the Egyptian-Jewish train running through the time tunnel. The Ben Ezra Synagogue is the most famous in Cairo for its genizah, which became a treasure worth more than gold for historical research and Jewish culture after it was discovered. The genizah included thousands of documents that were collected and preserved thanks to the dry climate and that sparked a revolution in the world of Jewish studies research, especially regarding the history of the Jews in the Middle Ages and their literary works. It seems that various entities came together in the same time and place, making the Cairo genizah such a significant treasure. Throughout history, Egypt was a place where various Jewish sages, scribes, and authors studied and wrote. Egypt saw commentators and poets such as Rabbi Abraham Ibn Ezra, Rabbi Yehuda Halevy, Maimonides, and others. Essentially, there is not one Jewish tribe or group in history that did not find a relic connected to its past in the Cairo genizah.

In the Jewish memory, Egypt was and will always be the crucible of the Jewish nation's birth and the place where the transition from slavery to freedom occurred. In Jewish culture, in the Jewish tradition evoked in Cairo, and especially on Passover, celebrated by Jews every year, there is a celebration of freedom that is passed down in the chain of generations.

After a sequence of three thousand years, there is no longer a Jewish town or significant Jewish community, in Egypt. In addition to the Cairo genizah, the renovated synagogues in Egypt, which have become museums, are a palpable testimony to an opulent Jewish past and a research tool for studying and commemorating generations of Jewish culture. This Jewish legacy provides a glimpse into a Jewish world that once existed and has since vanished.

Iran

25. The Heart That Was Left Behind – Tehran
Local Personalities: Mimi Cohen and Farangiss Sedaghatpour
Yishay Shavit

Each of us has a list of places and countries in our hearts that we dream of visiting one day. The enjoyment of making these dreams a reality and checking them off our list is what motivates us to travel to various distant countries and invest much time and effort in planning our trip. To be honest, these dreams are the fuel that keeps the entire global tourism industry running. At the top of the list of places that I dream of visiting is a country that I, as a resident of Israel, cannot enter – Iran.

As a child, I always loved staring at the photos featured in children's encyclopedias (if you are the right age, you probably know what I am referring to, and if not, just search for the Britannica Children's Encyclopedia). Since I grew up in Israel, the encyclopedias I had access to were written in Hebrew and emphasized the Jewish story. This was how I first became aware of the cultural and historical richness of Iran. I learned about King Cyrus, who allowed the Jews to return to Zion, and about his monumental tomb in Pasargadae. I gazed at the photos of the impressive stone reliefs in Persepolis, the glittering Persian capital city, and I fantasized about the day when I would visit the city of Shush, the home of Queen Esther, Mordechai, and King Ahasuerus. As I got older, I added a few more sites to my list of places to see in Iran – the opulent Golestan Palace in Tehran, where the leaders of Iran lived before the revolution, and the large, ancient mosque in Isfahan that influenced Muslim architecture from Damascus to Delhi. At some point, I even dreamed that one day, I would hike up to the top of Mount Damavand, the highest peak in the entire Middle East and the home of the ancient Persian gods.

But dreams don't always come true. Iran has remained an unreachable land for me. In the area where I grew up in the late eighties, there were many Jews who had immigrated from Iran. I remember that groups of children would sometimes laugh at the heavy, foreign-sounding accent in which they spoke Hebrew. But these insensitive children's jokes were not aimed at Iranian Jews alone. Immigrants from a range of countries were also laughed at by Israeli Sabra children who thought in those days that Israel was the center of the universe. Yet something about the Jews who came from Iran was different. Most of them came to Israel at the end of the seventies after the Islamic Revolution, while other immigrants had arrived in the early fifties. These were their first years outside Iran, and they were definitely still under the impression of the hasty exit they had made from their birthplace. A shadow of sadness was draped over their faces.

Jews lived in Persia (Iran's ancient name, by which it was known until 1935) alongside their non-Jewish neighbors for thousands of years. These relationships had their ups and downs, but unlike the situation in many European countries, the Jews were never overwhelmingly expelled from Persia. While they did not enjoy equal rights with the Muslim majority, and they were forced to pay additional taxes, they were exempt from military service and overall, their lives were comfortable compared with those of their Ashkenazi brethren. When the State of Israel was established, warm and friendly ties were forged between the Shah's government in Iran and the young state. Persian Jews benefited from this in many ways, both socially and economically. Today, it is difficult to imagine, but during the seventies, there was a daily flight from Tehran to Tel Aviv. Many Persian Jews took advantage of it to visit relatives in Israel and to do business. For a while, it seemed that the Jews of Iran had a golden future ahead of them.

Mimi Cohen née Tabibi remembers when the Iranian Jewish dream dissipated forever. She was nineteen years old when the Islamic Revolution began in 1978. She grew up in a Jewish home in the city of Tabriz, in the northwestern part of the country. In this region, most of the residents were members of the Turkish minority and spoke Azerbaijani. Mimi's mother tongue was different. She spoke the Jewish Persian dialect – a language derived from Arabic, ancient Persian, and Hebrew that was used by Jews in Persia for centuries. Her father owned a pharmacy in the city and was a cantor at the local synagogue, and Mimi went to the Muslim public school, where she learned how to speak Persian, among other things. She was not the only Jew in the class; fifteen other Jewish families who preferred to send their children to public school instead of to the French private school – out of fear that they would be converted – also sent their children to this school.

Mimi's life as a young Jewish woman in the seventies in pre-revolutionary Iran was generally pleasant. She remembers her trips to Tehran in the summer months, where she would spend time in the homes of her sister and brother who had moved there. During these visits, Mimi would often stroll through the alleyways of the large bazaar in the southern part of the city. This maze of about six miles of both narrow and wide streets makes up the beating heart of the traditional businesses of Teheran. These visits left a significant impact on the teenager from a city on the periphery and remained etched in her memory.

In 1978, the situation in Iran began to deteriorate quickly. Huge protests against the government began to fill the streets, and the violence escalated. Mimi especially remembers an incident in August 1978, during which about 420 people were murdered when the Cinema Rex theater burned down in the city of Abadan, in southwestern Iran. To this day, it is unclear who exactly torched the theater in this terror attack (which had the highest number of casualties of any terrorist attack in history at the time), but it can definitely be said that this event severely damaged the sense of security felt by many Iranian citizens.

Among the small Jewish community in Tebriz, rumors began to spread that Jews were going to be targeted and that supporters of Ayatollah Khomeini were going to be launching a looting and murdering campaign against the community soon. Mimi's family decided to take action. They sent Mimi to Israel, where she could live safely with her uncle, who had left Iran a few years earlier. A few months after Mimi left Iran, her parents began to receive explicit death threats. They sold everything they had at a loss, packed the Torah scrolls into their car, and drove to Tehran. After two very difficult years, they managed to reach Israel by the skin of their teeth.

Life in Israel was not easy for Mimi. While she did not miss her birthplace, she watched the developments there and the rise of Khomeini's supporters with concern and began to worry about her family. The challenges of integration in Israel didn't make things any easier. Israelis were sometimes snobbish toward her, and the nickname they called her – "Persian" – felt very insulting to someone who had lived her entire life in Iran being called "Jew." She felt that Israelis did not appreciate the education she had received and her talents, and after two years, she left Israel and moved to New York.

The city of New York was good for Mimi. She established a family and built a successful career. The years went by, and it seemed that Mimi had left her country of origin and her former life behind. She would not listen to Iranian music and didn't pay much attention to current events in the country. She completely disconnected from the place that had been her home for nineteen years and became Mimi Cohen, an American Jew.

Mimi's experience is not unusual. Many Persian Jews have a similar life story. A comfortable childhood in Iran during the Shah's era, the fear that constantly increased as the Islamic Revolution progressed, a

traumatic uprooting from their homeland, exile and loss of any interest in Iran or Persian culture.

Farangiss Sedaghatpour, Mimi's close friend, describes a strong
sense of alienation from her birthplace during the first few years after
the revolution. She did not want to remember the experience of being
unwillingly disconnected from her parents at the age of eleven due to
the sense of impending danger, or those difficult hours when she and
three Jewish friends at her school in Tehran hid in the attic while their
classmates gathered in the yard and screamed "Death to Israel." She
didn't want to be peculiar, different, foreign, "Persian." These feelings, shared by many Iranian Jews, led to the widespread conclusion
that the twenty-five-hundred-year-old Jewish community was on its
way out. The reign of the mullahs and the ayatollahs put a decisive end
to Jewish Persian culture.

One day in 2009, out of the blue, Mimi received a surprising message
on Facebook. A short time earlier, she had created a personal profile
and used her maiden name, Mimi Tabibi. A friend from Iran with whom
she had studied medicine (a degree she did not finish, since she was
forced to flee the country) found her and reached out. That innocent
message shook Mimi's world. The memories of her childhood in Tebriz
all flooded back, and she started to think more and more about her
former life. She began to miss her friends whom she had left behind,
but all the while could not ignore the tortuous road that her parents
had traveled when they were forced to escape from Tebriz.

That renewed connection via Facebook developed into more and
more childhood friends who all tried to convince Mimi to come back
to visit her homeland. They promised her they would do everything
in their power to make her feel safe. The promises and the nostalgia
caused Mimi to begin to check out the possibility seriously. For the first
time since she fled Iran, Mimi felt that she had to go back and see the
place where she grew up. Two years later, she had finally managed to

convince her family that she would be safe visiting Iran, organized all the trip details, and boarded a flight to Istanbul on her way home – to Iran.

The warm treatment she received at the airport in Tehran surprised her. Standing in the line at passport control, she kept her head covered with the traditional hijab. The clerk glanced at her passport and then said in a friendly tone, "You haven't been in Iran for thirty years – welcome back!" Her friend met her at the terminal exit, and after the initial excitement, the two got into the car and started to tour the country.

Mimi spent ten days in Iran. She dedicated the first part of the trip to Tehran, where she rode the subway, visited her brother's grave, and strolled through the large bazaar that she remembered from her childhood summer vacations. She chatted with the sellers in fluent Persian but felt that something in her had changed. The fear that someone would notice her and that the secret police were following her prevented Mimi from coming close to Jewish sites. She hoped to visit the Abrishami Synagogue, which is active to this day, but she didn't want to put herself in danger and was especially worried about putting others in danger. Therefore, she gave up on the idea and limited herself to visiting tourist sites only.

The visit to Tebriz, the city where she was born, was especially moving for Mimi. Due to the central location of their family home, it had been demolished, and apartment buildings had been built in its place. But Mimi managed to visit the school where she had studied and to see, albeit from the outside, the synagogue where her father had been the cantor. Before her return flight to Istanbul and New York, she even managed to visit the local pharmacy, whose owner remembered her father well and asked how he was doing.

When she returned home, Mimi shared all her experiences from her trip to Iran with her friends. Many of them could not understand what had brought her to put her life in danger and return to a country where the government could arrest her without a trial. She prepared a slideshow of the photos that she took and presented them to fellow

Persian Jews. They drank in every word she said. Their questions revolved around people and places they had known in the days before the Islamic Revolution. It seemed that all of those present felt a warm connection to Iran and to the cultural home that they left behind. Some expressed their concern for family members who belong to the Jewish community of eight thousand who are currently living all over Iran.

The warm sentiments toward Iran that were expressed by the audience didn't surprise anyone. While, as I already mentioned, during the first years following the revolution, many of the Jewish exiles turned their backs on their birthplace, as time passed, these sentiments began to change. In the mid-eighties, the Persian Jewish communities in New York, Los Angeles, Israel, and other locations became stronger. The members of these communities put significant effort into preserving the ancient culture of Persian Jewry, their language, and their customs.

Mimi's trip itself was a statement that she was not prepared to allow the Iranian government to suppress her Persian Jewish identity. I asked her if she could see herself moving back to Iran one day if the political situation allowed it.

Her answer was definitive: No! Neither she nor any other Persian Jew she knew had any interest in returning. They had moved on with their lives. Moreover, the Persian Jewish community is gradually integrating with the rest of the Jewish communities. The next generation is of course proud of its Persian lineage, but as time goes on, Persian identity is waning. Mimi's three children married Ashkenazi Jews, and the next generation will be more American and less Persian.

If so, I asked Mimi and her friend Farangiss, does this mean that Iranian Jewry is disappearing? In about fifty years, do they think that all that will be left of this rich Jewish culture will be a few frightened Jews living in the shadow of the mullahs' governments in Iran and some nostalgic memories? They remained politely silent for a moment, and when they answered, it seemed to me that I had offended them with my question. "We Persian Jews," they replied, "are connected to our homeland with an inseverable bond. We are the descendants of Mordechai and Esther, and we carry the Persian Jewish culture within us – it is part of our DNA. This connection to Persian culture will not be severed even if we never go back to live in our homeland. The mullahs' governments, as cruel as they may be, do not have the power to put an end to Persian Jewish culture."

What a wonderful answer! These two women seemed to me like fearless freedom fighters whose weapon is years and years of Persian Jewish culture and a sense of pride that only a strong community can impart to its members. This pride, as I understand it, is what inspired Mimi to travel to Iran and what gave Farangiss the strength to invest so much time and effort in organizing activities for the Persian community in New York and in writing Persian poems. Whatever the fate of Iran may be, the events cannot shake the sense of connection that the former residents of this country feel toward their culture. In this battle between the mullahs' governments and the Jewish exiles, which led to their expulsion from their land, the Jews have won.

Bahrain

26. Religious Tolerance in the Jaws of the Saudis – Bahrain
Local Personality: Nancy Khedouri
Ya'acov Fried

Bahrain, one of the smallest countries in Asia after Singapore and Maldives, is a collection of dozens of natural islands and a few artificial ones, opposite the western coasts of the Persian Gulf toward its "big sister" Saudi Arabia. Despite being an island, the country can be reached by car via a sixteen-mile bridge from Saudi Arabia, which is named after the Saudi King Fahd.

Thousands of vehicles cross the bridge daily via the official border crossing, halfway between the two countries. When the Saudis proposed construction of the bridge, Bahrain changed its traffic system from traveling on the left, like in Britain, to traveling on the right. This change was made in order to adapt itself to its sponsoring neighbor.

Until the eighteenth century, foreign empires from East and West controlled the region. At the end of the eighteenth century, a Sunni Arab tribe led by the Al Khalifa family conquered the islands. The descendants of this dynasty still control the kingdom. For decades, until 1971, Bahrain was a protectorate of the United Kingdom, which developed its energy industry in the fields of oil and gas.

The current ruler, Hamad bin Isa Al Khalifa, assumed the throne in 2002 and is responsible for the fact that this wealthy country is currently not only based on its oil and natural gas industry, but also on the development of the capital city, Manama, as a flourishing financial center.

About 70 percent of Bahrain's residents are Shiite Muslims. But the rulers of the dynasty are Sunnis, a situation that causes ongoing tension. In recent years, Shiite entities from the opposition, backed by Iran, attempted to change the status quo in Bahrain and led riots of the Shiite residents against the Sunni government. These incidents increase Bahrain's dependence on the power of its neighbor, Saudi Arabia.

Bahrain, which became a member of the United Nations and the Arab League immediately following its establishment, was once home to thousands of Jews. Over the past century, their numbers have gradually dwindled. Today, there are a few dozen Jews living in Bahrain who maintain close ties with the government, and some of them hold very senior positions. The government in this oil kingdom, in the heart of the Persian Gulf, grants freedom of religion.

About five years ago, the Jewish Federation of New York contacted me about organizing a leadership delegation to Bahrain, led by Rabbi Marc Schneier, who founded the Foundation for Ethnic Understanding in the United States and the Jewish-Muslim Foundation in collaboration with the king of Bahrain. In the preliminary conversation, the rabbi emphasized a few points: "I have been in close contact with senior officials from the Gulf states for many years. I cannot think of another country in the Gulf or an Arab leader in the Gulf who is willing and interested in recognizing Israel like the king of Bahrain. The king of Bahrain always spoke of his sincere desire to establish relations with Israel, he was the one who classified Hezbollah as a terror organization, and I think that there is no leader like him. He deserves recognition for his efforts to promote peace. The most important thing on our visit is for us to meet the Jewish community that works outwardly and with the explicit support of the royal palace."

I met Nancy Dina Khedouri, an attorney by profession who serves as a member of the upper house of the parliament in Bahrain, during the visit five years ago. "There are forty members of the upper house, all of whom were appointed by the king, Hamad bin Isa Al Khalifa. The lower house has the same number of representatives, voted into office by the public. I am proud of the special privilege that I have received to be a Bahraini, a Jew, a citizen of the Gulf, and an Arab." She shared, "I lovingly remember the Jewish holidays since my childhood. As Bahrainis, we were never separated from citizens of other religions. Days of joy and of sorrow always brought us together."

Khedouri continues, "Bahrain is the only country in the Gulf which has a synagogue. The building was constructed in the thirties by a Jewish pearl merchant from the famous Cartier family, who came from France for business reasons and discovered that the community had no house of prayer. The synagogue is not active today due to the small number of congregants and the fact that most are secular Jews. It occasionally opens on Jewish holidays, when Jews from Europe and the United States come to Bahrain as tourists. Last Chanukah, the king visited the synagogue and lit a candle with the members of the community. Following this gesture, his bitter rival Hassan Nasrallah criticized him sharply and expressed his suspicions regarding the Bahraini king's alleged ties with the Zionist state."

While Khedouri, the daughter of building engineer Eli Yosef Khedouri and Claudette Cohen, was born in Bahrain, she received her higher education in London. She holds a bachelor's in economics and English literature, as well as a degree in law, all from British universities. In 2010, she was appointed to parliament, and soon afterward became the head of the Committee of Foreign Relations, Defense, and National Security. A decade ago, Khedouri published her book *From Our Beginning to Present Day*. The book is a historical review of Bahraini Jewry and was published in English and Arabic. After its publication, the author was invited to the palace and presented a copy to the king.

Khedouri is also active in women's groups. "The legislation process in the parliament is a big challenge and requires intensive, sensitive, and Sisyphean work."

Khedouri isn't the first Jew appointed by the king to serve in the upper house. She was preceded by her cousin, Huda Azra Nunu, daughter of a well-known family of bankers, who filled this position for two years starting in 2006. But she didn't stop there. In 2008, in a political reality that viewed Jews as out of bounds and suspicious, Hamad bin Isa Al Khalifa appointed her as Bahrain's ambassador to Washington.

Jews are not strangers in the Arabian Peninsula. To this day, they can be found in Yemen, and the last remaining Jews from the Babylonian exile have not yet disappeared from Baghdad. Jews first immigrated to Bahrain at the end of the nineteenth century, in search of business opportunities. The pioneers came from Basra, Iraq; they were followed by Jews from Yemen and India. At its peak, prior to the establishment of the State of Israel, the community had over two thousand members.

Over the years, the Jews became a cornerstone of Bahrain's economy. The Halsachi family, for example, established the candy industry. The Nunu family led the banking system. A few of the Jews integrated into the educational system and became teachers. Many Bahraini children entered the world in the fifties and sixties with the assistance of the legendary Jewish midwife Ruth Moses, who was born in Turkey and earned the title "everybody's mother." The general public used the services of Rosa the seamstress, the first in the country to use a Singer sewing machine.

The atmosphere of religious tolerance is palpable as you visit the synagogue in Manama, located in the center of the old city next to a mosque for Shiite worshippers, a mosque for Sunni worshippers, and a Hindu temple. They are all within walking distance of each other, next to Al-Mutanabi Street, which bears the name of one of the greatest medieval Arab poets. In one of his poems, Al-Mutanabi says that his literature is seen by the blind, and his words are heard by the deaf.

Khedouri enthusiastically praises the king for his success in integrating between the different sects and especially for his efforts in advancing women. Hamad bin Isa Al Khalifa was the first to appoint a female minister to parliament (Dr. Alees Samaan, who received the health ministry) and allocated ten seats for women in the parliament. "I am proud that my country is an example to others of peaceful coexistence," Khedouri says with admiration.

The existence of a Jewish community in his country made the king's work easier, and the Jews were instrumental in his efforts to forge ties with the American government. He is following an organized plan, and a Jewish leadership delegation has been visiting and helping him in this area for five years already.

About a decade ago, Hamad bin Isa Al Khalifa contacted the Jews of Bahrain (most of them, about four hundred people, currently live in Britain) and invited them to come home. While none of them actually moved from London to Manama, his gesture positively contributed to relations between the palace and the Jewish community.

In 2013, Bahrain was the first Arab country to call out Hezbollah as a terror organization. Since then, the government surprised the world two more times. It condemned the murderous attack at a synagogue in Har Nof, Jerusalem, in which five worshippers were hacked to death and a policeman was shot. "The only ones who will pay the price for this are the Palestinian people," said Bahraini foreign minister Khalid Bin Ahmed. "It will be collectively punished, and it will suffer from more wrongdoings and more aggression." Following the death of Shimon Peres, Bin Ahmed published a moving eulogy. "May you rest in peace," he concluded.

An attitude of advancement of women, acceptance of Jews, and tolerance toward minorities in general is Bahrain's way of spreading a message of tolerance to the world, and this strengthens its relations with the West. Khedouri has stepped up to spread these messages via the media, as she benefits from the government's warm embrace of her community.

"We are blessed to have a kind king who grants the citizens freedom of worship and the right to pray as they desire," she said. "The Bahraini government views religion in a positive light. Sections 18 and 22 of the constitution allow every citizen to fulfill their religious commandments and enjoy freedom of worship. In our Jewish home, we have a mezuzah, and our Muslim friends respect it."

Neither during my first visit to Bahrain five years ago or my visit last year, after the signing of the peace accords between Bahrain and Israel, did I hear a word in my meetings with the Jewish community about the Israeli-Palestinian conflict. Khedouri and other members of the community also didn't mention anything about the kingdom's biggest problem, the status of its Shiite population. The Shiite majority in Bahrain is a strong opposing force that challenges the royal palace. In 2011, a violent revolt broke out that was only suppressed thanks to quick military assistance sent by Saudi Arabia. Bahrain's defense forces maintain an iron grip on the Shiite population. They suspect that Iranian intelligence is trying to incite rivals of the palace and they fear an uprising.

Therefore, it is no wonder that in his speeches, Hezbollah leader Hassan Nasrallah often attacks the kingdom. "Bahrain is heading down the path toward normalization with the Zionist entity," Nasrallah accused them last year. "But its oppressed population has not forgotten Palestine."

Following the signing of the Abraham Accords and after the peace agreement was signed between Israel and the United Arab Emirates, Bahrain also signed peace accords with Israel. The peace accords brought me on another visit, in order to sign tourism collaboration agreements with Bahrain.

I had a pleasant time in Manama, the modern capital, which felt similar to Hong Kong or Dubai, only smaller. When visiting Bahrain

Fort, I discovered artifacts attesting to life in the area as far back as 2300 BCE, and I wondered how life had been possible here in a world without air conditioning, when temperatures reach 50 degrees Celsius (122 F) in the summer months. On a trip to the desert, about an hour from the capital, the oil wells stood out in the landscape. I admired the rulers of Bahrain, who succeed in building an economy that is not only dependent on this energy source, for which the world is now finding alternative solutions. In addition to its oil wells, the kingdom built the world-famous Grand Prix Formula 1, which attracts many tourists to Bahrain every year.

I wondered what the reason was that specifically in this desert kingdom, a Jewish community had been allowed to exist and continues to feel welcome. There is no doubt that religious tolerance toward minorities is part of the backbone of the kingdom. Is the fact that a Sunni minority controls a Shiite majority part of the reason for religious tolerance toward Jews as well? In Bahrain, as opposed to Saudi Arabia, there are no Muslim religious pilgrimage sites, such as Mecca or Medina. Does this allow for less dogmatic practices? For years, the British government controlled Bahrain. Many of Bahrain's elite studied and still study in England. Does the broad education, including the influence of British academia on universities in Bahrain, help develop religious tolerance?

On my last visit, I discovered that over 90 percent of the tourists visiting Bahrain are Saudi Arabians. Bahrain is a huge tourist spot for Saudis, who enjoy music, restaurants, night life, mixed beaches, shopping at ultra-modern shopping malls, and the ability to buy alcohol – none of which exist in Saudi Arabia. The Saudis party while on vacation in Bahrain. To me, it seems that Bahrain is like a valve, regulating the pressure between the conservative Saudi rulers and the residents, decreasing internal tensions, and allowing the Saudi kingdom to continue its rule. While Bahrain is practically a protectorate of Saudi Arabia, the cultural backbone of religious tolerance is strongly maintained in the country. In my opinion, it is possible that Bahrain's religious tolerance is like a showcase that Saudi Arabia would like to display to the West, especially to the United States, as if to say, "Look at the cultural and religious acceptance in Bahrain; if you wait patiently, it'll reach us too…"

United Arab Emirates

27. The Birth of a New Jewish Community – Dubai
Local Personality: Ross Kriel
Ya'acov Fried

After the Abraham Accords were signed, direct flights began operating from Israel to Dubai. I flew there the day after the first flight. The CEO of the airline, who met me when we landed, shared his feeling that I had missed out by not landing on that first flight, when I could have experienced how the local residents, clad in jalabiyas, welcomed those on the flight singing "Hevenu Shalom Aleichem" in Hebrew. "That was an experience that I'll never forget," the CEO sighed emotionally.

Visiting Dubai was an opportunity for me to experience an attractive tourist destination that offers a captivating combination of ancient history, desert landscapes, Middle Eastern ambience and gorgeous international architecture, fascinating museums, and most of all, the feeling that the country has attempted to create the most advanced and unique place in the world.

The UAE is located at the southeastern edge of the Arabian Peninsula and is composed of seven emirates. Each of them is colorful and magical in its own right. During my visit, I couldn't stop enthusing over the ethnic diversity of the residents and the endless list of world records broken over and over again in the Emirates. The government in the country is monarchist, with each emirate controlled by a different royal family. The Emir of Abu Dhabi serves as president of the United Arab Emirates and supreme commander of the army. In contrast with other countries in the region, which had to wage fierce battles until they freed themselves of colonial control, the UAE did so without a struggle. While oil was the main catalyst for the large international investments that led to its exceptional success, additional huge industries were founded as well, including tourism at a level that is perhaps the most luxurious in the world. State leaders are dedicated to developing a range of industries and the country's infrastructure with their oil revenues, so that in the future, when alternatives are found for their black gold, they won't be dependent on that income. The Emirates are connecting to these alternatives already. For example, the city of Masdar in Abu Dhabi strives to become the first city in the world that barely emits any carbon and produces negligible amounts of waste. Their power sources will be solar and wind energy.

Wherever I visited, I heard people saying, "Here, we do everything big." The tallest building in the world is Burj Khalifa in Dubai. The airport in Dubai is the largest in the world. The aquarium in Dubai is the largest one in the world too. They have the largest picture frame in the world (492 meters), the world's largest woven carpet, and the only seven-star hotel in the world. The list goes on.

But more than anything else, the pleasant interfaith climate in the country surprised me. In contrast with other Arab countries, the UAE tolerates the independent religious lifestyles of all people, including the small Jewish community. This community was only founded about a decade ago and currently has about three thousand members, including hundreds of children.

During my visit, I discovered how this devout Muslim country is slowly opening its gates to Israelis and Jews, and even establishing kosher restaurants and hotels. Academics I encountered drew my attention to the name of the peace accords signed between Israel and the UAE (the "Abraham Accords"), testifying to the religious outlook at their foundation. Islam in the UAE is practiced differently from the way the same religion is practiced in other countries. The UAE and

Bahrain belong to the most moderate branch of Islam. The religious establishment that is an integral part of life in most of the other Muslim countries is not a strong force in the UAE, because politics and religion are kept separate.

In my conversations with government personalities and academics, I was told several times that the terrorist attack on the World Trade Center in New York, followed by the ISIS phenomenon, shocked the residents of the Emirates. The way they see it, someone who perpetrates such attacks in the name of Islam is a heretic. They wanted to show the face of true Islam, according to their beliefs, through messages that they spread within the country and through their international relations. At the same time, after the 9/11 crisis, the UAE decided to get involved in conflicts that took place in Yemen, Libya, and Afghanistan. They viewed this as the forces of good fighting against the forces of evil. The feeling is that in any Muslim country with a developing crisis, Turkey, the Islamic Revolutionary Guard Corps, and Qatar appear to fill the vacuum. The Emirati leaders established a moderate axis in the face of this radical one. A visit to the Emirates reveals, for example, that their traditional dress, which was devotedly preserved, is not connected to religion, but rather to preserving their ancestral heritage – and the proof is that women gradually removed the facial coverings.

Islam took a traumatic blow following the terror attacks of September 11, 2001, and the subsequent emergence of ISIS. The Emiratis felt that radical Islam had become the dominant voice in the world. This negative image led the UAE to deeply contemplate how Islam could restore its good, moderate name from the golden age of the Caliphates and present a modern version of Islam as an inclusive, tolerant religion. During its golden age, Islam was considered the most advanced civilization in the world. The UAE want to show that Islam can also be a moderate religion that goes hand in hand with progress and modernization. The country works to further this goal on two fronts – on the one hand, by ideologically opposing the radical axis (boycotting

Qatar and supporting wars in Yemen and Libya against radicals), and on the other hand, by accepting other religions and hosting over two hundred different nationalities within its borders. It is flying the flag of cultural pluralism.

This is also the answer to the question of how a Jewish community can live in a Muslim country with a sense of religious freedom. On a day-to-day level, the Emirati worldview is expressed through a series of unique institutions, such as the Ministry of Tolerance. Its existence is essential in light of the fact that close to ten million people live in the country, and only about 20 percent of them are local residents who hold citizenship. All the other residents are foreign workers who are not necessarily Muslim. The mass influx of foreign workers to the country began about forty years ago and has continued to increase. The UAE firmly established that foreigners living in the country will enjoy freedom of religion.

As part of this approach, the country built houses of worship for members of all religions, and 2019 was declared the year of tolerance in the UAE, during which the pope was invited to visit the Muslim country. This was a declaration to the entire world that in a country that practices moderate Islam, our hand is extended to other religions, and we are interested in forging connections on an interfaith basis.

The UAE led a process of change, in which religion is perceived to be able to mend rifts internationally, rather than serve as a catalyst of dispute and conflict. The peace accords between Israel and the Emirates, called the Abraham Accords, reflect this new approach. One of the local rabbis shared his excitement with me: "The Jewish presence and culture were invisible and unspoken in the country. Over the past ten years, Judaism became more visible and more outwardly present. When I returned here with my family about a year ago, on the eve of Rosh Hashanah, the airport employees welcomed us by saying 'Shalom' and asked curiously, 'Is your son Moshe named after Musa, and your son David named after Daud?' After the Abraham Accords were signed, the educational curriculum in the Emirates was changed as well, so that local students will also learn about Israel and Judaism. In the media, which is controlled by the royal family, portrayal of Jews has increased. Over the past year, we have seen programs about Jewish holidays and about Jewish culture and history."

One of the founders of the local Jewish community is Ross Kriel, who currently serves as president of the Jewish Council of the Emirates. Ross came from Johannesburg, South Africa, to work in the Emirates and was involved in the country's economic development. He shares that he never dreamed that he would be presented with the opportunity to lead the local Jewish community. He deeply feels that this has been the most meaningful endeavor of his life. Kriel moved to Dubai with his family a decade ago, to a place that had no minyan for prayers and where kosher food was only available inside the home. The first kosher food initiatives were established by his wife, Eli, after she cooked for a rabbis' convention that met in Dubai.

Kriel's first trips to the UAE were in 2008. Over the years, he discovered that the stereotypes and perceptions of this Muslim country were simply incorrect. He feels that anyone who comes to visit finds a harmonious environment that exists between Jews and Muslims. There are endless examples, he says, where instead of hatred, you discover fraternity, friendship, and collaboration. He expresses his surprise at the number of religious practices and rituals that Jews and Muslims share. The feeling of having a common tradition from our forefather Abraham, especially following the Abraham Accords, only further highlights how much we have forgotten, over the past several decades, the values shared by both Jews and Muslims.

As soon as Kriel moved to the UAE, he needed a minyan and a Jewish community, so he started holding prayer services in his home. He shared this with the authorities, and the group soon became a gathering point for Jews and an address visited by state officials.

The Jewish community of Dubai is a young community, in contrast with those situated in other Muslim countries such as Bahrain, Iraq, Syria, Lebanon, and Egypt. Jews reached the UAE only recently, for business, work, and involvement in the country's flourishing economy. The community never hid itself, but it maintained a level of modesty, not emphasizing its presence until recently, and mainly functioning with an approach of non-defiance. It is officially recognized in the UAE. Slowly, encouraged by the peace accords, Jews began celebrating their holidays publicly, providing interviews to the local media about various topics related to Jewish culture and even voicing their political opinions.

There are several active synagogues in the community today, including a liberal service, various informal Jewish learning groups, kashrut services, *shechitah* (ritual slaughtering of meat), and so forth. The Jewish Agency is even planning to send one or more educational emissaries to the community. The community members anticipate the founding of a Jewish center in the Emirates, permanent structures for the synagogues, and Jewish education for their children. The overall spirit of excitement, which grew stronger following the peace accords and the arrival of masses of Israeli tourists, also reinforced their hope that the community will continue to grow and develop.

During a few of my visits to the UAE, I felt that it was one of the safest countries in the world. I often heard people remark that "you can leave a suitcase outside, because the owner will be identified, and it will be returned. If you forget your cell phone in a taxi, it will be returned to you." I discovered a country with crime rates among the lowest on the globe. If the Jews who immigrated to the country were once only employees of international companies, there are now free-lancers there as well. Praying on Friday at the synagogue, surrounded by hundreds of community members, my eyes welled up with tears of joy. How did it happen – such an experience in an Arab country?

Over the years, over forty churches and Buddhist temples were built in the country. The first synagogue building is currently under construction. In this context, it is possible to understand the Emiratis' tolerance and acceptance of Jews and Judaism, and their motives to forge peace accords with Israel.

Thanks to the United Arab Emirates, the message of Islam as a tolerant religion is constantly becoming clearer. The country has recognized the study of Jewish culture and heritage and is even building museums that will exhibit Jewish history. However, it is important to pay attention to the delicate makeup of the relationship between various religions and the UAE. Tolerance is not a given. It is necessary to remember that the Emirati outlook is that the Jewish community, among other religions, should be allowed to flourish and exist in a respectful manner, as long as there is no concern that its existence or behavior could push aside or harm the "Emirati hegemony."

The Far Diaspora

India

28. The Jewish Gandhi – Cochin
Local Personality: A. B. Salem
Yishay Shavit

Abraham Barak Salem, a Jew in his late forties of slight build, with a beard and what was considered by his community as brown-toned skin, left his house with his three children. He was heading toward the Paradesi Synagogue, where he had prayed in the foyer his entire life. Walking down the street that would later bear his name, he greeted his many friends, Jews and non-Jews alike. They sat outside their homes, seeking some respite from the heavy heat and humidity that is characteristic all year round in the city of Cochin, South India (today Kochi, Kerala, in southwest India). A. B. Salem was a respected attorney and well-known politician in his locale, a pillar of the community. On his way to the synagogue, he walked by the old Jewish cemetery and glanced at the silent, mossy tombstones, some hundreds of years old. The question must have crossed his mind whether Jews of his own community would merit to be buried alongside the other Jews of Cochin.

Entering the synagogue foyer, A. B. Salem passed by Jews who looked just like him, wearing the same traditional south Indian garb. He didn't stop to join them in prayer, but for the first time in his life continued instead into the depths of the synagogue and sat down on the steps ascending to the bimah, the podium in the synagogue where the Torah is read. All eyes focused on him. From every direction, angry glares were shot at him – how dare he break the taboo that was hundreds of years old? How could a member of the *meshuchrarim* community, with dark skin, join the ranks of the white-skinned Paradesi Jews? There was utter silence when the reader, who was called up as the first reader to the Torah, passed Abraham by. That day, the social norms upon which the Jewish community of Cochin were based were turned upside down. The year was most probably 1928.

There are those who claim that Jews lived in southwestern India, in what is currently the state of Kerala, since the end of the Second Temple period. Others claim that the Jews arrived in this area as merchants as far back as the days of King Solomon, about three thousand years ago. One thing is certain: toward the end of the fifteenth century, when the Portuguese were navigating their way around the Cape of Good Hope and reached the Indian subcontinent, there was already a flourishing Jewish community in the city of Cochin that was thoroughly integrated into the local Indian culture. After the Jews were expelled from Spain, some Jewish merchants came from Europe to the area of the Malabar Coast in what is currently southwestern India. During the sixteenth century, they quickly realized the economic potential of the spice-trading business and settled in the region next to the local Jewish community, which was referred to as the Malabari Jews, meaning the Jews of the Malabar Coast.

Some Jews who settled in India came with their slaves (as unfortunately was the custom in the Middle Ages). Over the years, the slaves were freed. Their Jewish owners, who had released them from the yoke of slavery, were not prepared to accept them as equals, but the freed slaves viewed themselves as Jews for all intents and purposes. And so it was that the *meshuchrarim* (Hebrew for "freed") established their own community, alongside Cochin's two other existing Jewish communities.

The different communities were separated by their origins, their customs, and more than anything else by the skin color of their members. The Jews who had descended from the white-skinned European merchants were referred to as the Paradesi (meaning "foreign") Jews. They separated themselves from both the Malabari Jews and the *meshuchrarim*, two communities whose members were dark-skinned. They did not marry into these two communities and were mistrustful of some of their customs. As early as 1568, the white Jews established their own separate synagogue, the Paradesi Synagogue, and thereby created a separate community. The Malabari Jews, members of the ancient, established community, had many synagogues in which they could pray. But the *meshuchrarim* were left without a place to pray. The Paradesi community "graciously" agreed to allow them to participate in the prayer services in the new synagogue that they built. But there were a few conditions to their consent – the *meshuchrarim* were not allowed to enter the synagogue itself. They had to remain in the foyer. They were not allowed to read from the Torah, and they could not bury their dead in the same plot as the Paradesi Jews. Hundreds of years later, in the 1920s, Abraham Barak Salem, a member of the *meshuchrarim* community, started a revolution against these limitations.

I remember the first time I heard the story of the Jews of Cochin. It was 2003, and I was a twenty-eight-year-old Israeli backpacker making my way from Ernakulam to the Port Cochin area by ferry. Together with my partner Noa (who became my wife after this trip), we got off the ferry and tried to find our way to the modest hotel where we planned to rent a room. We did not have a written address for the hotel. Throughout our entire trip in India, which lasted eight months, we trusted our good luck. We would usually arrive in a region that we wanted to tour for a few days, walk around a bit to get a sense of our surroundings, and only then begin looking for a hotel with a clean, vacant room. Using this method, we had the chance to experience some unique moments that I will remember for the rest of my life. Today, I know that because of this method, we missed out on the amazing hotels that India has to offer, but that was the nature of our backpacking trip.

We got off the ferry on a street called Bazar Road. It was very different from any of the other streets we had seen in the many Indian cities we visited. It was broad, clean, and there wasn't much traffic. The distant colonial presence of the Portuguese and the Dutch was noticeable in the local architectural style. Despite the tourist market at the site, there was no sense of commotion or attempts at drawing the few tourists into the shops. Everything was slow-paced, perhaps due to the humidity that hung in the air or because of the local culture. We walked down the street, looking into the stores and asking the owners where we could find a nice hotel in the area. At the end of the street, we had two options – to turn left onto another large street or to turn right into a narrow, picturesque alley. I glanced at the signs noting the street names, and my heart skipped a beat. The wide street on our left was called Jew Town Road, while the alley to our right was called Synagogue Lane. It turned out that we had reached the region that had once been the beating heart of Cochin Jewry.

We turned right into the alley. After a short walk, we found ourselves standing in front of the Paradesi Synagogue. This is the oldest standing synagogue in India, the place that Indira Gandhi visited in 1968 during the celebrations commemorating four hundred years since its establishment. The doors were open. We placed our backpacks in a corner, took off our shoes, as is the custom in all synagogues in India, and entered.

Today, I know that all the synagogues in Cochin share the same structure. In all of them, there is a bimah shaped like a keyhole in the center of the sanctuary, with a women's section in the back, supported by two large pillars, on the second floor. In the heart of the women's section, there is another bimah from which the men read from the Torah on Shabbat and festivals. In this way, the community emphasizes the central place of women, while still honoring the Orthodox custom that only men read from the Torah. Even had I not known this on my first visit, it would have still been possible to feel that this synagogue is extraordinary. My eyes were drawn to the hundreds of porcelain tiles adorning the floor. Each one of them was different! The ark was huge and its wooden embellishments very impressive. I opened my book to learn about the site; it was an old book about Cochin Jewry that I bought at one of the bookstores we visited on the trip. This was essentially the first time I heard about the different groups among the Jews of Cochin and the discrimination that the *meshuchrarim* suffered.

A few hours later, after we had already found a room in a quaint hotel in the area, I found myself, to the dismay of my partner, glued to the book. It wasn't that I was a stranger to racism within Judaism. I just couldn't believe that discrimination based on skin color could be morally justified within a Jewish community. That was not the Judaism that I knew! I tried to glean any possible piece of information about this issue from the book, but to no avail.

A few days later, Noa and I decided to spend an entire day on a boat on the Kerala backwaters, a unique network of lagoons and lakes. We boarded a public bus that stopped not far from our hotel and traveled to the city of Alappuzha. It was a typical Indian bus. Unlike the spacious tourist buses, the two seats on each side of the public bus were very narrow in Western terms, with enough room to seat about a person and a half. I chose to stand. We were the only tourists on the bus, so we became the main attraction for the other passengers. The driver played music from a famous Bollywood film at full volume, and one of the passengers tried to teach me the corresponding dance moves. An hour after boarding the bus, I was sad to see that we had reached our destination. As a parting gift, my dance partner gave me that day's edition of the *Times of India*.

Holding the newspaper in one hand, we got onto the boat and sailed straight into paradise. Sailing in the endless backwaters of Kerala feels like drifting into a travel advertisement. Large coconut trees on the shores of the blue lagoons, tiny boats, fishermen spreading their nets straight from the huts where they live, children swimming in the water. An infinite encounter of blue skies and green vegetation. Tranquility for the body and soul. After a few hours of never-ending staring at the wonder of nature, I decided to glance at the newspaper in my hand. My eyes were drawn to the matchmaking ads. In India, to this day, most marriages are not for love, but rather prearranged matches. The parents decide who their child will marry. Finding a bride or groom is not only under the authority of the parents but is also considered their duty. Many Indians believe that the match must be a worthy one, meaning with a family from the same caste. Almost all dating ads included this piece of information.

The term *caste* is not a Sanskrit term. In traditional Indian culture, the terms *varna* and *jati* are used, but for purposes of this discussion, I will use the more familiar English term. The belief that a person is born into a certain caste that defines what is permissible and forbidden for the individual is over three thousand years old. A caste cannot be changed, so social transitions are not possible. In traditional Indian societies, the castes not only define with whom a person may establish a family, but also the profession in which they will work, the place they will live, and even the well from which they may drink. Discrimination based on caste is illegal in modern India, but as the dating ads in the newspaper testify, this worldview still has a decisive impact on everyday lives. Thus, as I sat on the boat in the heart of the paradise of Kerala, I started to ponder the possibility that the division into social groups and the discrimination that existed among the Jewish communities of Cochin originated from that same caste perception. Many years later, when I was much more familiar with India, its culture, and the Jews who lived there, I realized that this initial inkling had been correct.

India is the only country in the world where Jews historically never experienced anti-Semitism. Anti-Semitic incidents were unknown, and there was no discrimination or persecution based on religion. Think for a moment about your own Jewish community or another Jewish community in your surrounding area. How was it historically impacted by anti-Semitism? Did people move to the community as a result of persecution elsewhere? Were organizations like the JCC founded because Jews were not accepted into certain clubs? Were the various Jewish Federations established, among other reasons, out of the need to fight anti-Semitism? It can certainly be said that without anti-Semitism, Jewish communities would have developed differently. In India, though, Jews were always part of the society around them. They lived next to their Muslim, Christian, and Hindu neighbors. They influenced those around them and were influenced by them.

One of the ways in which the Indian environment influenced the Jews of Cochin was in their internalization of the caste perception. The Paradesi Jews were eager to emulate the hierarchical caste system within India and perceived the Malabari Jews and the *meshuchrarim* as inferior due to their skin color and their origins. They did everything in their power to influence the non-Jewish environment to accept this worldview as well.

There were significant social and economic benefits available, and in order to obtain them, the Paradesi Jews had to differentiate themselves from those dark-skinned Jews, exactly like the members of the higher castes in the society that surrounded them were doing. They refused to marry Jews who were not members of their group, didn't permit their burial in their plot in the cemetery, and didn't allow them to pray next to them in their synagogue. Thus, a singular Jewish community developed in Cochin where discrimination based on social group and skin color was accepted for hundreds of years.

The influence of Indian society on its Jewish community never stopped. In the 1920s, with the uprising of the Indian nationalist movement, many Jews were swept in by the new winds of the time. They learned the teachings of Mahatma Gandhi and of the nonviolent protest that he organized, a struggle that focused on the idea of satyagraha, holding firmly to truth, without compromising. They read the newspaper reports about Gandhi's fight against discrimination based on castes and were deeply influenced. Abraham Barak Salem was profoundly moved by these social winds. He was active on behalf of India's independence, participated in national conventions of the movement, and was personally familiar with its leaders. From his perspective, the struggle for India's independence was no different than the struggle for the soul of the Jewish community. This approach is what led him to leave his home and enter the Paradesi Synagogue. This is what spurred him to break the social taboo that discriminated against him because of his origin. This is what won him the nickname "Jewish Gandhi."

The Jewish community of Cochin barely exists anymore. Most of its members moved to Israel in the fifties. Today, there are fewer than ten Jews in the city. A. B. Salem convinced many that they should leave their homes and move to the newly established Jewish country. He was a Zionist with all his heart and soul, but he was also an Indian patriot. He never left his beloved city, and when the day came, in 1967, he was buried in the local cemetery next to the street that bears his name. The same street on which he walked to reach the synagogue.

29. Keeping the Flame Alive in the Heart of India – Delhi
Local Personalities: Yechezkel Yitzchak Malkar and Sarmad Kashani
Yishay Shavit

Rabbi Nachman of Breslov used to say that wherever he goes, he is essentially going to the Land of Israel. While I'm not a Breslover Chassid, I can definitely see the beauty in such a statement. Throughout my travels around the world, I do the same, with a slight change: wherever I go, I search for the people of Israel, for the local Jewish community.

I try to find what I like to call the "Jewish flame" that illuminates my world in a slightly different light. That is how I found myself sitting on a rickshaw, the local version of a taxi, in the middle of one of the most crowded streets in Old Delhi, searching for the tomb of a Muslim-Jewish Sufi mystic.

Delhi is one of the largest cities in the world. Its metropolitan area has a population of 28 million, as of the writing of these lines. It is intense and complex, a city of contrasts. I love this city. There is something about Delhi that is hard to find in many other urban areas in the world: rich historical depth mixed with a plethora of cultures and languages, gushing life that is impossible to stop. It was home to the leaders of the Mughal Empire, who turned it into one of the wealthiest cities in the world, where millions of people now live from hand to mouth. The books written about this city could fill an entire bookcase. I have read many of them, and I can promise you that they don't discuss the Jewish people.

Whatever way you look at it, Delhi's story does not include Judaism. Members of the three largest Jewish communities in India lived primarily in the cities on the coast of Cochin, Mumbai, or Calcutta. Very few Jews came to Delhi throughout history, and they did not leave a significant mark on the city. How, then, could I fulfill my custom? Where would I find the "Jewish flame" to illuminate this huge city for me? Some research was necessary. I asked friends, people who were deeply familiar with India, and then I heard for the first time about Sarmad Kashani.

To my great surprise, the rickshaw driver wasn't surprised at all when I asked him to take me to the *dargah* (the temple built above the tombs of the righteous) of Sarmad. The driver simply got onto his bike and started pedaling with determination. He was familiar with the site and how to get there. At first, we kept driving down Chandni Chowk, the main street of Old Delhi, one of the busiest streets in the entire world. Suddenly, the driver turned sharply off the street, crossing just five centimeters in front of a wagon hitched to a huge ox, and entered the narrow alleyways of Kinari Bazar. It is difficult to describe what I saw there, simply because there is nothing parallel to it anywhere in the world. Thousands of shops selling every sparkling item you could possibly imagine, from diamonds and gold to wedding apparel and down to cheap, colorful, and useless souvenirs. The rickshaw driver weaved his way through a mix of smells that had no connection between them. One moment, we smelled the enticing aroma of the *gulab jamun*, the sweet Indian dessert, and immediately afterward, we passed by a putrid sewage canal.

The people around us were wearing a huge range of clothing styles that testified to their different origins. There were Kashmir merchants, homeless Bihar children, women who were obviously members of the middle class of Delhi, local Muslims with thick beards, Sikh men from Punjab, and many, many more. Authors of travel books who claim that visiting India is an attack on your senses surely visited Kinari Bazar. I still don't know how the rickshaw driver did it, but after about ten minutes of pedaling through the market streets, he stopped next to a half-red, half-green building at the foot of the Jama Masjid, the large mosque of Old Delhi. When I gave him a surprised look, he announced, "Sarmad Dargah." We had reached our destination.

Sarmad, the seventeenth-century Sufi mystic, was born in Iran to a Jewish merchant family of Armenian descent. He set out on many trading trips that led him, among other places, to the Indian subcontinent. His life story is not fully known, but it is clear that at some point, he converted to Islam. In addition, we know that he fell deeply in love with a young Hindu man named Abhai Chand, with whom he traveled from city to city throughout India. Sarmad became a mystic and at some point even stopped wearing clothing. He would walk around naked as the day he was born, started writing poetry, and translated the Torah into Persian. Upon reaching Delhi, he became an acquaintance of the Mughal emperor Shah Jahan (builder of the Taj Mahal) and his eldest son Dara Shikoh, who were happy to learn the principles of the Jewish faith from him. After Aurangzeb, another one of Shah Jahan's sons, assumed the throne, Sarmad was no longer favored, and his head was cut off on the steps of the mosque. The legend is that the holy Sarmad bent over, picked up his severed head, climbed up the steps, finished his prayer, and only then returned his soul to his Maker. He was buried in the *dargah* built at the site where the entire incident took place.

Sarmad was a man who broke boundaries. Essentially, one can say that he had no boundaries at all. A merchant who became a mystic and came out of the closet at an older age, a man who walked around naked on the fringe of society, but also felt at home in the palace of the greatest ruler of the world at that time. When asked, he defined himself as "a Sufi, Catholic priest, Buddhist monk, Jewish rabbi, a heretic, and a Muslim." I was pleased to discover that those who visit his tomb today are also people whose religious affiliation is hard to classify. Both Muslims and Hindus visit the *dargah*, recite a short prayer, and ask for success in life. Some even catch a quick nap at the site. How many of them know about the saint's Jewish roots? It's hard to tell.

Can I say that I found the Jewish connection to Delhi? The flame that will change the light of the city for me? For a few years, I thought so. What's wrong with this colorful story? A nude Jewish-Muslim saint walking around with his decapitated head in his hands. I liked the universal message of Sarmad, which suited my worldview. I stopped searching. Until I met Yechezkel Yitzchak Malkar, the leader of the Yehuda Chaim Synagogue in Delhi.

I first visited the Yehuda Chaim Synagogue in 2015. It is located in one of the most central areas of New Delhi, not far from the embassy's road and from the Rajpath, the boulevard leading from the residence of the president of India and the parliament building, where the main parade in honor of Republic Day takes place. In short, the political heart of all of India, a region that I am very familiar with as a tourist and a tour guide. But I never knew that there was an active synagogue in the area. I arrived there in preparation for a trip that I was going to be guiding. The head of the community, Yechezkel Yitzchak Malkar, welcomed me warmly and told me a few things before the prayers began. He noted that in all of Delhi, there are no more than fifteen Jewish-Indian families. Fifteen families in a city of 28 million residents! The Yehuda Chaim Synagogue, built in the fifties, serves them and the few Jews who find themselves in the city on a Friday night, mostly diplomats and their families, as well as tourists. When I asked whether it was a Reform, Conservative, or Orthodox synagogue, I didn't receive a clear answer. The prayer book was Orthodox, and the prayer service started out that way as well, but very quickly, Yechezkel began to display great flexibility and essentially led the prayers in his own unique, cheerful way, without being too strict or rigid.

After the prayers, I felt a bit confused. What exactly had that prayer service been? What was this community's story? Who was Yechezkel Yitzchak Malkar? I tried to think logically, but still came out empty-handed. In the end, my curiosity got the best of me. I decided to apply an ancient Jewish strategy – chutzpah. I walked up to Yechezkel, whom I had just met less than an hour earlier, and started asking him questions. The answers I received came straight from his heart and opened up a window for me to understand Indian Jewry.

It turned out that Yechezkel was born to a family from the Bene Israel community in Pune. In 1980, he arrived in Delhi for work reasons and immediately started looking for other Jews in the city. He quickly became the leader of the tiny local community. Despite never having been ordained as a rabbi, Yechezkel leads the prayer services, makes sure the synagogue operates properly, and lives next to it. He maintains ongoing contact with the community members and serves as the spokesman and ambassador of Judaism in India's capital. Jokingly, he said that he fills all the community positions other than being the shochet and the mohel.

Due to the tiny size of the community, it is important to him that everybody feel at home at the synagogue. Therefore, the prayers and the customs are generally traditional, but in fact very flexible. Yechezkel never converted anyone to Judaism, but he feels comfortable conducting weddings between couples in which one spouse is not Jewish. In general, he feels comfortable in a multi-religious environment. He noted that there are nine religions in India, and despite the fact that Judaism is the smallest of them, the ocean of knowledge will never be full without their drop of Judaism. In this spirit, he lectures at interfaith events and writes for the *Times of India*, where he has published over a hundred articles. He has met and hosted some of the most prominent personalities in India and even lectured before them. His goal in life, he told me, is to maintain the Jewish flame in Delhi – to be an eternal Jewish candle among the millions of other candles in the city.

Yechezkel's sincere answers boosted my self-confidence, and at some point, I mustered up the courage to ask him personal questions. Yechezkel didn't shy away, telling me about his father and his sister, who immigrated to Israel, and about his visits there. He spoke of his three children, his two daughters who moved to Canada and Australia and got married there. His son, Noel Malkar, who lives in Delhi, is involved in music and has no intention of following in his father's footsteps. If so, I wondered, what will be the fate of the Delhi community when Yechezkel no longer has the strength to lead it? It seemed that Yechezkel read my mind. He decided to end the conversation by saying that he refused to join his family in Canada or in Australia. Someone, he said, must keep the flame constantly burning.

I left the synagogue with a good feeling. Here, I had found another Jewish angle to life in Delhi. Another flame. After a while, I began to see the similarities between the two flames, that of Sarmad Kashani and that of Yechezkel Yitzchak Malkar. Both were people who didn't toe the line. Both didn't let external social requirements define their lives. Both were people who represented Judaism in the capital of one of the largest and most important countries in the world. The similarity between the two that attracted my attention more than anything else was the religious flexibility and willingness to conduct a multicultural and deep, genuine interfaith discussion. Was it possible that this flexibility was characteristic of Judaism as a whole? After all, this culture was capable of adopting different ideas and beliefs for thousands of years. Perhaps this was a form of testament to Jewish adaptation to its surroundings in a place where Jews never experienced anti-Semitism or persecution? Whatever the reason may be, the lesson that I learn from the stories of Sarmad and of Yechezkel is that if Jews want to keep the eternal Jewish candle burning in India, they must be flexible. India, as I mentioned before, is an attack on all the senses, on all our preconceptions. If we lower our mental defenses, if we allow ourselves flexibility of thought, India-style, I believe that we will better understand this country and its tiny Jewish community.

China

30. A City of Refuge – Shanghai
Local Personality: Nina Admoni
Mickey Medzini

I always wanted to visit a city of refuge. The biblical concept fascinated me, and I imagined a city where every person can feel safe. A city free of worries, fear, or persecution. A city of peace. The precise explanations of my teachers at school, who said that the biblical cities of refuge were only intended to shelter those who had accidentally murdered another person, didn't alter the picture I had created in my mind. The very fact that there were such cities in the past, cities of peace, made me see the world through a more optimistic lens. When I grew up, I realized that these thoughts were just youthful fantasies and that the world is a harsh place. But then I heard the story of Nina Admoni, who, together with her husband, was a friend of my father's. Nina shared with me about the period she spent in Shanghai.

Over sixty years after leaving Shanghai, Nina Wertans (today Admoni) is still afraid of thunder on winter nights. They remind her of the American bombings of the city toward the end of World War II in 1945. Nina was born in Warsaw, Poland, and was seven years old when the war broke out there. Her parents decided to flee. They drove their family car until they reached the city of Vilnius in Lithuania. There, they tried to find a way to reach safe shores. At the end of 1939, no such way was apparent. Even if the Jewish family succeeded in moving through Western Europe or through the Stalinist Soviet Union, which country would accept them? The United States? The limitations on the number of immigrants permitted to enter the US, Nina's parents thought, made that route impossible. As Jews whose country had just recently been conquered by the Nazis, they searched for a city of refuge.

Just when it seemed that there was nowhere to run, Nina's parents heard about another surprising option. In their despair, they knocked on the door of the Dutch consulate in the city and obtained fictitious visas to the island of Curaçao, which was under Dutch control. These were given to them by Jan Zwartendijk, the local consul. Using these documents, they were admitted to the Japanese consulate, where the vice consul, Chiune Sugihara, gave them transit visas to Japan (both of these consuls, who operated against the instructions of their governments, were later honored as Righteous Among the Nations by Yad Vashem and the State of Israel). With these documents in hand, they bought tickets for the Trans-Siberian Railway, and after about twelve days, during which they crossed the entire Soviet Union, they reached the port city of Vladivostok. The family boarded a ship and disembarked at Kobe, Japan. There, they started to search for additional possibilities.

It was at this point that they learned that the route to the United States was blocked to them, because they had not been included in the quota of Polish immigrants. Seven-year-old Nina, who had been torn from her childhood and crossed vast expanses and many countries, grew up overnight. She learned, like many other Jewish children during that period, that people like her weren't welcome anywhere. Jewish blood was cheap in Nazi Europe, and there was nowhere to escape. After six months, the family had to leave Kobe. They sailed to the only place that was open to them – the city of Shanghai. Nina and her family were taken in there by representatives of the Jewish community, who helped them and about two thousand other Jewish refugees find a place to live and acclimate in the city.

In 1940, Shanghai was a very special city. Even in the nineteenth century, the Western superpowers realized the inherent commercial potential of the local port, and after the Opium Wars, a peace agreement was forced upon the Chinese that included, among other terms, an imperial approval for Europeans to settle in the city. As a result, a French quarter and an international quarter were established in this region, and the port was given the name "the Bund." The foreign residents there were subject to European rather than Chinese law, a fact that attracted merchants from all over the world. Among the foreign residents, there was a group of Jewish merchants from Iraq who were referred to as the Baghdadis. Some of them belonged to very wealthy families, such as the Sassoon family ("the Rothschilds of the East") the Kadoories, and the Hardoons. These families laid the foundation for the Jewish community of Shanghai, the same community that helped Nina's family. Essentially, to this day, it is not difficult to spot the footprints left by these Jews along the length of the Bund fairway. A good example is the Fairmont Peace Hotel, one of the most beautiful and best hotels in all of China. It was the first high-rise in the East, built by Victor Sassoon.

In 1940, Japan controlled the city, having conquered it a few years earlier from the Chinese. On the eve of the Japanese attack on Pearl Harbor, foreign residents in the city still enjoyed a high level of independence, and the Japanese authorities gave them a free hand. This unique political status was what enabled European Jews to find refuge in Shanghai.

I first visited China in 1992, not many years after this huge empire opened to the West following many years of isolation under the control of Mao Zedong. While this was my first trip, it wasn't the first time I encountered China and its culture. My grandfather, Moshe Medzini, lived in the city of Harbin in northern China for a few years and made his way to Israel via Shanghai. My father was one of the founders of the Center for East-Asian Studies at Hebrew University of Jerusalem.

All my life, I had heard stories about China, but nothing prepared me for the culture shock I experienced in Shanghai.

Today, Shanghai is one of the most modern cities in the world. Its skyline is taller and more beautiful than the skylines of most American cities, and the city is the financial and commercial center of one of the largest empires in the world. Upon exiting the airport, you can take the high-speed train to the center of town. Traveling at a speed of around 310 miles (500 km) per hour doesn't really give you a chance to take in the landscape outside the window.

This wasn't the situation in 1992. While then, too, it was impossible to see anything out the windows of the old bus I rode from the airport to the center of Shanghai, the reason was different – the number of people crowded into that bus exceeded the number of passengers that fill a New York subway car during rush hour. There was not a centimeter free, so it was impossible to even get close to a window, let alone see the landscape.

I don't know how, but in the end, I managed to get off the bus exactly at the stop I wanted – outside of the Old City of Shanghai. The number of bicycle riders was absolutely amazing. It seemed to me that the entire city was out riding their bikes. Millions of people, millions of bikes! I admit that it took me some time to successfully cross the street and enter the narrow alley that housed my hotel. The hotel was permitted by the authorities to host tourists. Here, it was still possible to detect the traditional China of the past, with food stalls selling different types of food that I had never seen before, produce sellers offering their unfamiliar goods, and meat sellers whose products were still alive. Many people on the streets were dressed in their pajamas, a custom that was popular among the residents of Shanghai during those years.

After a few days of getting acclimated in China, I decided to visit a local synagogue. I knew there had been six synagogues in Shanghai in the past. Some brief research told me that there were only two now.

I decided to go to the Ohel Moshe Synagogue in the Hongkou district. Walking through the streets of the district, which had been completely renovated over the previous few years, was a very interesting experience, but the comfort and cleanliness that characterized the streets made it difficult to imagine the distress of that period. In 1992, the three-story synagogue building was neglected. Yet the former glory of the Jewish community of this city was still evident. The synagogue was built by the second wave of Jews who arrived in the city. These were Jewish refugees who fled Russia for fear of Communism, after the Bolshevik Revolution. Many of them were merchants, and some of the more successful ones donated money on behalf of the community. Thus, the building was purchased and converted into a synagogue during the twenties.

Nina's family was forced in 1943 to move to the district where this synagogue was located. During the first two years of their lives in Shanghai, the family lived in the French quarter, and Nina's father even found employment with a Russian commercial company (despite joining the Axis powers in World War II, Japan refrained from declaring war on the Soviet Union). Thus, Nina's family was able to live a modest, quiet life. The Japanese government, which controlled Shanghai, did not give in to Nazi pressure regarding "the Jewish question." While they halted Jewish immigration to the city after Pearl Harbor, no anti-Semitic laws were enacted. But in 1943, German pressure increased, and the authorities decided to transfer all the city's Jews who were of German or Austrian origin or who had no mother country (such as the Jews of Poland, whose community had ceased to exist), to the Hongkou district, which was referred to as the "Jewish ghetto."

Although the fenceless ghetto of Shanghai cannot be compared to the ghettos of Europe, life still wasn't easy. While schoolchildren like Nina were given full freedom of movement, adults who wanted to go to work outside the quarter had to request transit permits from the authorities – and these were provided sparsely. Poverty increased, followed by hunger. The Joint Distribution Committee saved the day by providing the city's Jews with food and money. This was no mean feat, because at this stage, the United States and Japan were at war, and special permission was required from the American government to dispatch food to enemy territory.

At school, Nina met the children of other Jewish refugees who had come to the city a few years before her own family. These were Jews who had fled Germany after Hitler rose to power, especially after Kristallnacht, as well as Jews from Austria who had escaped after the Anschluss. When I think of the conversations that Nina and her friends, from various countries in Europe, must have had, all at the beginning of their adolescent years, I imagine they talked about what life was like as refugees. *What did we leave behind in the land that we were forced to flee? How did we first hear of Shanghai? How did we manage to get here, in unthinkable ways? What are our dreams for the future?* Conversations of young refugees, for whom Shanghai was a city of refuge.

During the last weeks of the war, B-29 planes bombed Shanghai. A few bombs fell not far from Nina's home in the Hongkou district. She never forgot the fear that these bombings caused, and as I already mentioned, throughout her life, Nina was afraid of the sound of rolling thunder on winter nights, which reminded her of those difficult days. But after a short period of time, the attacks stopped – Japan surrendered, and the war ended. Nina's family started to collect information from home, and when the extent of the destruction became clear to them, they realized that there was no reason for them to return. They managed to reach the United States and settled down there. While studying at University of California, Berkeley, Nina met a young Israeli named Nahum Admoni. The two married and moved to Israel, where they developed successful careers – she in the corporate sector and he in the Mossad, where he rose to be the director-general during the eighties. It is worth mentioning that during Nahum's service as head of the Mossad, the organization was responsible for bringing the Jews of Ethiopia to Israel in Operation Moses.

Since 1992, I have returned to China many times, both privately and as a tour guide. On almost every trip, I manage to visit Shanghai. Every time, I am surprised yet again by the speed at which the city changes. The millions of bicycles were replaced by luxury cars, the streets are broad, the shops modern with inviting lighting, and the economy is flourishing. It gives you the impression that Shanghai is the place to be in the twenty-first century. In my opinion, anyone who wants to understand the revolution that China has undergone over the past generation must visit this city.

In 2007, a new site joined my map of places that I visit with tourists in Shanghai – the Ohel Moshe Synagogue. The synagogue that I visited on my first trip to the city was renovated and well maintained and preserved. Its three stories now house the Shanghai Jewish Refugees Museum , which tells the stories of three communities of Jewish refugees – from Russia after the revolution, Germany after Hitler's rise to power, and Poland after the outbreak of the war – over twenty-five thousand Jews for whom Shanghai was a city of refuge. The humanistic message that the Chinese government would like to convey to tourists visiting this museum cannot be taken for granted and is another reason to visit the site.

After Mao Zedong established his government, following the Communist Revolution, there was not much left of the Jewish communities in Shanghai, but public interest in them only increased over the years. Jewish and even non-Jewish tourists visiting the city are exposed to the story of these communities, and this encourages local investment in preserving and developing the site. Recently, a project was launched to save tombstones from the old Jewish cemetery. This task, led by a Jew named Dvir Bar-Gal, turned out to be very challenging. The rate of the city's development is astronomical, and historical sites are often sacrificed for this accelerated growth. Despite all the challenges, thanks to this project, it is possible today to see part of Shanghai's Jewish past.

When China opened up to the West in the nineties, the community was reborn. Researchers estimate the Jewish population in Shanghai to be about ten thousand, half of whom are Israelis. Like Jews in many locations, they established community institutions such as a school and synagogues. Most of them came to Shanghai for business reasons rather than for its Jewish heritage. But a short visit to the Jewish Refugees Museum can teach us all that the city of Shanghai was always kind to Jews. My childhood dream came true – I visited a real city of refuge.

Uganda

31. The Conservative Jews of Uganda – Mbale
Local Personality: Rabbi Gershom Sizomu
Ya'acov Fried

Joanne Moore, whom I have known for many years, is a Jewish woman from Virginia who has been working with international humanitarian aid organizations for decades. We have spent many hours together discussing the complexity of African culture in general and social changes in particular. We have also discussed in depth some of the neglected Jewish communities in Africa, which have always fascinated me. I am sharing here Joanne's powerful and personal account of how she first came to Uganda and what she discovered.

I first arrived in Africa in the summer of 2001 as part of the worldwide campaign to fight HIV, which had spread through the continent like wildfire. In Kampala, the capital city of Uganda, I participated in a convention for local and international organizations that focused on programs to prevent the spread of AIDS among women in general and among mothers and girls specifically. It was at this convention that I met Julie, a Jewish colleague from the United States who later became a close friend. She told me about her brother, a Conservative rabbi in the United States, who had been working for several years on finding the Jewish tribe in the depths of Uganda.

That day, we watched a live broadcast of the Twin Towers collapsing. All at once, the convention became surreal. One minute we were talking about the existence of a Jewish tribe here in Uganda; the next we were watching on the screen the collapse of the Twin Towers and what seemed like the end of the world. It felt like straight out of a science-fiction movie. We planned our upcoming trip to find the lost Jewish tribe. I was absolutely terrified; what would the world look like after this attack? The thought that kept crossing my mind during those next few weeks was that perhaps Uganda was a much safer place to be than New York.

After a few weeks, I traveled with my friend Julie and her brother to Uganda to meet with the Abayudaya tribe. We got into a jeep and rode on red dirt paths that wound between quicksand swamps. Masses of people made their way to the marketplaces. Women wearing colorful clothing carried large baskets on their heads, with small babies wrapped in thin fabric tied to their bodies. Children carried vessels of water and shouted to us, "*Mazungo*" (white man). The men rode their bicycles on the paths, which were dotted with red mud houses with straw roofs. There were green banana groves in every direction. While we were driving, I heard the story of Uganda's soil for the first time, and especially the statement that the soil is so fertile that if you eat an orange and throw the seeds on the ground, new trees will immediately grow on their own, without any human intervention at all.

On the way to the Abayudaya tribe, we passed through the city of Jinja, which is located on the coast of Lake Victoria, one of the tributaries of the White Nile. Excitement overcame me as I realized that I was traveling to look for a lost Jewish tribe and passing a tributary of the Nile River on the way – the same Nile from which Moses was drawn as a baby. The story of his leadership is the strongest symbol for me of the process of our birth as a nation.

After a few hours on winding dirt roads, we reached the city of Mbale in eastern Uganda, where the seeds of Judaism began to sprout about a hundred years ago. The small, white homes in the village had a darkish tint and fragile concrete floors. Most of the homes had two rooms with minimal furniture, faded couches, low stools in the main room, and another room meant for sleeping that featured a pile of mattresses on a thin mat. The homes of the Abayudaya were easily identifiable by their doors and windows, upon which Stars of David and other Jewish symbols had been drawn with chalk. We entered one of the homes. A white sheet was spread across the main wall, proudly featuring the letters of the Hebrew alphabet. The woman who lived there bashfully peeked at us from the other side of the room, and it was clear that she was pleased to have Jewish visitors. This was the beginning of my first visit to this small, resolute community that clung to Judaism and survived against all odds.

The story of this community in eastern Uganda began in 1913, in the village of Nabugoye. The military leader of the eastern province in Uganda under the control of the British Empire, Semei Kakungulu, reached the conclusion that the New Testament did not express the will of God and that he must honor the words of the Old Testament in their literal sense. He left the Protestant church and joined the Bamalaki, an African Christian sect that was beginning to gain popularity in Uganda, expressing his protest against British control through his religious principles.

The Bamalaki sect synthesized ideas from both the Old Testament and the New Testament. They restored Saturday as the day of rest, prohibited the consumption of pigs, and permitted marriage to more than one woman, finding justification from the Old Testament for all of these changes. Kakungulu, a charismatic personality, gathered support and followers who began to fulfill commandments according to their interpretation of the holy Scriptures, with no connection to other Jews or any other community. When he heard that there were Jews who live according to the Bible, he wanted his followers to learn from them how to practice the Old Testament. Kakungulu sent letters to three Jewish communities, in Jerusalem, New York, and Johannesburg. He attached a map noting the location of his community as well as a request that the rabbi or emissary who would come to them possess two important traits: the ability to speak English and a willingness to focus on teaching them how to live their lives according to the literal meaning of the Old Testament.

The ceremony in which Kakungulu circumcised himself and his sons, like our forefather Abraham, constituted an expression of their acceptance of the commandments of Judaism. He called their group Abayudaya (the tribe of Jews). Hundreds of his soldiers and supporters joined the community that he created. He wrote their first book of instructions, called Ebigambo, which included quotes from the Bible, while simultaneously training teachers and instructors at the synagogue he built in 1923, which began to function as an educational center.

Kakungulu's call for religious and educational assistance from Jewish communities around the world was answered several years later, when a mohel (Jew trained in circumcision) named Yosef arrived and stayed with the community for over a year, teaching the members the laws of kashrut (Jewish dietary laws), Sabbath and festivals, as well as Jewish traditions and sources. He even trained one of the members of the community to be a mohel.

In 1928, at the age of fifty-nine, Kakungulu passed away after a severe illness and left behind a Jewish community of about two hundred members that occupied several miles of land.

Kakungulu's vision did not fully come to fruition, because the community faced challenges in many areas. He did not leave behind a strong foundation of Jewish culture, and the leaders who followed him were plagued by disputes and strife. In addition, discrimination and intolerance from the general population in Uganda prevented community members from finding employment. The community did not have the resources to establish a Jewish educational system, and many chose to send their children to schools run by Christian missionaries. Many children of the community's founder and members of his extended family became Christian, while others chose to give up their children's education entirely in order to protect and preserve their Jewish identities.

These processes led to many intermarriages and the dwindling of the number of Jewish young adults in the community. Yet the desire of the community members to protect and strengthen their Jewish identities did not disappear despite the huge challenges that they faced.

Toward the end of the sixties, members of the community tried to contact the Israeli embassy in Uganda in hopes that they could send their children to receive a Jewish education in the State of Israel. At the same time, however, the dictator Idi Amin rose to power. He put an end to all relations with Israel and even prohibited all religious activity in Uganda other than Islam and Christianity. At his order, synagogues were closed, praying was forbidden, and anyone who chose to continue to pray did so secretly. The years of Idi Amin's rule weakened the Jewish community even more.

After Idi Amin's fall in 1979, the new leadership of Uganda proclaimed religious freedom, which enabled the community to resume a Jewish lifestyle and save whatever was left. In 1980, the community consisted of about fifty young people. J. J. Keki was a charismatic figure in this small group: "We realized that if we didn't take drastic steps, we were doomed to extinction. I initiated and established the Young Jewish Community (YJC) youth movement as an educational platform to preserve and revive Jewish life here. We understood that if we didn't connect with Jewish communities around the world, our situation would deteriorate economically, socially, and religiously. Our Jewish identity cannot exist while we are isolated from the greater Jewish family of international communities." Keki was sent as a representative of the youth movement to the synagogue in Nairobi, the capital city of Kenya, in order to study the organizational structure of their community. About a decade later, he and his two brothers initiated the establishment of a collective settlement as a model for collaboration, at the center of which they built Moses Synagogue, whose construction was completed in 1995.

In 1992, an American student named Matthew Meyer visited the community and shared its existence with Kulanu, a Jewish-American organization dedicated to helping Jewish communities around the world. A delegation from Kulanu, including rabbis, reached Uganda in 2002 and performed a festive ceremony of immersion in a ritual bath for members of the community. The members were recognized by the Conservative movement, which was very active in bringing them donations and volunteers who assisted in the areas of health, economics, and Jewish education. About four thousand members of the Abayudaya chose to undergo a Conservative conversion performed by five American rabbis of the movement. The pinnacle of this process was in 2008, when Gershom Sizomu, the leader of the community, was ordained as a rabbi after five years of study at a Conservative rabbinical seminary in the United States. It is important to note that an additional group of several hundred people requested an Orthodox conversion, which was performed by Rabbi Shlomo Riskin during various visits to the region. Today, Rabbi Gershom Sizomu serves as the community's leader, in addition to being an active member of parliament in the country.

The Abayudaya live a lifestyle of tolerance, respect, and good neighborly relations. Small stone and mud houses are scattered throughout the villages, which have slowly begun to show the influence of modernization. It is still possible to identify the homes of the community members with ease according to the Star of David and other Jewish symbols drawn proudly on their doors, walls, and windows. The community runs a Jewish school, several synagogues, and various cultural events.

On Friday mornings, the buzz of Sabbath preparations is palpable in the village. From backyards, which are used as kitchens, the aromas of various dishes waft through the air. School ends earlier than usual, and village members who have moved to the city return to the village before the Sabbath. As sunset approaches, everyone dons festive

Sabbath clothing and begins to walk toward the synagogue, which is at the top of the hill. The Sabbath prayers are sung with an African beat in a mixture of Hebrew and Luganda, the local dialect, accompanied by tambourine and guitar music. The vocal capabilities of the community members are unbelievable, and their harmonies are moving and mesmerizing.

The reality of Judaism by choice, of an isolated Jewish community choosing to live a Jewish lifestyle throughout the years despite the challenges and even seeking to convert in order to feel part of the Jewish people is a phenomenon I have never seen anywhere else in the world. Judaism is not a missionizing religion. The community leaders contacted American rabbis to seek conversion out of a sense of commitment to the Jewish lifestyle. The rabbis who converted them shared that they sensed that despite the difficulty involved in maintaining a Jewish lifestyle while isolated in Africa, the community members were completely dedicated to this endeavor. The distance and the isolation make it very difficult for the Jewish community to develop, both physically and spiritually. But this is a choice that they step up and make every day – to be part of the Jewish tribe and family, despite the temptations of modern development that continue to challenge the community's existence.

Rabbi Gershom Sizomu adds: "We are living in a world of Jewish values. We get up every morning with a sense of responsibility for our continued growth and development." Rabbi Sizomu's grandfather was an officer under Kakungulu's command in the army, and their relationship was one of trust, friendship, and closeness. After Kakungulu's death, his grandfather continued to be a prominent educational and religious figure in the community. Rabbi Sizomu decided to pursue rabbinical studies in the United States and Israel for about five years and returned with a vast sense of commitment to lead the community. He could have opted for a life in the United States or Israel, but he chose to continue to contribute to this cause. The community invests in education in general, and especially in teaching Jewish values. It is not difficult for the community's leaders to leave Africa today and move to North America, but they are motivated by an exceptional sense of dedication to the continued Jewish existence of the community. The members essentially make the decision every day to be a Jew by choice.

"To us, Judaism is our culture. The Sabbath prayers, the singing, the elementary school and the high school that we run, the health clinic for new mothers, the collective organizational structure, and the learning programs are our Jewish culture and lifestyle," Sizomu explains. "I believe that the actions of the forefathers are a symbol for their children. I returned from the rabbinical program to come home to Uganda and lead a process of teaching a new staff to serve as the spiritual shepherds of the Jews in Uganda, in nearby Kenya, and in other tiny communities throughout Africa. I experienced the way that fear and insecurity controlled the entire country during Idi Amin's era. That terrifying regime did not allow us to live as Jews. He also did not allow us to engage in *tikkun olam* [improving the world] on behalf of the general population. Today, our schools, health clinic, and collective organization are open to the non-Jewish population as well. We are dedicated to *tikkun olam* as part of Jewish culture."

Visiting the Abayudaya tribe in the heart of Africa and participating in their local prayers was a unique and extraordinary experience for me. I can't even begin to describe the intensity of the prayers. During Kabbalat Shabbat, we sang the psalms from the prayers with children whose names were Sarah, Rebecca, Rachel, Samuel, and Joseph. Angelic voices filled with emotion and purity rang out in the synagogue. I sat next to a little girl who sang in Hebrew and seemed to be staring at me, as if to check whether I knew the psalms too. It is no wonder, I mused, that a collection of the community's songs was produced by a leading music company in the United States and even won prestigious prizes.

The next day, we celebrated the bat mitzvah of one of the other girls at the synagogue. Rabbi Sizomu asked her softly and sensitively about the meaning of commitment to education and congratulated her for joining the adult members of the greater Jewish family. She read from the Torah and sang the haftarah (a short reading from the Prophets that follows the Torah reading in a synagogue) in the traditional liturgical tune. I couldn't contain my emotions at the sight of an entire room of people who look different from us but share the same tradition, roots, and common destiny. And all of this was taking place not far from the Nile River, where Moses was drawn out of the water.

Rwanda

32. Justice, Justice Shall You Pursue – Agahozo-Shalom
Local Personality: Gideon Herscher
Ya'acov Fried

"Why Rwanda? It's a place of genocide, violence, filth, and it's unsafe too," I was told. "Okay, it might be one of the only places in the world where you can see gorillas in their natural habitat. But seriously, are you sure that justifies the long journey to Africa?"

The year was 2009. It was neither the exciting experience of spending time at the gorilla reserve in the heart of the jungle – where I could examine Darwin's theory on the origins of man up close for the first time in my life – nor the trip through the countryside with its heavenly landscapes of green hills rolling from horizon to horizon between blue lakes that had brought me to Rwanda. I had come because of a beloved friend.

A few years before my visit, I learned of a vision that was shared by Anne Heyman and my dear friend Gideon Herscher to establish Agahozo-Shalom Youth Village. Today, Gideon is one of the senior officers of the American Jewish Joint Distribution Committee (the Joint), and at that time, he was at the beginning of his professional career. Anne Heyman, a philanthropist who contributed to the Joint, conducted a series of conversations with Gideon, dedicated to the subject of helping Rwanda following the horrible massacre that had occurred just a few years previously. "As Jews, what can we do for Rwanda?"

The shared vision that developed reveals the immense potential that is realized when a motivated philanthropist like Anne joins forces with brave leaders like Gideon. With Gideon's help, the Joint provided Anne with an initial work plan before setting out on a journey to research and familiarize themselves with the complex situation in Rwanda. At the top of the vision paper, the following lines were quoted from the Talmud about the Jewish obligation to do good for the entire world: "Whoever can prevent his household from committing a sin, but does not, is responsible for the sins of his household. If he can prevent sin among his fellow citizens and does not, he is responsible for the sins of his fellow citizens. And if he can prevent sins in the world, he is responsible for the sins of the whole world" (Talmud, *Shabbat* 54b).

Rwanda, the most crowded country in Africa, is at the center of the Dark Continent and borders with Burundi, Uganda, Tanzania, and Congo. While it does not feature a seaport, it does have many lakes and is part of the drainage basin and sources of the Nile River. Rwanda has a balanced tropical climate, with moderate temperatures that make visiting the country pleasant all year round.

Twelve million citizens live in this country, which is the size of New Jersey. A large portion of Rwandans live in communities with a few thousand members. Most of them are Christian, with a small minority of Muslims and followers of other religions. There is a network of roads between the villages, but it is not rare for the road to suddenly end and become a dirt path.

Kigali is Rwanda's capital city and the economic and cultural center of the country. Most of the government buildings are found here, next to cultural, sports, and art centers. Walking through the streets on foot, I felt very safe. I especially enjoyed the colorful Kimironko Market with its fabric shops. I couldn't resist the temptation, and I entered a tailor's shop. That evening, a package was already waiting for me at my hotel, containing a jacket and two pairs of trousers sewed according to my measurements. I continued to wander through the city's many museums and galleries. I was especially excited by the galleries displaying artwork created as part of community projects, from which part of the proceeds were given back to the community.

I visited the Kigali Genocide Memorial, originally constructed to provide a proper burial for the hundreds of thousands of bodies of Rwandans murdered and left throughout Kigali after the war. Later, exhibitions were created to tell the story of the murder of the Rwandan nation, with examples of similar cases of genocides around the world, including the Holocaust of the Jewish nation.

In April 1994, the leaders of the extreme majority from the Hutu tribe in Rwanda launched a campaign to eradicate the Tutsi minority. In less than one hundred days, over 800,000 people were murdered. The horrific consequences of the genocide continue to impact Rwanda to this day. Rwanda was left destroyed, and hundreds of thousands of survivors underwent intense trauma. Justice, social responsibility, and reconciliation were not at the top of the country's priorities during those years.

Humanitarian aid organizations stepped in to rehabilitate the country's feeble economy. Child mortality rates were among the highest in the world, and the average lifespan was forty-one years. This was the most densely populated country in Africa, and they had few natural resources and primitive industry, with 90 percent of the population engaging in basic agriculture.

In the conversations between Gideon Herscher and Anne Heyman, the feeling was that the Jewish nation could not stand idly by at the sight of such severe suffering and poverty, especially in light of the Jews' own history in the Holocaust, which at that time had occurred just forty years earlier. Such a feeling was also in keeping with the Joint's ethical philosophy and agenda.

Anne still had memories of racial prejudice from her years in South Africa. She possessed moral sensitivities that she expressed, among other things, by establishing a program at Tufts University called "Moral Voices," to focus on various aspects of social justice. She was active at the university with other Jewish students, through the local Hillel organization, in developing social sensitivity within the Jewish world, as well as among the non-Jewish community. The Joint and Anne definitely saw eye to eye when it came to the Jewish value known as *tikkun olam* (repairing the world), which is the key to *tikkun halev* (repairing your wounded heart).

"*Tikkun olam* motivates Jews all over the world to get up, take action, and help rehabilitate communities dealing with severe crises – from crimes against humanity in Bosnia and Darfur to natural disasters in Sri Lanka and India," Gideon told me. "*Tikkun olam* obligates us to do our best to heal and lend a supportive shoulder to communities in pain, regardless of their religious affiliation or ethnicity. Jews are responsible for ensuring that the concept of 'Never Again' stays on the table in Jewish communities and reverberates all over the world."

Anne traveled with Gideon to get a closer look at the reality of life in Rwanda. They encountered the frightening results of the massacre, which left about a million orphaned children, from whom the hope for a better future in their country had been robbed. Gideon shared about their trip: "We met the president of Rwanda and representatives of several local organizations that had been assigned the task of caring for the orphans. Some of the orphanages were being run by sixteen-year-old children who were orphans themselves. In your wildest dreams, you could never fathom how dangerous and violent such an arrangement can be."

Anne and Gideon returned from their visit to Rwanda with the feeling that any serious investment in the future of the country had to be focused particularly on the urgent and critical needs of those orphaned children. "Our earliest ideas included establishing a youth village that would include a school," Gideon explained. "The Agahozo-Shalom Youth Village project strove to provide a comprehensive and focused solution, as part of the efforts to help the orphans. It was a youth village planned and built as a partnership between American, Israeli, and Rwandan communities. The village would provide a safe living environment for the orphans, where they would be protected from abuse, neglect, and exploitation and would also receive support – no strings attached – as the beginning of their process of rehabilitation."

Gideon shared that the developers "wanted to open a school in the village that would allow the children to expand their horizons, shape their futures, grow their skills, and improve their ability to function in the community, and to even become leaders themselves. We dreamed of a school equipped with upgraded computers and art centers, which would also offer vocational training and university scholarships. Anne worked tirelessly to ensure the health and well-being of the orphans and of the community living next to the village by establishing a health clinic on its premises."

The village was established in Rwamagana in eastern Rwanda, where the largest population of orphans was living. "When we started planning the village, we chose to cooperate with the Yemin Orde Youth Village, under the leadership of Dr. Chaim Peri, who had extensive experience in the absorption of Ethiopian Jews in Israel. We reasoned that graduates of Yemin Orde, who are significant contributors to the fields of education, health, agriculture, communications, and business in Israel, would be able to mentor the teachers in Rwanda. We believed that the fact that they experienced their own challenging immigration and absorption process and came from Africa as well would help them return to Africa and be agents of change."

Professor Reuven Feuerstein, founder of the Feuerstein Institute and clinical, developmental, and cognitive psychologist, joined Dr. Peri and the Yemin Orde staff. Professor Feuerstein and his institute have researched and developed educational processes for deprived populations in Israel. Their successful results with populations that had undergone trauma and the fact that Professor Feuerstein was intimately familiar with the effects of the Holocaust on orphans in Israel made him and his team a source of inspiration, support, and guidance for the managers, teachers, and employees at the village.

The Agahozo-Shalom Youth Village, whose African name means "the place where tears are wiped," was established a few years after the idea was born. An Israeli manager was appointed to run the village, based on the idea that Israelis had extensive experience in absorbing immigrants, including many adolescents who arrived in Israel without their families, beginning from the Holocaust period and including the waves of immigration from Russia and Ethiopia. The feeling was that it would be appropriate to adopt the Israeli model for treating trauma among orphans at the village as well. The vast sums of money needed to establish and operate the village came from donations contributed by Anne Heyman and the Joint.

The site, which housed about five hundred boys or girls, resembled a kibbutz, including housing, dining rooms, study centers, public buildings, and an agricultural farm. Israeli companies such as Netafim and organizations such as the Jewish National Fund (JNF) also contributed. A local staff of teachers and counselors, dorm mothers, and volunteers was formed and they built a unique curriculum. Parallel to this, dozens of teachers, counselors, and social workers were brought to Israel for continued education programs, including at Feuerstein's institute and at Yemin Orde, for exposure, study, and continued training. Professor Feuerstein and his team created trauma therapy plans.

"In retrospect," Gideon Herscher shares, "Professor Feuerstein was the one who introduced the educational approach that says even when you experience trauma and a scar is left, it is possible to open up a window and develop a perception of a different reality. What you see right now is not necessarily the reality you will see a few seconds from now. At any given moment, many alternative possibilities could open up in your life." According to Feuerstein, a Holocaust survivor himself, "Even after experiencing trauma, it is possible to think and live differently from your current perception of reality. Cognitive changes are possible. The mental and educational process is a transition from the frozen state of trauma to a perspective that sees a better future and hope on the horizon."

I came to the village to get a better idea of this wonderful project brewing in the heart of Africa and to pave the way for a Jewish leadership delegation from the United States. These leadership delegations would have a chance to really see the impact of philanthropic investments by American Jews and the huge contribution of Israeli bodies dedicated to education and society, which changed the lives of the orphans at the village for the better. While at the village, I was exposed to the personal losses of many of the children and staff members. Everywhere I turned, I was moved to tears by how sensitively the children behaved and their thirst to listen and learn. I saw the innocent look in their eyes and the community life that had been created. Two ideas echoed in my heart throughout my visit, everywhere I went. The first was the sign on the village that read "See far – go far," and the second was the village motto, "Restoring the rhythm of life." As Gideon said with all his heart, "That was the theme that guided us along every step of the way. These kids' rhythm had been tragically disrupted, and the challenge was to restore that to the extent possible."

I left a few days later feeling that while I didn't know if it was possible to fully heal from trauma, I was now sure that it was possible to continue to function and live a better life, alongside the trauma.

Anne Heyman passed away after a horseback riding accident a few years ago. She dreamed, and she revolutionized the lives of thousands of orphaned children in Rwanda, in cooperation with the Joint. I feel that in the hearts of many of us, members of the Jewish nation, Holocaust survivors and their contemporaries and children, there is a desire to melt and break down the pain of our personal memories. Survivors often have a feeling of intergenerational pain, as if they are carrying the pain with them in their spines. I share Gideon's feeling that Anne sensed that the pain and memories of the Holocaust would be soothed by taking action.

"Rwanda gave Anne the opportunity to do so much good. She would bawl every month on her visits to the village. Five hundred children anticipated her arrival. She loved them, and at the same time urged the management, the parents, and the entire staff to aim for excellence; from the children, she expected motivation to learn and to act. Perhaps her sobbing was part of that liberation of the painful memories. Taking action relieved the memories. The difficult past and the present met in a space of hope."

Gideon and I are true soul friends. We have held endless conversations and discussions contemplating many different questions, including that of our purpose in this world. We both share the idea that when people embark on a journey outside their comfort zones, especially when this is accompanied by action that promotes social justice, like at Agahozo-Shalom Youth Village, several things are liable to be aroused or occur inside the traveler's heart.

The collective Jewish memory does not stop at Jewish boundaries. We are thirsty to heal our painful memories, such as the trauma of the Holocaust. Sometimes, the thought arises that perhaps doing good for someone else will make the painful memories duller or even cause them to disappear. "The pain of the Holocaust memories makes me feel that I need to do something," Gideon told me. "It is very possible that Anne was unable to live with the pain of those memories, and so she decided to go to a different painful place. Her approach was, 'I will go to a painful place, help them with my experiences, and in this way, perhaps heal my own painful memories.'"

On personal journeys to distant locations around the world, outside of Western civilization, we step out of our comfort zones. We sense the different smells, the changing colors, and our entire consciousness is shaken. Something dramatic happened to me on my trips to distant locations, such as Rwanda. Emotions such as compassion, love, and the ability to listen, my perception of the value of life, a smile, and the power of a hug, underwent an earthquake. I felt that my heart was giving commands to my brain. It was an opportunity to separate between important and unimportant, to be authentic, and to let my heart be vulnerable on the one hand and courageous on the other.

When the youth village first opened, there was a ceremony that was attended by the president of Rwanda, ministers, heads of state, donors, the managers of the village, and the students. "I saw that Anne was nervous," Gideon related. "The students arrived in very poor physical and mental states. She became very anxious and asked, 'Did we do the right thing?' I remember that I stood there and said to her, 'We've been given a one-time opportunity; we have the privilege of making a real difference.'"

The following poem was written by one of the orphans at the village for the school graduation ceremony, which was attended by Anne Heyman a month before her death. Anne excitedly shared the poem with Gideon just a few days before she passed away. Gideon read it in his eulogy for Anne.

> Hello grandmother Anne Heyman,
> You stand like a man
> You speak like a president
> You defend like a royal person
> You smile like an angel
> You really deserve to be a hero
> I call you a soldier.
> Our country does not grow by chance
> It is by the spirit of hard working
> We never sit and wish, we dream and act
> We are committed to making a progressive development
> And show the world that we can.

Gideon concluded his eulogy with the following words: "Anne, you showed the world that indeed, we can."

Suriname

33. In the Heart of the Jewish Savanna – Suriname
Local Personality: Rene Fernandez
Ya'acov Fried

I landed in Paramaribo, the capital city of Suriname, after a short flight from Belem, the gateway to the Amazon region in northern Brazil. The flight from Belem to Suriname was like a psychedelic journey in deep green above the rainforests. In Suriname, I met up with a friend who had decided to encircle the continent of South America in a yacht and invited me to join him for part of his trip. The weather was stormy, and instead of sailing along the length of the Atlantic coast, we headed out for a short trip on the river that goes inland. It took me a while to get over the fact that the water is not red, and that the red name actually refers to the color of the huge red leaves that have fallen off the trees and cover the bottom of the river. We headed back to our port of origin in Paramaribo to wait for the storm to pass. When we heard that the ocean was not going to be any calmer for at least two days, I went to the marina office to check out touring options in Suriname itself.

The bulletin board in the marina office was covered with suggestions of hikes in the thick of the jungle, but my eyes rested on one in particular: "Visit Jewish Savanna." Throughout my life, wherever I travel, I always research and try to check out in advance the Jewish aspect of the location. This was the first time that the Jewish aspect "looked for" and found me first. I had never heard of any Jews or Jewish life in Suriname. I called the number on the advertisement and reached a woman who introduced herself as the guide and a Jew herself. She mentioned during our conversation that the communities of the Caribbean in general and of Suriname in particular had a captivating Jewish history, and that I could hear all about it during this trip into the depths of the savanna.

The next morning, we started the trip by sailing in a tiny motorboat through a narrow river channel, as the skies above us loomed darkly and sprinkled us with bothersome raindrops. After sailing for about an hour, we reached a small place to dock in the thick of the savanna. We got into a mud-plastered jeep whose original color was indiscernible and drove down a bumpy dirt road even further into the Surinamese rainforest.

The rainy season in Suriname is usually over toward the end of January, but it was already late February, and the tropical rain had turned the jungle floor into a sticky brown paste that even our trusty jeep had difficulty driving across. The trail wound between enormous trees with ferns wrapped around their trunks and huge bird of paradise flowers that were as tall as a person. We were less than sixty miles away from Paramaribo, the capital of Suriname, but the poor road conditions and the swampy mud made what was meant to be a short trip into a journey that took hours.

We did the last part of our journey on foot. The screeches of parrots and monkeys could be heard in the background. When an unlucky snake crossed our path, the jeep driver, who was accompanying us, smashed its head with a stick. After a short walk, we reached a clearing in the forest where flat marble stones were spread across the ground. The guide took out a brush that she had brought with her and cleaned the stones. Among the thick, wet grass, I spotted Hebrew letters.

The letters were slightly unclear after being exposed to the tropical climate for hundreds of years, but they were still readable. "Here lies the honorable and learned Shmuel Roblis," and the name Shmuel Haramati appeared on the second tombstone. I knelt down in the mud and excitedly exposed more and more inscriptions written in lyrical Hebrew.

Not all the inscriptions were legible, and not all the names were decipherable; many tombstones were cracked and broken. But the etched stones told the stories of many: Rachel Yeshurun, who passed away in May 1762, "for she struggled severely during childbirth"; Abraham de Aguilar, who passed away in July 1767 and "now lies on the dust of the earth"; and many small gravesites belonging to children. Most of the tombstones also included eulogies inscribed in Dutch and Portuguese, which were commonly spoken by the Suriname community at that time.

In those days, it was not difficult to gather a prayer quorum to recite the Kaddish prayer next to the graves of those who rested under the tombstones, where the huge, vibrantly colored butterflies now hovered. The Jews constituted about half of the white population in Suriname in the eighteenth century, and due to the many Jews who populated the bank of the Suriname River, this region is still called the Jodensavanne to this day. Many of them were farmers, the owners of sugar plantations, and they gave their farms Hebrew names such as Sukkot, Hebron, and Carmel. A large number of these Jews were Dutch, the descendants of Jews expelled from Spain and Portugal who moved to this new land in the sixteenth and seventeenth centuries. Further down the muddy path, we visited the remains of the Bracha v'Shalom Synagogue, which was built in a similar format to the Portuguese synagogue in Amsterdam. Even today, it is possible to see that it was built of red bricks, which is characteristic of Dutch construction.

No one knows exactly when the first Jews arrived in Suriname and the Caribbean shores. The first Jewish inhabitants were a group of Jewish Anusim from Portugal who used rare exit permits from the country during the sixteenth century to escape to other European countries and from there to Central and South America. The first group apparently arrived in 1652 from England. Another group came in 1656 after a long journey of wandering. They originally moved from Europe to Brazil, which had been transferred from Portugal's control to the sovereignty of Holland. But when Brazil returned to Portuguese hands, Joseph Nunez de Fonseca, also known by the name David Nassi, led the community on a long journey throughout the New World. After a few attempts at settling in various locations, the community settled down in Jodensavanne (Jewish Savanna). Toward the end of the seventeenth century, Ashkenazi Jews also began to arrive, mostly from Germany and Holland. In 1735, they founded an independent Jewish community in Paramaribo, and a quarter of the sugar plantations in the colony belonged to its members.

According to Rene Fernandez, a businessman and head of the Jewish community in Suriname, there was never any anti-Semitism in the country. He shares that many non-Jewish residents wear a Star of David around their necks, because they believe that it is an amulet for blessings and good luck, and many boast a Jewish father or grandfather. Back in 1665, when the British controlled the region, Jews were given a bill of rights equal to those of the British residents of Suriname, and these rights were maintained even after the colony was conquered by the Dutch in 1667.

The Jewish residents in Suriname dealt with many challenges: the distance from the civilization with which they were familiar, the difficult climate, unfamiliar diseases, the isolation and sense of foreignness among the local residents (native-born American Indians and black slaves brought from Africa to work in the sugar plantations). Like most of the whites in the region, the Jews had slaves too. However, they did not play an active role in the slave trade. This was not due to their sense of justice, but rather because the Dutch company in control of western India had a monopoly over this enterprise. In the adjacent Jewish communities, there were cases of Jews who were given permission to trade and own slaves. But throughout the Caribbean area, the number of slaves that one was permitted to own was limited, in order to prevent the residents from becoming large plantation owners.

Rene Fernandez is very involved in the economic, social, and political life in Suriname and the Caribbean. His family has lived in Suriname for many generations, and he holds the title of Knight of the Order of Palms, one of the most important titles in Suriname. Fernandez is actively involved in preserving the Jewish heritage and sites of the region. He relates that he recently submitted a special request to the European Union for sponsorship of the efforts to rehabilitate the cemetery and the synagogue in Jewish Savanna.

Although he is not observant, Fernandez makes sure to hold a Shabbat dinner and pray on Shabbat at the Neveh Shalom Synagogue in Paramaribo. On the Shabbat that I joined him with the handful of elderly men who gathered to pray, we did not have a prayer quorum. The tiny community of about 150 has not been able to afford a rabbi since 1969.

Today as well, all religions enjoy tolerance and fraternity in Suriname. Muslims, Christians, Hindus, and Jews live alongside each other, and the Neveh Shalom Synagogue actually shares a courtyard with its neighbor, a large mosque. It was built at the beginning of the eighteenth century and renovated in 1992. It is a wooden structure that was painted white, in the style of the colonial mansions that were popular in the Caribbean at that time. Like most of the synagogues in the Caribbean area, such as the synagogues in Suriname, Jamaica, St. Thomas, Curaçao, or even Amsterdam, the floor is covered in sand. When I entered, I took off my shoes and wondered, why build a synagogue with a floor made of sand?

There are those who claim that this is reminiscent of the days when the fathers of the crypto-Jews would gather together to pray in small groups in cellars whose floors were covered in sand, in order to mute their footsteps for fear that the Inquisition officials would hear them. Another explanation is that the sand represents the temporary nature of the exile, which will eventually end and herald the return to the Land of Israel. There are also those who claim that the sand represents the Sinai Desert, where the Israelites walked for forty years before reaching the Promised Land. In the same way, the crypto-Jews were forced to wander "the deserts of the Christian world" until returning to the Jewish faith.

Neveh Shalom is the synagogue of both Surinamese Jewish communities, the Sephardic and the Ashkenazi, which united in the eighties due to the small size of the local Jewish population. This put an end to years of quarreling between the two communities, about which the people of Suriname like to tell the famous joke about the Jew who ends up on a deserted island and immediately builds two synagogues: one to pray in, and another where he will never set foot. At the end of the eighteenth century and the beginning of the nineteenth century, members of each community were in fact prohibited from participating in the prayer services and ceremonies of the other community, and until 1813, marriages between members of the two communities were forbidden. Ironically enough, these communities bore the names Neveh Shalom (sanctuary of peace) and Tzedek v'Shalom (justice and peace).

"When I was a boy," Fernandez relates as he sits in the garden of his elegant home, and a pleasant breeze blows between the palms and tropical plants, "both synagogues were full on the holidays. Now, both of the communities are gradually shrinking." He views himself as a Surinamese Jew and jokes that he is a "mixed child" – his mother is Ashkenazi, while his father is a descendant of one of the well-known Sephardic families. In 1975, when the Dutch left Suriname (then called Dutch Guiana), many of the members of the upper middle class abandoned the country, including quite a number of Jews. Most moved to the Netherlands, and a minority immigrated to Israel. In 2010, an eighteenth-century synagogue from Suriname was fully uprooted and placed on display in the Jewish Culture and Art Wing of the Israel

Museum in Jerusalem. Fernandez, however, remains loyal to his birth-place and says, "Suriname was and is my home."

A visit to what remains of the Jewish communities in the Caribbean – in Suriname, Jamaica, St. Thomas, or Curaçao – is a moving and somber journey through numerous cemeteries and tiny communities. Despite the diversity and differences among each island and community, there are quite a number of common characteristics. It is no coincidence that Jewish communities developed primarily on islands that were under the sovereignty of the Netherlands, Denmark, and Britain. The Netherlands and Britain were Protestant and the enemies of Spain, and they happily took in the Jewish exiles, who brought with them money, connections, and an education.

Some claim that it is no accident that Columbus arrived in the New World in the same year that the Jews were expelled from Spain and that it was heaven's way of ensuring that the exiled Jews would have a safe haven. Keeping with this idea, in the prayer books of Jamaican Jews, there is a special prayer that is not found in any other prayer book outside the Caribbean: a prayer of thanks to Christopher Columbus for discovering the island that provided security to the Jewish people and enabled them to flourish. According to some theories, Columbus him-self was the descendant of conversos, and there are those who even think that he was a crypto-Jew himself. There are also those who claim that there were a few crypto-Jews in his crew who descended at the coast of Jamaica, which was a Spanish colony at the time. According to this claim, they established covert Jewish communities that came out of hiding only after the British conquered the island in 1655.

Whether the claim is true or not, it is well known that there were Jewish communities that lived in hiding in the Caribbean, sometimes under the protection of the Columbus family, which controlled Jamaica. Diego, Columbus's son, gave the "New Christians" (conversos) special permission to settle in Jamaica. They were referred to as "Portuguese," and the Spaniards hated them. After the British threw the Spaniards out of Jamaica, they allowed the "Portuguese" to stay. There are testimonies that Antonio de Carvajal and Simon de Caceres, the founders of the Jewish community in England, provided British officials with information that helped them conquer Jamaica. It seems logical that the Jews in Jamaica were the source of this information.

Jewish life in the Caribbean cannot be separated from the historical events that occurred in the region. In the sixteenth and seventeenth centuries, the Caribbean underwent an accelerated process of colonization, during which the Jewish communities also grew. Spain and Portugal, who had arrived in the region first, took over significant parts of Central and South America and the islands in the Caribbean Sea, but as Britain, France, and Holland became stronger, they took over more and more islands.

Due to their knowledge of the languages and their far-reaching connections with Jewish communities in other Caribbean islands and in Europe, America, the Middle East, and even the Far East, the Jews' attempts at international trade were very successful. The colonies faced quick-paced development, and the capital and technological knowledge that the Jews possessed were welcomed with open arms. Thanks to this environment, a different style of Jewish life developed in the Caribbean than in other areas of the world. Here, Jews were not required to define themselves by prejudices, and they therefore did not isolate themselves from the general population. In the nineteenth century, the Jewish presence in the Jamaican parliament was so dominant that it was only natural to close it on Yom Kippur.

Many Jews moved to the islands from Europe after World War II, and yet, the Jewish communities remained tiny. The Caribbean Jewish communities underwent a process of rapid assimilation with intermarriage. About two years after my visit to Suriname, I visited Jamaica and took part in the Shabbat prayer services at Shaare Shalom Synagogue, along with about fifty community members. They were Sephardic and Ashkenazi; white, black, and mixed; Jews who prayed fervently and

Jews who didn't know how to read Hebrew; spouses of Jews, converts of various ethnicities, and others at different stages of their conversion processes. I again stood on the sandy floor, as customary in the communities of crypto-Jews and their descendants, in the style of the synagogue in Amsterdam. The tiny communities dispersed throughout the Caribbean Sea have almost disappeared, and the synagogues with the sandy floors are almost the last testament of the Jewish Anusim who escaped the Inquisition in Spain and Portugal.

Epilogue: There Is Us

Ya'acov Fried

In all my travels to Jewish communities around the world, the strongest feeling I've had is amazement. On many of my trips, I felt like a small child who was exposed to a wondrous invention for the first time. My travels throughout the Jewish world led to new discoveries – encounters with complex realities that I didn't necessarily understand but that always made my heart beat faster.

While writing this book and meeting the local personalities, that feeling of amazement in my heart only grew with time. My fellow authors and I felt, during our writing journey, that we had been granted unique opportunities to meet inspiring personalities who are involved in or who are creating this amazing reality. The encounters, the visits, and the writing process caused us to reflect on our personal identities and lives and on our Jewish identities. They also increased our self-awareness and stirred us to deeply contend with our inner selves.

It is our privilege to share our journey of emotion and love with you, the reader. *The Beating Heart* was born and evolved out of a sense of partnership and Jewish responsibility and the desire and passion of the local personalities and the authors to share their unique realities. Each community's story is a piece of the Jewish mosaic that belongs to us all.

The opportunity to process our feelings created a common beating heart. Every subject that we explored proved and demonstrated that a home in general, or a Jewish home, is not a physical place, but rather a place to which we are emotionally connected. We also discovered deeper layers of our own Jewish identities.

Usually, the experience aroused within us, the authors, a feeling of development and change. In each of the Jewish communities around the world that we wrote about, we felt at home. What a wonderful feeling. To just be myself. A feeling that I am not watching a play, but rather actively involved, in a purely authentic way. It was amazing to feel my heart beating in tandem with the hearts of other Jews all over the world. However, there were also cases in which my inner voice expressed a sense of concern that I might lose part of my identity. This happened mostly upon encountering communities that had been abandoned or were extremely assimilated. In these cases as well, I inevitably understood that it wasn't exactly a feeling of lost identity, but rather a magical catalyst and opportunity for developing my own Jewish identity.

We invite you, the reader, whether you experience the destinations by reading or visiting, to view these places from a perspective of amazement. We invite you to approach the places described in these pages with a sense of curiosity, realizing that you may discover things you never knew or imagined, and that you might even find yourself changed.

Looking back on the Jewish journeys we conducted and on the writing process, we discovered that in order to experience unfamiliar things, it is necessary to identify the obstacles that are preventing us from experiencing freely. What are those obstacles? On the one hand, we are all subject to cultural codes and patterns, as each one of us is "the image of his native landscape." On the other hand, a journey through the Jewish world that is sparked by curiosity and the desire to see the unique aspects of the common Jewish destiny, as expressed in each community, is often met with mental and cultural blocks that make it difficult to understand and become intimately familiar with the destinations.

We tried to illuminate and slightly dissolve these obstacles in our writing. A clear example is Poland – a challenging country to visit, to put it mildly. The dominance of the memories of the Holocaust and our associations of a trip to Poland with touring concentration camps create a mental block that prevents us from seeing other important elements. Therefore, we tried to evoke the rich history of Poland's Jewish heritage, the Jewish culture developing there today, and the complexity of the relationship between Poles and Jews.

Many tourists who visit Jewish heritage sites believe that they cannot feel the historical experience because they are not proficient in Jewish texts. In the essays about the German communities and the essay about Ukraine, we present ways of confronting this challenge.

The culture gaps between the tourist from North America, who is exposed to Ashkenazi Jewish culture and to the Western world, and destinations in the Jewish world with a different culture, such as the North African world or the Far East, are tremendous. There is a tall wall separating them. Therefore, in the essays about Morocco, Tunis, Cairo, and India, we endeavored to shine light on elements that could help bridge the culture gap and topple the wall.

Undoubtedly, some Jewish readers may feel uncertain about learning about populations with weak Jewish identities. In some of the essays, the reader is invited to discover this type of Jewish identity, such as the challenges of crypto-Jews in Portugal who "came out of the closet," or in the isolated Jewish community of Azerbaijan, and of course, the challenge of assimilation in the Jewish communities of Italy and France, among other places.

I believe that the Jewish world has some sort of deep cultural genetic code that every member of Western culture carries within, even in the absence of religious tendencies. This is expressed in the historical developments that occurred within the communities, in their struggles for religious and personal liberty, and in the Jewish texts that gave rise to Western culture. Furthermore, the vast human mosaic that has evolved and developed in Jewish communities throughout history until today provides a golden opportunity to deepen one's understanding of the reality of our world.

Many of us perceive social justice as a central component of our Jewish identity. Throughout history, and today as well, it is clear that the Jewish nation has been a leader of social justice, with astonishing expressions of mutual responsibility. In this book, we tried to grapple with the idea that we are sometimes so focused on ourselves that we fail to see the other side. In the essays on Greece and Rwanda, we presented different angles of social justice. In Greece, we highlighted the local population's operations on behalf of refugees who are not Jewish, and in Rwanda, Jewish activism on behalf of the local residents.

During your journey through this book, you will encounter weird and wonderful communities, cities, and countries. The magic that may happen is an opportunity for personal, inner discovery on intellectual, emotional, and hopefully spiritual dimensions – all while breaking down stigmas and preconceived notions. We believe in the Jewish approach that the spirit is inseparable from the intellect and emotion; every deep learning experience inevitably reaches the spirit as well and therefore both influences and is influenced by it.

Based on my experience, I would like to share with you three tools that could be of use to you during your trips to these destinations, in order to transform them into trips of discovery. The first tool is to try to speak with the older members of your family. Clarify your family's roots prior to their arrival in North America. Where were they from? What was their lifestyle before they arrived? Why did they immigrate? How did they deal with the cultural and religious openness of the United States?

The second tool is reflective. Try to create as many opportunities for personal encounter as you can during your trip. An encounter is an invitation to come into contact with identities that are different or shared. Try to clarify what you share and what makes you feel part of one nation. Try to understand the Jews you meet, and perhaps this will also help you better understand your own selves.

The third tool is the "owner" tool. I suggest that you walk through the different Jewish communities feeling that you are the owners of your identity. Make room in your heart for the strange and unclear things that you will see. Don't hurry to judge what has been revealed to you. Let time take its course in processing the inner experience.

Remember! You could have been me, and I could have been you, had our families made different decisions before immigrating from Europe to their country of choice. In this spirit, I believe that you may discover a new family. There is no them; there is you, there is I, and most of all, there is us.